THE ART OF MEMORY

History and Social Science Series

General Editor: Greg Dawes
Series Editor: Carlos Aguirre

The Art of Memory

An Ethnographer's Journey

Stefano Varese

TRANSLATED BY MARGARET RANDALL

FOREWORD BY LYNN STEPHEN

Raleigh, North Carolina

Library of Congress Cataloging-in-Publication Data
Names: Varese, Stefano, author. | Randall, Margaret, 1936- translator. |
Stephen, Lynn, writer of introduction.
Title: The art of memory : an ethnographer's journey / Stefano Varese ;
translated by Margaret Randall ; introduction by Lynn Stephen.
Other titles: History and social sciences series.
Description: [Raleigh, N.C.] : Editorial A Contracorriente, 2020. | Series:
History and social sciences series | Includes bibliographical
references.
Identifiers: LCCN 2020035408 | ISBN 9781469661681 (paperback) | ISBN
9781469661698 (ebook)
Subjects: LCSH: Varese, Stefano. | Anthropologists--Latin
America—Biography. | College teachers—United States—Biography. |
Indians of South America—Peru—Social life and customs. | Indians of
Mexico—Social life and customs. | LCGFT: Autobiographies.
Classification: LCC GN21.V365 A3 2020 | DDC 301.092 [B]—dc23
LC record available at https://lccn.loc.gov/2020035408

ISBN: 978-1-4696-6168-1 (paperback)
ISBN: 978-1-4696-6169-8 (ebook)

This is a publication of the Department of Foreign Languages
and Literatures at North Carolina State University. For more information
visit http://go.ncsu.edu/editorialacc.

Distributed by the University of North Carolina Press
www.uncpress.org

To the memory of my mother Pina,
to the sixteen years we lived together,
to everything I owe her.

CONTENTS

MORE THAN A TRANSLATOR'S NOTE

Margaret Randall

R ENDERING AN ENGLISH TRANSLATION of Stefano Varese's *The Art of Memory. An Ethnographer's Journey* was both a challenge and an immense pleasure. A challenge because, as is always true when translating the work of someone in a field with which I am not an expert—in this case social anthropology—there's more than literary language to consider. A pleasure because giving life in another language to such an important book was something I enjoyed immensely. I believe the last half of the past century was extremely important in terms of the experiences that have shaped us: politically, socially, and morally. I also believe that few books have done that half-century justice. This is one of them.

Stefano is an old and valued friend. As I worked, I could often hear the author's rich cadence. Having a ready back-and-forth with him throughout the process was also immensely helpful, and I am as grateful to him for that as I am for our friendship. This translation brought me back to the mid-1970s when Stefano and I worked briefly together in the Peru of progressive president Juan Velasco Alvarado—times of change and great hope. When Stefano asked me to be the English translator of his memoir, I was elated. I knew I was about to embark on an exciting and meaningful journey.

Before going further, I want to emphasize that this is an extraordinary text, unique among the many being published today. Stefano Varese, internationally known social, political, and cultural anthropologist born in Italy, coming of age in Peru, and professor emeritus from the University of California—Davis, acquired wide recognition with his groundbreaking *La sal de los cerros*, first published in 1968. He had produced a good deal of important work prior to that book and has continued to produce a good deal since. Stefano has the rare ability to be able to seamlessly combine the personal with the professional, weaving them together in a fully realized account. I believe *The*

Art of Memory. An Ethnographer's Journey occupies a central place in his oeuvre—and collectively for us, his readers.

Stefano is an important authority on the Indigenous peoples of the Amazon and throughout Latin America, as well as on the state of ongoing conquest that has decimated and attempted to erase the continent's first peoples. He has been part of a number of think tanks and academic groups that look at the treatment of Indigenous peoples and their treatment by anthropologists as well as governments. His speaking and teaching credits make up a very long list and he has won many important awards. Yet the recognition he values most is not to be found on his formal curriculum vitae. It includes such honors as those bestowed by the Asháninka people of Chanchamayo, in the central Peruvian rainforest (a Meritorious Medal for his work in retrieving and reevaluating their cultural identity), and Cuba's prestigious Haydée Santamaría Medal (named for a heroine of that country's revolution and one of the truly great women of our time).

Stefano's brother, Luis, who worked for the government of Ecuador, once told him the following story: When he introduced himself as Luis Varese to an Indigenous leader of the Ecuadorean Amazon that leader, Valerio Grefas, said: "How strange that you have the same name as my son, Distefano Varese," to which Luis responded: "That is my brother Stefano's name. Why did you call your son that?" Grefas said: "Because Stefano Varese is the most important defender of the Amazonian people." For Stefano, this is the sort of praise he values above all others.

I am not surprised. In this book, among many other gems, are Stefano's stories of doing research among the Campa-Asháninka of the Gran Pajonal, long before foreign academics and evangelical missionaries entered the territory with their insulting dogma and exploitative practices. One of the great beauties of this book is Stefano's ability to go beneath the surface, in search of those hidden stories and personal motivations that are ultimately responsible for mapping history and the choices we make within that history. He presents Indigenous belief systems and customs with the sensibility only those who have lived with those who espouse them—and himself experienced their power—can convey. His power of translation, in the most profound sense of that term, is simply unequaled. Indigenous legends and stories come to us here in a language as evocative and respectful as it is knowledgeable, woven seamlessly in and out of the memoirist's own life experience.

This book also offers truths that are particularly relevant to the times we inhabit today, these chaotic and dangerous times in which so many of us here in the United States feel trapped by the rise of neo-Fascism with a president who is at once raving, chaotic, rooted in sociopathic illogic, and profoundly dangerous. Battling our current situation, it behooves us to think about the rise of an earlier Fascism in western Europe as well as an experiment in social change here in the Americas that has never received the attention it deserves, the Velasco Alvarado administration in Peru.

In this memoir, from the position of an active and deeply committed participant, Stefano explores the human dimension of these events as well as the larger political relevance. In these pages, the author brings his parents, siblings, friends and colleagues to life, and explores his own sociopolitical development inscribed against a backdrop of the major political and cultural forces of a turbulent century. The brief Velasco Alvarado revolution (1968-1975), in which Stefano took part, is posited in memory against his childhood growing up in a small Italian village among anti-Fascist partisans during World War II. The author's ability to contextualize experiences of social change enriches this powerful narrative. And this is a book that reaches high, to speak of the author's friendships and working relationships with some of the great minds of the late 20th century — in fields as disparate as philosophy and cybernetics — and into the depths of his own psyche to courageously lay bare family secrets that will be gratefully received by many readers because they will feel familiar, mirroring as they do our own experiences of abuse, personal negotiation, and redemption.

Rarely have I encountered a memoir that so skillfully — and revealingly — blends the personal, the public, and the deep recesses of cultures still little known among Western readers. It is often said that memoirists write the story that best positions them or a cause they espouse. *The Art of Memory. An Ethnographer's Journey* is never so self-serving. It presents people, places, and events with moving nuance; the author and his cast of characters — some intimate friends and family, others among the luminaries of our time — are never only "good" or "bad," never entirely "right" or "wrong." They are only and always human.

Stefano was born in Italy and spent his early childhood in an area occupied by Mussolini's Fascism. As a young man, he traveled to Peru with the intention of spending time with his father who had abandoned his mother and preceded him there. He ended up staying, and that Andean nation gave him his education, both formal and in the field. It was in Lima, in 1973, when left-leaning populist General Juan Velasco Alvarado was in power, that Stefano and I first met. (By way of disclosure, the book includes a few paragraphs about our meeting.) We were both working at the Center for the Study of Popular Participation, a joint project of the progressive Peruvian government's National System of Social Mobilization (SINAMOS) and the International Labor Office of the United Nations Program for Development (UNPD/ILO). Stefano was Research Director of SINAMOS, and I had been invited to carry out a three-month research project that involved interviewing women and assessing their needs in the new sociopolitical context. We became the sort of friends who may not see one another for years but, when they reconnect, do so as if no time has passed. We traveled to the Amazon country together and Stefano, who already had considerable anthropological experience, was a valuable mentor. And in the light of later events, we both believe Peru's Velasco Alvarado administration to have been an historic moment that hasn't received the attention it deserves.

But, *The Art of Memory. An Ethnographer's Journey* does not end in the turbulent 1970s. It continues through Stefano's exile from Peru, life in Oaxaca, Mexico, and many years of teaching at the University of California—Davis, from where he retired as professor emeritus. Later parts of the narrative include important political analyses from a man who has experienced the inner workings of several social systems, as well as more personal stories of parenting, family and friends. The reader is left grateful for such an honest— at times even raw but always compassionate—window on humanity's struggle with meaning.

As I say, this is an extraordinary memoir. In deeply moving prose, Stefano takes us from his World War II childhood, with all its questions, to a new world where the questions may be less obvious but are just as complex and relevant. The cultural impact of Fascism is something we would do well to revisit today. And the complexities of conquest and colonialism always deserve a fresh look.

This book weaves intimate experience—some of it painful, much of it joyful, all of it intensely interesting—with the philosophical attitudes that have shaped several generations. *The Art of Memory. An Ethnographer's Journey* addresses race, class, gender, sexuality, culture, and even notions of "good" and "evil" without ever losing itself in New Age superficialities or platitudes. The author's personal story moves seamlessly through the story of his time. This is a book I value deeply, feel privileged to have been able to translate for an English readership, and one to which I will return often.

Albuquerque, New Mexico, Summer 2017-Winter 2019.

Lynn Stephen

UNIVERSITY OF OREGON

I FIRST MET STEFANO VARESE in Oaxaca, Mexico in 1984 as a graduate student. Stefano was the director of the Oaxaca Regional Unit for Peoples and Indigenous Culture and also of the Grupo de Apoyo al Desarrollo Étnico de Oaxaca. I visited Oaxaca for two months in the summer of 1984 and returned to live in Oaxaca from the summer of 1985 until the end of 1986, and again for several months in 1987. During this time, I was conducting fieldwork for my doctoral dissertation in the Zapotec community of Teotitlán del Valle, about 45 minutes from Oaxaca City where Stefano lived.

I approached Stefano as a fellow intellectual and asked to be able to talk with him periodically about my fieldwork. He quickly introduced me to the amazing group of linguists, anthropologists, geographers, ethnobotanists, and theatrical and visual communicators who were, as he notes in this book of memoirs, engaged in "ethnopolitical activism in 40 communities in Zapotec, Mixe, and Chinanteca ethnicities." This group of young people became my friendship circle and I went to many public events, parties, and on trips with them throughout Oaxaca and to Guatemala. What I was learning at the time through my interactions with Stefano's model of engaged, activist anthropology was to think about my own research in relation to questions of Indigenous autonomy, territory, and the great variety of knowledge transmission channels that the Indigenous peoples around us in Oaxaca used.

As someone who together with others dedicated myself to activist, engaged, and collaborative anthropology foregrounding the "saberes" (knowledges) and knowledge systems of Indigenous and Afrodescendant peoples in the Americas, reading *The Art of Memory. An Ethnographer's Journey* has been a homecoming. Full of activist intellectuals, anthropologists, and others who I either know through reading their work or through personal interactions, this book carries an essential message for our times: we and every living thing and all of our collective ancestors are all connected now and into the future. We have a contract with the cosmos to care for all that is on our planet now and into the future.

It is in the intersection of Oaxacan Indigenous thought, action, social, ethical, and political ways of being that my mind and soul connect with Stefano Varese. His work—which at one point he describes as breaking the anthropological, biological, and pedagogical molds that for almost ten decades contributed to the concealing and suppressing of Indigenous knowledges, creative imagination, and profound ethical values—is path breaking. Varese was a pioneer not only of activist research in Oaxaca, long before later generations took it up there and elsewhere, but of an entirely original and powerful approach to the study of Indigenous cultures and peoples that could not be dissociated from an engagement with their lifestyle, cosmovision, and livelihood.

Perhaps it is true that great ideas often occur simultaneously in different places. As Stefano Varese put together his team at Culturas Populares in Oaxaca in 1979, Colombian sociologist Orlando Fals Borda was carrying out his program of Participatory Action Research (PAR), which rejects the hierarchical distinction between researcher and researched and promotes a dialogical, self-reflective, and participatory approach to knowledge production. Fals Borda remained committed throughout his life to the oppressed and rural poor in Colombia usually labelled as "peasants." In 1977, he helped to organize a conference on PAR in Cartagena. Varese's project started just two years later in Oaxaca, also incorporating a dialogical learning process that centered Indigenous epistemologies and used them to challenge modernist ideas of development and progress.

Stefano's trajectory as an engaged intellectual, however, did not start with his arrival in Oaxaca. Born in 1939 with his childhood spanning World War II in Italy, Varese arrived in Peru in 1957 to live with his father and stepmother. His world included a religious education, a family steeped in literature and music, and his father's jewelry business, which sent him on trips up and down the Peruvian coast to sell to regional jewelry shops. Completely uninterested in the family business, young Varese used the trips to learn about the peoples and communities he passed through. He lived first in the center of Lima and then for ten years with his father, stepmother Rita, and siblings in the chic neighborhood of Miraflores. Later the family moved to a house his father built in the neighborhood of Chacarilla. He enrolled to study Ethnology in the Universidad Católica, Peru's pre-eminent private university. He studied religious history and ethnology and was strongly influenced by Liberation Theology and literary criticism through his teachers. He received a Bachelor of Science degree in Ethnology at the Catholic University in Lima, Peru in 1966 and a Doctor of Philosophy degree in Anthropology in 1967 from the same university.

Woven together with his discussion of his education is also an intimate portrait of how Stefano developed as a teenager and young man, intellectually, sexually, and emotionally in open and honest prose. At several points in the book he battles with a painful event in his childhood. This experience surfaces like a dark monster from the deep at several points in his life and bleeds into what he sees as ten years of lost and wandering sexual encounters and relationships before he met his wife Linda. His struggles with painful memories and how to move past them are described in almost surreal terms. His belief in dreams and that they are sources of knowledge—something he learned from his Indigenous interlocutors—follows him through life and connects with other lessons learned from being in an otherworldly state after consuming teacher plants under the guidance of a shaman.

Varese's doctoral dissertation, published as *La sal de los cerros (Notas etnográficas e históricas sobre los campa de la selva del Perú)* in 1968, was based on both a close reading of Franciscan archives and his own fieldwork. It is worth noting that the literature on Peruvian native communities of the Amazon was at that time almost non-existent. A pioneering work, *La sal de los cerros* provides an intimate look at the daily life and cosmovision of the Asháninka and documents their expulsion of Franciscans during the colonial era in 1742 and control of their territory until 1848. Stefano observed the reciprocal exchange of gifts and objects of value. Through his interactions with Asháninka families, he learned to decipher the ethical and social function of the Indigenous institutions that makes it possible to have cultural cohesion connecting thousands of families spread over a vast territory, who visit, participate in feasts, hunting and fishing expeditions, and exchanges of goods. Once two people engage in a sacred reciprocal exchange, the other has become nosháninka, "my people, my brother."

The same year that *La sal de los cerros* was published, the Revolutionary Government of the Armed Forces took power on October 3, 1968. The government expropriated and nationalized Standard Oil and passed an agrarian reform law coupled with expropriations of large landholdings on the coast that were to be changed into cooperatives. Plans for land reform for lowland Indigenous Amazonian peoples were less clear.

In his first post-Ph.D. job in 1970 with the office of the Peruvian Revolution's Agrarian Reform, Varese immediately sought to apply the knowledge from his fieldwork among the interlinked Asháninka peoples. The territory, water, forests, mines, symbolically sacred places, and plants of the Asháninka and other Indigenous peoples must all be understood together, he argued. As he writes here, "the ethnic community's full jurisdiction over the totality of its surroundings must be within the scope of autonomous development of the Indigenous peoples." Varese was largely responsible for placing the Amazonian communities at the center of intellectual and policy debates during this period.

Stefano's proposal for how the Peruvian government should approach its engagement with Indigenous peoples bears a resemblance to the Zapatista Army of National Liberation's (EZLN) initial proposals for Indigenous autonomy and territory in Chiapas in 1994 and Mayan peoples' demands for control of territory and autonomy in Guatemala during the same time period. Stefano defined Indigenous communities as social entities linked by networks through a shared territory. In the lowlands of Peru a community, he writes, is "historically constructed as a network of blood and political relationships that exist as discreet groups of a few nuclear or extended families in a large territory they consider as belonging to the group. Relationships between people in the same linguistic/dialect group tend to be friendly, but always tense and competitive, often mediated by fights, attacks, deaths, or renovated by rituals of alliance. Matrimonial links, or links created by political kinship and horizontal relations of three ascendant generations, can become a community." Networks that are historically constructed are held together by reciprocal relationships built on politics and kinship that extend over vast territories that are collectively owned—this picture of Indigenous peoples produced a serious challenge for a model of agrarian reform that was posited on individual plots for peasant subsistence farmers. While Stefano did not get far in getting titles assigned to communal lands and territories in Peru, the model he proposed came with him when he was exiled to Mexico in 1975. While he was working on revolutionary agrarian reform in Peru, in January of 1971, Stefano attended a unique meeting of fourteen Latin American social anthropologists who together crafted a document known as "The Declaration of Barbados," named for the Caribbean country where the meeting took place. The declaration was signed by Stefano Varese and nine other male anthropologists and Nelly Arévalo de Jiménez (the only woman). Three other anthropologists did not sign the statement for fear of reprisals in their home countries. The declaration called for "the liberation of the Indians," specifically "the creation of a truly multi-ethnic state in which each ethnic group possesses the right to self-determination and the free selection of available social and cultural alternatives." A number of the anthropologists Stefano met there became important connections, particularly Guillermo Bonfil Batalla of Mexico.

In the book that follows, Stefano identifies this meeting as the moment when his activism expanded beyond Peru and allowed him to connect to other people engaged in similar efforts in the region. He was already engaged in activism with Amazonian Indigenous communities through his participation in the Velasco government. The Barbados meeting expanded his horizons and brought a wide international perspective to his attention. The dialogue and ideas that emerged there tied him to a generation of primarily male anthropologists committed to Indigenous autonomy and self-determination. The Barbados connection with Bonfil Batalla was directly responsible for Varese being offered a position at the National Institute of Anthropology and History in Mexico, first in the capital and later in Oaxaca. Bonfil Batalla, a very important intellectual in Mexico, was one of the thinkers behind the ideas of Indigenous autonomy and the notion of how to consolidate pluricultural states. He was also a major critic of the model of state *indigenismo*, a set of paternal policies institutions and laws that the Mexican government had promulgated in relationship to Indigenous peoples. Bonfil Batalla and Varese met at the crossroads of activist anthropology, Indigenous autonomy, and the necessity to redefine the state's relationship with Indigenous peoples. Stefano went on to travel as part of a delegation from the Latin American Studies Association (LASA) in 1985 to Nicaragua where the revolutionary Sandinistas were at war with the Indigenous and Afrodescendant populations on the Pacific Coast. There, Stefano and his fellow delegation members witnessed another historical struggle for autonomy: that of the Miskito, Sumo, Rama, and Garífuna Indigenous communities and Afrodescendant "creoles." The revolutionary left has often not understood or seriously tried to incorporate the territories, social organization, and governance and justice models of Indigenous peoples into their development plans. Nicaragua was no exception. Varese and other anthropologists who became familiar with the autonomy model proposed by the Indigenous peoples of the Pacific coast of Nicaragua used it as a blueprint for discussions about Indigenous autonomy in Mexico and elsewhere. Ultimately, a number of governments in Latin America changed their constitutions to recognize their countries as pluri-cultural, multi-lingual states—Colombia, Ecuador, Bolivia and, in the case of Guatemala and Mexico, what we might call pluri-cultural "light." When the EZLN in Mexico and communities such as Cherán in Michoacán and organizations such as the Regional Coordination of Community Authorities—Community Police (CRAC-PC) in Guerrero implemented autonomous forms of governance and justice, they faced heavy opposition from the state. And as Charlie Hale, Rachel Seider, Shannon Speed, Nancy Postero, and others have written about, "multicultural neoliberalism" has been a way for states to recognize the demands of Indigenous movements for inclusion and recognition of their cultures and institutions and wrap it in a narrative of progressive neoliberal development that has resulted in intensifying inequalities and the ransacking of Indigenous territories for extractive industries, extending a new kind of settler colonialism into Latin America.

As noted above, Stefano's book is much more than a memoir of an engaged intellectual. It is also a very honest introspection into his life and that of his family. Significant parts of the book are about members of Stefano's family, but most importantly about Linda, his wife. Much of what Stefano has written about and his ability to travel, to research, to take jobs in different places and to have a family is because of Linda's tremendous intellectual, emotional, and economic support. Stefano makes clear their shared ideas and intellectual projects as well as the key role she played in maintaining their family. Varese also openly explores the challenge he and his wife faced once they realized that their son had Asperger's syndrome, a developmental condition characterized by difficulty in reading social cues and in language development. What was even more difficult than the diagnosis of Asperger's was trying to figure out what was happening to André as a young child in Mexico where there was no knowledge of his condition. He acknowledges the importance of the specialized education Linda gave their son André while working full time as a bilingual high school teacher.

Like many anthropologists of his era, Stefano's professional world was predominantly male. Most of the intellectuals he recognizes as a student and as a maturing and seasoned anthropologist are men. There are some women but they are few and far in between. After reading *The Art of Memory: An Ethnographer's Journey* it made me wonder what kinds of lessons Stefano learned from Indigenous women—he mentions a few, but not much as major influences—and from women intellectuals in Mexico. Lourdes Arizpe, Margarita Nolasco Armas, Mercedes Olivera Bustamante, and other women were also pioneering figures in Mexican anthropology in areas linked to Stefano's interests. Anthropology in the U.S. and also in Latin America is now dominated by women, but their contributions are still only slowly being recognized in the canon of activist anthropology as well as the anthropology of Indigenous autonomy. As more recent work on gender and Indigenous autonomy by scholars such as Aída Hernández Castillo, Shannon Speed, María Teresa Sierra, and Mariana Mora has shown, Indigenous women do have distinctive visions of what autonomy and Indigenous rights mean—refusing to split gender and Indigenous rights from one another.

For me, the final pages of this book offer the most important insights. They come from Varese's model of how to do social science. "The coming together of activism and social science," he writes, "my way of practicing anthropology, opened multiple windows of perception which might otherwise have remained obscured by modernity's obsessive epistemology of materialist empiricism." While the last pages also incorporate the lessons learned from teacher plants such as ayahuasca, Stefano closes by focusing on two different models for how to understand the world—clearly endorsing the one he has learned from Indigenous peoples through the years. The first is anthropocentric modern Western cosmology—"the separation of humanity from nature, man's hierarchical position at the top of an unquestioned universal order, hierarchy accompanied by commercialization of the universe." The second model brings important lessons to us in our emergency era of climate change: "The Indigenous world—that cosmocentric world—is inhabited by animals and immaterial beings committed to a cosmic conversation that recognizes in each entity an interlocutor with intelligence, free will, feelings and awareness of its own teleological participation." We urgently need this cosmocentric worldview to ensure the survival of our planet.

Stefano Varese has written an intellectually important memoir that broadens our understanding of the social movements, cosmologies, and struggles for autonomy and rights of Indigenous peoples in the Americas. At the same time, he also writes about his own life and development with honesty and sensitivity. Stefano's embrace of the challenges in his own life also marks his relationships with others—from his family to fellow anthropologists and students to the many Indigenous men, women, and children he worked with for over five decades. He models a deeply humanistic anthropology, activist participatory research, and institution building in Peru, Mexico, and the United States. This exceptional memoir shows how to write about oneself and others with beauty and sincerity.

ACKNOWLEDGMENTS

I N THE BEGINNING I imagined this book in a mixture of Italian and Spanish. It took seven or more years to write it in a continuous alternation between academic writings, in the required English language of the university world, and the Spanish of my commitment to the Latin American Indigenous people movement and my own memory. It has been an exhilarating and exhausting dance especially demanding for my wife Linda and my son André, who had to withstand my absentee-presence and my constant exonerating excuses not to participate in my domestic life. To both of them I owe everything. Vanessa and Isabella, even from the distance, helped me to remember and to imagine. And here follows a long list, surely incomplete, of all the people that during the last decade have influenced and participated somehow in the organization of this manuscript. To my friend and poet Margaret Randall I owe the English translation. I am grateful to Frédérique Apffel-Marglin, Carlos Ferrand, Guillermo Delgado, Norma Klahn, and Róger Rumrrill for their sometimes too enthusiastic and generous commentaries, but I am especially thankful to our friend Nancy Price who, from the perspective of an Anglo-American reader, pointed out some imperfections in the cultural translation that my wife Linda had already caught in her partial reviews of the manuscript. My friend Arnold Bauer was able to read some of the earliest pages in Spanish, returning to me some encouraging commentaries. Ben Orlove, Andean anthropologist and author of the biography of his father, insisted very early that I should continue with my memoir even if such an effort would never benefit my academic career. To Miriam Wells, with whom for years I shared many miles of running along the parks and oaks of Davis, I owe a special thanks for having insisted on picking my memory during those early morning runs. I am thankful to Inés Hernández-Avila, Nimipu-Tejana poet, author, and professor for the innumerable times she offered her advice and assistance, and to Lynn Stephen, a dear friend over the years, for accepting the invitation to write a foreword to this book.

The publication in English of my memoir would have not happened without the obstinate insistence of my historian friends Chuck Walker at the University of California—Davis and Carlos Aguirre at the University of Oregon. Chuck Walker and Carlos Aguirre, among the most prestigious Latin Americanist and Andeanist scholars, are honoring me with their friendship and trust. Gracias, amigos del alma.

Davis, December 2019

CHAPTER I

Sechura

ꙮ

THE FOUR-ENGINE PROPELLER PLANE seemed enormous to me.
It was my first flight. The year, 1956. The month, maybe October or
November. My mother Pina and sister Ilaria had accompanied me
by train from Turin to the Malpensa airport in Milan. Everything began to
dissolve in a haze on this three-day journey across the Atlantic, the American continent, and south to the Pacific, to the Peruvian coast on the Sechura
desert. I don't know if it was my head that felt confused, or my emotions:
that intense feeling of guilt that overcame me from the moment I announced
to my mother—with all the impetuousness of my seventeen years—that I
wanted to travel to Peru to get to know my father. That hapless, traitorous,
and adulterous man who had abandoned me, my sisters Giliola and Ilaria,
and my mother when he fled with his lover Rita, according to my mother a
Genovese secretary of doubtful moral character.

I remembered only a few things about my father Luigi: a warm and tender
hand one Genovese winter, as we walked to a parish where he would enroll
me as a cub scout, and the horrific shudder at seeing a rat scurry from the
drain of the "Turkish bath" where I'd placed my feet so I could urinate. That's
what they called those places in Italy, because everything primitive and exotic
came from the Ottoman Empire, like "Turkish grain" or the Indigenous corn
of the Americas they attributed to the Muslims. Later I remembered recur-
ring visits to a doctor who subjected me to misty inhalations intended to cure
my persistent bronchitis. Papá read me pages of Emilio Salgari in the waiting
room, perhaps instilling a love of adventure in my young mind.

I didn't remember anything about his deserting us aboard a Genovese ship
going to Argentina with the secretary who was his lover. I had only vague images of dark scenes, with passionate shouting and heavy telephones thrown

My mother Giuseppina Druetto Ivaldi
(b. Turin 1912- d. Turin 1968), circa 1934

impetuously by my mother Pina at the illustrious head of the criminal lawyer Luigi Varese Guerci-Lena, reduced to the role of an ingrate caught in the
adulterous act. My mother's cycles of desperate wailing followed me throughout my childhood and adolescence, and in those years of my youth I didn't
know if they were tears of rage, pain, or guilt and remorse for not having been
able to keep my father Luigi in her arms. He who had chosen my future stepmother's exotic promises of tropical Italian love.

Years later I would understand the desperate loneliness and opaque emp-
tiness of that abandonment, the humiliation my mother endured when she
had to return, defeated, to her father's house, and the challenge of reinventing
herself alone: a young woman facing the difficulties of becoming an itinerant
schoolbook representative and saleswoman. Toward the end of her life my
mother, Giuseppina Druetto Varese, was honored by a youthful Italy with the
title of Cavaliere della República and a gold-plated medal, a little breastpin
with the country's tricolors and a certificate I suppose was meant to recognize

My father Luigi Varese Guerci-Lena
(b. Genoa 1907- d. Lima 1987), Genoa, circa 1936

her contributions to the new nation's young mercantile economy. I have them all in my closet in Davis, California, except for the certificate, lost in exile along with those other ritual objects that still give meaning and memory to the honorable and lonely life of Giuseppina, my mother.

CHAPTER 2

To Lima

☸

THE THREE-DAY FLIGHT TOOK me from Italy to Shannon, Ireland, and from there across the Atlantic to Halifax, Nova Scotia and then south. I think I remember Miami, and then Panama, Colombia, Ecuador, and finally Talara: the International Petroleum Company's oil town, the *gringo*'s gateway to the Sechura desert that extends from north to south for ninety miles between the Pacific Ocean and the western Andean range and loses itself in more than six hundred miles of desert sands.

I knew nothing about Talara or the Sechura desert, and even less about the U.S. company, International Petroleum, with its workers' camp and the homes of North American technicians segregated from the rest of the town. I returned to it in subsequent years on occasional visits as a traveling salesman of jewelry designed and fabricated by my father's shop, Joyería Vasco.

My father and his wife Rita had tried to organize a surprise reception for me on the flight from Panama to Talara. Once aboard the plane, the young and beautiful Panagra stewardess, an Italian-Peruvian by the name of Chiara Mazzoni, was supposed to have welcomed me in Italian to this new world, letting me know that not all of that which was Italian was lost to me: "Ciao, sono Chiara, sono un'amica di Luigi e Rita. Benvenuto in Peru. Magari uno di questi giorni ci possiamo vedere a Miraflores e fare qualche cosa insieme."[1] Luckily a new shift of stewardesses had come aboard, because from that very first moment my shyness would have frustrated my reputation as a young buck in questions of the heart.

---

1. "Hi, I am Chiara, I am a friend of Luigi and Rita. Welcome to Peru. Maybe one of these days we could meet in Miraflores and do something together."

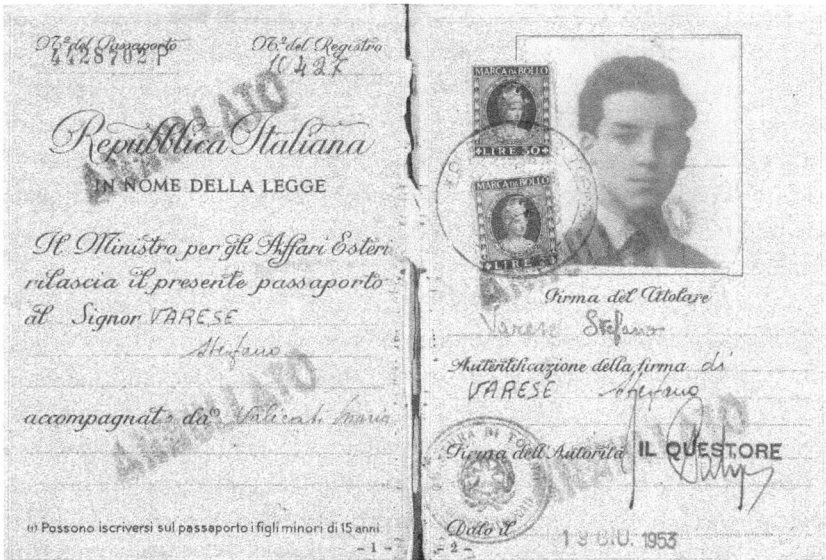

My first passport

Talara's landing field was a spot of red sand better equipped to receive a train of pack horses than an international flight. There was my father, leaning against a one-story building with a flat roof. His suit, which at first seemed white, turned out to be the color of straw, and his sunburnt skin, especially on his head of thinning hair that, years later, I recognize each morning in my bathroom mirror made me believe, in my innocence, that I had arrived in the tropics of my fantasies and absent father. I don't remember the embrace, nor what I managed to say or hear. But I liked what I saw and delighted in what I felt. I stored those first moments in my memory without realizing that I had begun the long and subtle process of reinventing myself as the son of a new father, whose old hazy and turbulent image was already beginning to dissolve among the Sechura sands.

At the edge of the field, hugging the lane, an extravagant American car awaited us. It was the taxi and its chauffer who would drive us along the Pan-American Highway to Lima, more than six hundred miles to the south.

On the way to the city of Piura, in the middle of one of the dune fields, my father told the chauffer to stop the car by the side of the highway. Astride a sandy hill, pointed in the direction of the desert and with its four wheels sticking straight up in the air, was a truck that seemed to be napping. Beside the truck, stretched out on the hot sand, was the driver—the owner of his time—who, with a bottle in his hand and the best of all possible judgments, told my father he was going to drink the pisco that had caused the accident until it was gone: it alone was to blame. Papá translated his conversation with the truck driver, as well as our chauffer's few comments, into Italian, and told me there was nothing to do but let the wise trucker get on with his drinking.

A few hours later we arrived in Piura, at the Tourist Hotel on a drowsy tree-filled square, and at the restaurant where my Peruvian culinary education began. Stuffed avocado, fried bananas, pulled pork, *chifles*, and cold beer. Finally, brewed coffee and Inca Corriente cigarettes that Papá offered me instead of the Camels from Italy I had in my pocket, explaining that dark tobacco was much better than the pale American kind. My proclivity for dark tobacco was born in those next ten years of Peruvian life, while my father took up a pipe and finally swore off smoking altogether. I felt an immediate gratitude for the adult treatment my father offered from the moment of my arrival, without asking anything in return.

I think it was a year later that my father got me adult legal status, and suggested I consider becoming a Peruvian citizen. During those early years of my life in Peru it didn't occur to me that my independence and autonomy guaranteed my father and his wife Rita my loyalty and roots in the country, and thus distanced me from my mother and Turin. Enthusiasm for my newfound freedom momentarily overshadowed my profound nostalgia for Mamma Pina, Ilaria and Giliola, and also for Nonna Massa and Nonno Luigi,[2] Zia[3] Lella, and all my childhood friends, the tree-lined avenues, parks with their statues, elegant arcades on Via Roma, baroque palaces, snow-capped Alps, winter skiing, and boating on the Po River.

I think I remember that we spent those first nights on our way to Lima in Piura and Chiclayo. Peru's northern coast seduced me. The desert and its oases of tropical vegetation excited my imagination. The distant hills devoid of human presence, arid pampas, rapid ocean sunsets, solitary beaches, mysterious coves, and the Andes one always intuited to the east, impressed

---

2. Nonna and nonno are Italian for grandma and granpa
3. Zia is Italian for aunt

My maternal grandparents Massa and
Luigi, Turin, circa 1930

My paternal grandparents Amelia and Cesare, Genoa, circa 1930

From left: Uncle Carlo, grandmother Amelia, my father Luigi, and my grandfather Cesare, circa 1914

From left to right: Uncle Carlo, grandfather Cesare's brother (?), my father Luigi, grandfather Cesare, Genoa, circa 1910

themselves upon my European consciousness like the seeds of a "new world" that I would later reencounter in my New World readings and my own life in that land.

At last we arrived at Pacasmayo, and from there went on to Chepén, to a small sugar cane *hacienda* (or was it rice?) run by an Italian immigrant my father knew. Somewhere I have a photo of my first horseback ride on the *hacienda* grounds: in the black and white image is a very thin young man beneath an overly large straw hat and with a somewhat uncertain and timorous gaze atop a trotting horse.

At that time, I knew little about the agricultural situation on the coast, nor about the profound injustices that allowed me the luxury of riding a horse through those cane or rice fields without having to ask permission of anyone: me, the young light-skinned foreigner who wasn't even aware enough to ask myself why those dark and shabbily dressed men bowed their bare heads as I passed, their hands clutching their hats to their bellies.

A decade later, accustomed to Peru by then, I would return to those great coastal properties, first as a guest of the wealthy Aspíllaga family at its Cayaltí *hacienda*, and a couple of years after that as part of a committee evaluating the agrarian reform program of the Revolutionary Government of the Armed Forces. The cane laborers were still there, with the same submissive gesture, not knowing exactly what the Revolution expected of them. And I continued to be possessed by a sense of unresolved guilt for having participated, indirectly, in the expropriation of the Cayaltí *hacienda*, and thus having betrayed my loyalty to the class that should have placed me on the side of the large landowners and not in the ranks of the peons and their military defenders. It's true, my father was the artistic jewelry maker, the refined Italian who with his creations of gold and precious stones attended to the tastes of the country's oligarchy, but whose bond and responsibility lay elsewhere, and at home we understood this without need of explanation.

I think it took us another day to travel by car from Chiclayo to Lima. In Pasamayo, near the northern entrance to Lima, Papá once again sent out persuasive signals about his wife Rita and his children Luis and Chiara being my new family now. During those last miles of Pan-American Highway approaching Lima, in the back seat of that huge American car, surprised by the vision of hundreds of exotic faces, automobiles shiny as Sunday shoes or decaying in heaps, and big windowless streetcars that made seafaring sounds, I no longer remember if I could discern a pathway between the seduction of the new and the rapidly fading past that up to then had been my only existence.

The doorman of the white multi-story building on Colmena Derecha[4] was black and wore a black uniform. The elevator was much more modern than the elevators in Turin or Genova I had seen growing up, and the house that opened out beyond the third-floor door was a sublime mansion in my eyes. Rita, Luis—from that moment on he would always be Gigi—and Chiara were waiting with a mix of smiles, languages, and accents I couldn't grasp. Was it the Genovese of my infancy? An immigrant Italian? Was it Lima's Spanish spoken rapidly and without its final s's, that I would discover over the next few months? Or was it, rather, the uncertain combination of contested emotions, doubts, regrets, shames, and hopes that overwhelmed that initial meeting, imbuing it with a sense of drama that made it a bit unreal, even humorous? Rita was shorter than my mother Pina. Gigi and Chiara were as blond as my sister Ilaria, and Doña María, the nursemaid who accompanied my Peruvian family for the next thirty years, had a lovely olive colored smile that made me think of my half-sister Giliola. Papá—more than a patriarch—seemed like an orchestra director intent upon smoothing over any possible dissonance. And so, on that summer night in Lima, my new American life began.

4. Colmena Derecha was the popular name for Nicolás de Piérola Avenue. That part of "modern" downtown Lima had the earliest tall buildings of more than four floors, perhaps six or eight, considered skyscrapers at that time. And so, people started to call that part of the Avenida "the right side of the colmena", or beehive, where many people lived in close proximity.

Casaregis Beneath the Bombs

🜊

MY OTHER, EUROPEAN, LIFE had begun in Italy, in Genoa where I was born at the end of July 1939, of a Turinese mother and Genovese father. For the next sixteen years, I had no father.

I know little about my early ancestors, and not much more about the more recent ones, although the Fascist bureaucrat who attended to my father Luigi when he went to record my birth at the civil registry in Genoa claimed to know more than my father about our family's origin. My father says that when he put my name down as Stefano Carlo Varese, the man announced triumphantly: "Jew Race!" In the fall of 1938, Benito Mussolini's Fascist regime, with the reigning house of Saboya's consent, had dictated its first measures against Italian Jews. In July of that same year, in servile submission to the policies of Nazi Germany, several pens in Fascist service had promulgated the deplorable manifesto on racial purity, followed by more systemic efforts to provide historic and "scientific" underpinnings to the supposed "purity of an Italian race of totally Aryan origins."

By the summer of 1939, that shameful anti-Semitic legislation was complete. And the Italian and Genovese world received me with those laws on their books. When my father responded that, as far as he knew, we were a Catholic family, the bureaucrat replied: "But think about the Varese clothing store, over there on Scurería Street by the port: that's the Jew Varese's store!" He was talking about my father's father, my grandfather Cesare, whom I barely remember with his round glasses and timid smile.

Once in Peru, Papá told us that he had to go to the city archives and look up the Varese family genealogy and that of his Lombardic mother, Amelia Guerci-Lena, of noble extraction, as far as possible all the way back to the 18th century. I have never seen my original birth certificate, but I don't think

Grandmother Amelia and grandfather Cesare,
Genoa, circa 1930

it bore the infamous note "Of Jew Race," which on the other hand appears on those of thousands of Italians with surnames such as Levi, Segre, Montalcini, Fermi, Modigliani, Padova, or Mantova, denouncing their possible Jewish origins.

Varese, like other Jewish Italian surnames, is the name of a northern Italian city. Names of geographical places were taken by Sephardic Jews when they arrived in the north of Italy after their expulsion from the Iberian Peninsula. Perhaps that little Fascist bureaucrat was more educated than Papá thought. My memory of this anecdote holds a bitter irony because the cousins of Rita, my father's second wife, who were most probably not Jews, ended up in Nazi forced labor and extermination camps in Poland. They managed to survive and return to Genoa as toothless skeletons on the verge of death.

The doubts about my possible Jewish ancestry, though, have stayed with me as I've gotten older, and my Greek nose turns ever more toward the south-western Mediterranean, to end up in irrefutable likeness with all good Near Eastern noses, and its comrade earlobes on either side in a definite Semitic aesthetic. I suspect that my mother Giuseppina—Pina as everyone called her—and my father Luigi, rushed to take me to the nearest baptismal font at who knows what Genoa church to give me up to the Holy Mother Church and make of my small body and flaming spirit a good receptacle for Catholicism, thus saving me from the ugly onslaught approaching from Germany to the north.

A newborn, I knew nothing, nor could I imagine any of this terrible history until I was perhaps ten or eleven years old, around 1949 or 1950, when I sought refuge in the bookstore of my maternal grandfather—Nonno Luigi Druetto—and, learning to read, made a huge effort to conquer my dyslexia. I devoured the written versions of the war stories by my grandmother, who was baptized Massaua by her railway-man father. He was anticlerical and a "colonizer" of Abyssinia, and had her re-baptized Margherita by the priest who would later marry her to my grandfather Luigi. Nonna Massa—that's what her husband called her—practiced her Garibaldi-style anticlericalism by way of humor and raunchy jokes that told tales of priests and nuns more given to eroticism than mysticism and with generous invitations to enjoy that wine that was so good for you precisely because it was " . . . the blood of Christ."

In my childhood imagination, Nonna Massa's anticlericalism seemed like a sort of tacit allegiance to Judaism and, without doubt, to Nonno Luigi's antifascism. For months, he'd hidden in the *infernetto*—the bookstore's subcellar—a legendary Jewish man whose name could not be mentioned even once the war ended. But Il Nonno, with the discrete generosity of an ex-socialist turned "liberal," had also made room in that same basement, and given work as well, to Frantz, a thin and pale German soldier who remained in Piemonte behind the enemy lines.

I remember Frantz well, working in the bookstore, carrying piles of books from one place to another, speaking an Italian that seemed as grotesque as it did mysterious to my eight-year-old ears. The image and memory of soldier Frantz of the German Wehrmacht grew to immense proportions in my mind when, at one of the Christmases right after the war, my mother and maybe also I Nonni gave me a German war rifle with its barrel opportunely plugged. I immediately identified it as the rifle that had belonged to Frantz, the German soldier who was doubly a traitor: to the Third Reich, for having deserted, and for having sought refuge in the shop of an ex-socialist protector of Jews.

Among all these retrieved memories, and the versions I have been able to glean from my older siblings, I now come across some archetypical Italian images and flavors inculcated in me by Nonna Massa. "Stefi—she would say in her Turin dialect—go down to the cellar and fill these bottles with red wine. And whistle the whole time you're down there!"

My grandparents bought wine in great round glass demijohns, wrapped in straw and with a large cork. I had to pour the wine into bottles—*fiaschi*—to serve at the table. I loved doing this because of its social prestige as much as for its technical challenge. I descended into the basement with the bottles, a red rubber hose, and a well-tuned whistle that even today issues from the right side of my lips. My tacit agreement with Nonna Massa was that the only time I would stop whistling was when I had to breathe in air, so I could transfer the wine to the *fiasco*. My love of good wine and my whistle have remained with me to this day, in a kind of recurrent commemoration of my grandmother Massa.

IN 1939, MY FATHER must have been thirty-two when the German army invaded the Czech Republic, and Poland a few months later in September. Mamma, who gave birth to me in July, was twenty-seven, my sister Ilaria was two and a half, and my half-sister on my mother's side, Giliola, would have been around nine.

Ilaria and I were born at the house in Genoa, on Via Nizza, and we must have lived there until the middle of 1940, when Mussolini declared war on France and occupied the coastal zone in the southern part of the country. It was the culmination of the Fascist bourgeoisie's imperial dream, that had begun in 1935-1936 with the colonization of Somalia, Eritrea, and Libya, and the military conquest of Abyssinia and Albania, in an effort to revive Italy's colonial empire that the House of Saboya had proposed in 1914 with the annexation of Eritrea.

Between 1940 and 1941, my parents, siblings, and I moved to the apartment on Via Casaregis. I begin to have memories of the tree-lined street and elegant, almost aristocratic palace, and of the apartment that one entered by way of an elevator made of dark wood, etched glass windows, and black wrought iron work that enclosed it in a cage that seemed a bit crude to my child's eyes.

My father Luigi as Captain of the Italian Army,
Prato Sopra la Croce, circa 1942

My memories can't really be from those years, when I was barely two, but from when we returned to that house after the war had ended and I was six. On the other hand, the first house I can evoke with certainty is the one on the Levantine coast of Liguria, the house across the street from Cavi di Lavagna Beach, built on one of those embankments in that region of the Mediterranean coast as generous in cliffs and inlets as it was frugal in flatlands.

Now I suppose that Papá moved us to the house on Cavi sometime in 1942, when the port of Genoa began to suffer bombings by the English naval fleet. I don't think this move by Attorney Luigi Varese Guerci-Lena's family could be called a "*sfollamento*," nor could we be called "*sfollati*," refugees from the war. It must have had more to do with a concession obtained by my mother Pina after the dramatic pressure to which she subjected Papá. Now that I look back, I imagine the arrangement must have had some benefits for my father in his complicated activity as a criminal lawyer, Army captain assigned to Genoa's anti-aircraft guns, and his young secretary's illicit lover.

The few times we left Cavi, we did so on a railway apparatus about which I was passionately enthusiastic. There must be some technical name for that marvelous adult toy which—made to run by two men who raised and lowered a mechanism in the form of a balancing pole—moved it along the train tracks, through black tunnels that served as bomb shelters and homes for the homeless. The platform only had room for a few people and their belongings. For me, those trips, or escapes through the tunnels that protected us from the bombs, were marvelous adventures replete with sudden mysteries that must have been the reasons my mother approached them with such an acute sense of drama, shrieks, cries, and the ulterior narrative that always acquired heightened intensity in Papá's presence.

One morning, Cavi's antiaircraft sirens began their long and undulant lament. Mamma took me by the hand and dragged me running from the house. I think my half-sister Giliola had hold of my other hand. We didn't go along the side street, Via Aurelia, the one built by the Roman emperor, but across a hillside covered in ancient olive trees. Desperately, we ran over that hill, beneath the trees, parallel to the sea where we could begin to make out the English planes. Antiaircraft sirens aren't noise. They are music. It's a sad high-pitched lament that announces a destiny of death or salvation. Those sirens remained engraved in my ears for years, their sound revived by American war movies that began to circulate after the war and that I, as a young boy in Turin, saw every chance I got.

Little by little, the noise of the English planes became one with the music of the sirens and distant explosions. Mamma, in her desperate flight, shouted Ilaria's name, and we would finally see her running toward us on the hill through what must have been one of the town's narrow streets. I clearly remember her two blond braids and skinny legs. The four of us ended up hidden under one of the olive trees until the planes flew by, the siren changed to a more optimistic tone, and the view of blue sea and olive groves showed its friendly face once more. Mamma broke into desperate cries, Ilaria and Giliola too.

I, on the other hand, would have to endure a lesson right there and then about that little boy I'd see with his arm amputated above the elbow because he hadn't taken refuge in time during a bombing. Later we learned that perhaps it hadn't only been bombs that had caused such destruction of hands, faces, arms, and bodies of the region's children, but also those little toys and ballpoint pens that fell from the sky attached to small parachutes launched by the Royal Air Force and finding their way into camps, beaches, and curious hands, exploding when you took them from their cases.

It isn't possible for me to accurately reconstruct the chronology of all that happened during those months we lived on the coast. I know that one day, from atop a stone wall that separated Via Aurelia from the sea, I watched in astonishment as the corpses of sailors that had washed ashore were plucked from the beach. I don't know if they were Italian or English or German. The swollen bodies floated like balloons on the sea's placid and undulating surface. They offered no resistance to the soldiers and townsmen who pulled them in using those long hooks with which they pulled fishing boats to dock. They snagged them by their uniforms and brought them onto the sand in a silent ritual interrupted from time to time by orders barely murmured by those in command, perhaps out of respect for the dead. I don't know why I, a three to four-year-old child, was there observing that ceremony of war.

I suspect that after two years of conflict, people had come to see war realistically, devoid of patriotic rhetoric but rather as the stupid and brutal barbarity it is. Mamma, despite her innate propensity for drama, must have resigned herself to allowing us to see and feel the evil in all its crudity, free of Fascism's artifices and propagandistic lies. I don't believe Papá shared Mamma's educational bent in this respect, as much because of his bourgeois background as because of his passive adhesion to Fascism's reasons for going to war.

On the other hand, Zia Gina, my mother's younger sister and wife of Colonel Franco Angioni, who had by then joined the Allied Army, professed a basically practical and opportunistic idea of war's educational value. One night when aunt Gina and her two sons were with us at the Cavi house, we heard a banging on the door. I have a clear recollection of Mamma going to open it, and seeing, from the floor where I was playing with some little toy soldiers, three German military men, possibly officers, with their green uniforms and polished black boots, standing at attention and asking permission to enter. Coincidentally, a German apple strudel sat on the table. I remember very well aunt Gina telling me to take one of my green toy tanks with the Nazi cross painted on its sides, a tank simulating one from the German Panzer Divisionen, and roll it across the floor.

For years, I thought those German officers had just happened to come to the home of two beautiful Italian women—aunt Gina was particularly good-looking with her blond hair and a body I admired even as a child—and not by invitation. But the apple cake gave the plan away. I remember feeling a certain sense of fear that night, perhaps more because of the excessive physical presence of those elegantly uniformed men than for the discretely seductive role they played as members of an occupying army.

From that same stone wall that circled the house, or maybe another, I was involved one day in one of my efforts to imitate my older sister Ilaria. I fell to the ground on my head, and all I remember is coming to in a darkened room, voices murmuring who knows what prayers, damp cloths on my forehead, and the slow return from some distant and nebulous consciousness to which I have gone over decades due to migraines and vertigo.

I didn't make the connection until much later, in the early 1980s, when a homeopathic doctor in Oaxaca, whose reputation is seriously questioned by the city's reasonable inhabitants, held a pendulum over my forehead, and concentrated with closed eyes as it followed its circular motion. Then he said: "You suffered a fall as a child, causing severe damage to your head. You had a cerebral concussion. I am going to cure your migraines." And, indeed, he did. But he was unable to cure the vertigo I suffer to the present, or the malignant cancer that one day decided to take up residence in my organism to remind me of human frailty. Or maybe it wasn't that homeopathic doctor's inability in the face of those two ills, but rather my lack of faith in his therapeutic powers when confronted with the catastrophic ideology that in our culture accompanies illnesses as pernicious as cancer.

Around 2000, already living in California, my endemic vertigo and occasional migraines conspired to express themselves less painfully but more menacingly. It was a young doctor at the University of California—Davis who told me, with his grave German accent, that what I was experiencing as rhythmic blues in my left ear, was a fistula. If it was situated in my brain, it would have to be sealed off so it couldn't develop into an embolism. If, on the other hand, it was located on the brain's outer wall, it could coexist with me in some sort of friendly relationship for the rest of my days. The fistula chose the second option.

Friend fistula
I thank you for my years of vertigo
This new circular time
And the calm rhythm that puts me to sleep and wakes me
And the memory of future, its circular finite and infinite
And more than anything, friend fistula, I humbly salute your sincere voice.

ON SEPTEMBER 3, 1943, the Allies landed in southern Italy. On the 8th, Italy surrendered, the Germans established their defensive Gustav-line south of Rome and declared those officers and soldiers who had given up to the Allies to be their enemies. The Italian officers and soldiers who remained close to the German lines were captured, deported, and a majority executed by Wehrmacht and SS troops.

My uncle Franco Brivio, whom I would get to know years later in Peru, managed to escape on a Croatian fishing vessel and, crossing the Adriatic Sea, make it to a place just south of the city of Bari, behind the Allied lines. It was on this flight that Franco began to establish himself as a great fisherman, surviving that crossing by eating the fish he captured by throwing well-aimed hand grenades into the sea.

There, in southern Italy, fighting with the Allies, was my other uncle, also named Franco but of surname Angioni, a Sardinian career officer and artillery colonel who wore the Royal British Army uniform. I met Colonel Franco, the father of my cousins Paolo and Stefano (whom we called Nené), in 1945 when he arrived in Turin riding an American jeep, with his chauffer and military assistant, wearing the stunning Allied Forces uniform and the arrogance of a career officer who had survived several battlefields, the Saboya monarchy, and the Fascist takeover that had trained him as an officer in defense of the Imperio del Fascio.

At the beginning of June 1943, the Allies got to Rome after defeating, in long and bloody battles, those German troops that continued to resist, retreating slowly toward the northern part of the country. Mussolini, freed from prison by German SS parachutists, reorganized his government in the north, establishing the "Italian Social Republic." This was known as the Saló Republic. There he joined the Germans in their war against the Allies, especially the civil war against *i partigiani* (the partisans). All of Italy threw itself into a delirium of terror and barbarity.

Cavi di Lavagna, situated along the Via Aurelia—the imperial Roman road linking Rome with the lands of Gaul—was about to become a difficult and dangerous place. Both the retiring German troops and advancing Allies would pass that way, bombing bridges and buildings and counting on the partisans' sabotage. German and Fascist reprisals came quickly, against the partisans and anyone suspected of supporting them. The terrifying news of Rome's Ardeatina Trenches had arrived. It is possible that people had also heard of the massacre in Boves, a town on the border between Piemonte and Liguria, where an SS colonel had ordered ferocious punishment for those suspected of helping a small group of partisans. The entire town was destroyed and burned, and the people, including the priest, murdered. News came via the airwaves, and I remember Papá's order never to tune into the BBC again.

At the beginning of 1943, Papá moved the whole family to Prato sopra la

Partigiano friend of my mother Pina murdered by
Nazi-Fascists, Prato Sopra la Croce, circa 1942-43

Croce, a small village deep in the Ligurian Alps, reachable only by corriera—
bus—or truck. The house that received us—and this time truly as sfollati
(refugees)—was made of stone and wood with a roof of pietra di lavagna, the
flat black slate used as roofing in Italy's northern mountains.

I began my second wartime childhood in this lonely village, surrounded by
chestnut trees, narrow streets of stone and mud, and pathways filled with poi-
sonous nettles. Those pathways wound into the mountains along streams that
meandered toward other mysterious forests where *i partigiani* lived: those
tall young men, some with coarse beards and others with blond hair and blue
eyes, like the son of one of Mamma's friends who died just then at the hands
of the Germans and whose black and white photograph I still retain in some
memory box.

From time to time, the partisans would come to the house to ask for food
in exchange for the English parachutes of smooth white silk that Mamma
would hide under the pile of wood she used for cooking and keeping us warm.
Later she would dig those parachutes out and use them to make us boxer
shorts. But only boxer shorts: secret garments hidden from German or Fas-

My father Luigi visiting us in Prato Sopra
la Croce, circa 1943

cist eyes. I felt a certain pride in that invisible anti-Fascist and rebel uniform linking me with those mysterious men of the forest.

Papá would sometimes arrive on his bicycle from the nearest town, Borzonasca, from which there was still bus or truck service to Genoa. I remember those arrivals well: festive for me, Ilaria and Giliola, and a bit recriminatory for Mamma because she must have suspected the relationship developing between him and his secretary, the youthful Rita Scotto Ivaldi.

Years later I learned that Papá traveled with two *lasciapassare* (identity cards), the official one issued by the German Fascists and another "illegal" one from the partisans. Knowing his legendary state of distraction—a trait I inherited—I've often asked myself how it was that he never made the mistake of showing the Germans the partisan *lasciapassare* or the Fascists the guerrilla one.

But he always arrived safe and sound, bringing with him some food, delicious precisely because it was so scarce. One morsel I remember well, not for its taste but because we happened to be eating it when Mamma heard the planes and, with her customary drama, made us leave the house and go into the forest. Papá argued that there was nothing to bomb in Prato sopra la Croce, so why were we interrupting our meal. In the long run, for Attorney Luigi Varese Guerci-Lena there was a certain etiquette that had to be preserved, even in moments of crisis. I remember we ended up eating those splendid potatoes with basil garlic pesto beneath the chestnut trees in a kind of picnic forced by the rigors of war.

I LOST MY INNOCENCE twice in Prato. The first time when I came home one afternoon after the village children and I had been playing at tossing live machinegun and rifle shells at a fire in the forest. Distracted by the feeling of excitement caused by the explosions, I didn't notice that one of those kids had stolen my shoelaces—a priceless commodity in that time of scarcity—perhaps with the intention of taking the shoes as well. I managed to begin the walk home when I heard piercing screams.

I ran as fast as I could in my unsure shoes, trying to distance myself from those screams and reach my house, when I tripped on the opening to a *cortile di campagna*, a passageway as we would call it in Mexico. I remember it very well, its floor of mud and stones, with two-story houses on either side constructed of stone and lavagna, black coals piled in one corner and a group of people standing around a thick plank to which a pink-skinned pig was tied, gushing blood from its recently slit throat. There was a metal bucket filling with blood, around which women and children were moving excitedly, almost dancing with joy. I stopped, immobilized for a few seconds, long enough so those images and their sounds remain engraved forever in my unconscious. I got home, minus my shoelaces, guilty of having taken part in the explosion of unspent shells, and deeply hurt by that vision of barbarous slaughter in which—I was beginning to believe—I had participated.

My second loss of innocence took place a few months later when two young girls from Prato, maybe twelve or a little older, took me by the hand and led me into the chestnut forest that ran up hill behind our house. There, laying on the grass, the two girls accompanied my naïve fingers over their undeveloped places, while they caressed that part of my own body whose awakening I had already discovered. With inspiring erotic elegance, the girls had me smell my exploratory fingers, insisting, I believe, in the aphrodisiac qualities of aroma therapy. I suppose I remained a virgin, and those two initiators of my sex life found the adventure wanting, since they never again invited me anywhere after that afternoon.

In my travels through nostalgia, I sometimes stumble on that pathway of nettles, the two young girls in the chestnut forest and an immense sadness at the death—announced by its screams—of that animal of opaque but rosy skin spilling its blood and life into the peasant bucket. I never returned to Prato, to the stone house with its wood-burning stove and ash-covered washstand—there was no soap during the war—or to the British parachutes hidden beneath the woodpile and those infantile skirts and pants. I refused my sister Ilaria's invitation to accompany her when, a few years back, she returned to the village in search of forgotten memories.

For me the war must have passed in relative indolence in that corner of the Ligurian mountains. For Mamma and my sisters, it was a different story. One day Ilaria and Giliola set out running with me to the village's little main square. A small military ambulance had arrived and several wounded emerged, among them Mamma, walking with crutches and dragging one leg enveloped in bandages. The *corriera* in which she was riding from Genoa on her return to Prato had taken a direct hit from some allied shells and Mamma, along with the other passengers, had thrown themselves into the roadside ditch for protection.

That sight of Mamma as one of the "war wounded" coming out of a military ambulance was an event of epic proportions in the midst of my usual rural tedium.

NOW THE WAR WAS real for me. It was palpable not only in the image of that green and white ambulance with its large red cross, and in Mamma's injured leg and crutches, but also in the rumors that began to circulate around Prato and which Mamma's grandiose stories confirmed.

Advancing upon northern Italy, already close to our village, was an army of black soldiers—Africans or Moroccans or Algerians, in any case black—sent by the Allies as a vanguard force to punish the Italians. Young women would be their initial targets. My sister Giliola, thirteen or fourteen, with her long black braids and olive skin, would naturally be the African 'barbarians' first victim. And so, with the proverbial African and maternal sword of Damocles threatening, Giliola had to spend the last weeks of our time in Prato living in closely watched vigilance as she feared savagery.

It wasn't the black hordes catching up with us in Prato, but our whole family that, in May or June of 1945, came out of hiding and arrived on the Levantine coast, at Cavi di Lavagna, where we met up with the Allied troops.

In Cavi, seated on the stone wall of my earliest memories, my sisters and I began a long, shy friendship with, and inexplicable admiration for, those soldiers: black, blonde, mulatto, North African, and Brazilian, who gave us unimaginable and exotic morsels to eat. Chewing gum. Chocolate bars. The strange and mysterious sweet and salty taste of peanuts, those nuts with which I fell in love, and that would accompany me throughout my life. The first cans we saw and heard, with their muffled sound and the whoosh of tired air escaping to entice our childhood hunger. Engraved on my infantile mind is the image of a huge black soldier in his U.S. Army uniform, seated beside me on the wall, trying to teach me the secrets of chewing gum. An immense and friendly mouth, with its crown of white teeth, the red tongue that seemed to have a life of its own as it transformed the gum into a complacent wad of sugar and mint.

During those days in liberated Cavi I think I learned my first lessons in The American Way of Life. I fell in love with those soldiers, their uniforms, jeeps, height, smiles, friendship—who knows if simulated or sincere—and, without being aware of it, their music. I would reconnect with this love years later in my passion for jazz and, later still, for a variety of Afro-Latin American musical genres I must have heard hummed or whistled by some Brazilian or American soldier on that wall in Cavi de Lavagna.

CHAPTER 4

Vita Nuova

𓆎

I SPENT THE FIRST SUMMER of my life in the southern hemisphere between the beaches of Lima, the spas of the Sur Chico coast, and the cultivation of laziness in the streets of Miraflores and San Isidro. I had no plan to do anything useful or particularly creative. I only wanted to travel, go fishing with my new cousin Marco, and pal around with his sister Maura who, young as she was, fell in love right away with the exotic guy who couldn't yet speak Spanish.

I lounged naively through those months of sun, heat, and blue sky I still imagined to be eternal in these southern tropics. I didn't understand why my new extended family of Italian immigrants was so intent upon absorbing the sun and heat, and why they already seemed so nostalgic about a blue sky that would soon turn to gunmetal gray saturated with cold humidity (Lima's drizzle), that indifferent rain that soaks without wetting and penetrates one's bones with its unrealized fantasy of becoming the sort of rain that falls upon all normal geography.

"I'VE TOLD YOU, STEFANO — my father said—, the Incas instructed Francisco Pizarro to build Lima on the shores of the *río hablador*, the Rimac River, more or less close to the Pacific Ocean but inland enough to avoid God Pachacamac's rage. That little island of rock and sand off Lima's southern beaches is Pachacamac, a god who rests calmly in the sea since the beginning of time, awaiting the return of the other gods. The Spanish invaders gave the Incas this advice — my father continued — that is revealed in the curse of having to live in this colonial city with its insufferable climate and depressing temperament." Seven years later, in 1964, the Peruvian writer Sebastián Salazar Bondy published his *Lima la horrible*, a book in which he painted to perfection that cursed Indigenous wisdom and the eternal complaints of European invaders and their creole descendants.

March marks the end of the coastal summer, the beginning of winter, and the new school year. My brother Gigi would return to grade school at the Pestalozzi Swiss School, and Chiara, if I remember correctly, attended some sort of school-like crèche or stayed at home with her *nana* María and mother Rita. The educational crisis of my Peruvian half-siblings began to reveal to me my father's deeply-rooted Catholic culture as well as his commitment to a permanent, critical, and secular experience.

Rita and Papá wanted to enroll Gigi at the Jesuit school, an institution with a good academic reputation that was also close to home. But one of its requirements was insurmountable. There was no certificate attesting to his parents having been married in the Church. Papá was a bigamist and Rita a simple concubine. There wasn't another religious school in Lima, or all of Peru, that would accept "children born of sin." On the other hand, the Pestalozzi Swiss School, as well as the German Humboldt, the English Markham, or U.S. Roosevelt, although firmly on the periphery of Western Christianity, had accepted the idea that the Middle Ages had ended and the gains of the French Revolution and Enlightenment were here to stay, not only in institutions but in people's consciousness.

With the beginning of the school year I began to experience a certain discomfort. All my numerous cousins on my stepmother Rita's side were in primary or secondary school by now, and some, like Marco, were already preparing themselves to go to the university, while I took refuge in my failed Italian education. I countered my father's insistence that I study with a fabricated passion for work, any sort of work. In Turin I had been forced to repeat the third year of secondary school when I failed Latin. Then I failed another year in the program at an Institute of Business Administration (*ragioneria*), this time because I couldn't pass mathematics and accounting, two courses I hated with a vengeance. My mother and paternal grandfather Luigi had wanted to turn me into an illustrious bookseller and businessman.

It was my father, with his Italian formation as a criminal lawyer and student of Roman Law and Philosophy of the Law, and above all with his passion for intellectual work and the arts, who was finally able to very subtly point me back to the classroom.

IT WAS IN APRIL, I think, that I began a deliberate program of work and study of the Spanish language with a student from the Jesuit School, a young man by the name of Manuel Calcagno. He was the son of a Chilean opera singer and a very good teacher of Spanish as spoken in Peru, as well as of Peruvian literature.

With an excellent pedagogical sense, Manuel alternated between Peruvian and Spanish literature and comic strips, those illustrated weekly children's stories, including the Chilean Condorito, the U.S. Little Lulu and, if I remember correctly, translated versions of Donald Duck and Mickey Mouse. Perhaps, little by little and without realizing it, I was being colonized by Yankee imperialism, as Armand Mattelart and Ariel Dorfman would argue fifteen years later in their book *How to Read Donald Duck* (1971).

As a result of those months of reading and conversing with Manuel, the Spanish language took possession of me to the extent that it became my second "mother tongue," claiming superiority over my Italian (Mamma's Piedmont dialect and Papá's and Rita's Genovese speech), the French I had studied as a child in Turin and the Aosta Valley when I went skiing with the Alpine soldiers, and the English I'd learned on my summer trips to England.

The house in Lima, nevertheless, was a truly polyglot space in my new intellectual life. My father and his wife spoke Italian to one another and zeniese (Genovese) when they didn't want the children to understand. They alternated between speaking Spanish and Italian with us, and read books, magazines, and newspapers in Spanish, Italian, and French.

CHAPTER 5

My *Linguas Francas*

卐

I N PERU, THERE ARE regional Spanish dialects—the languages of the
Kingdom of Castile and Aragon—brought over by the Spanish invaders
in the sixteenth century. I thought that in Spain, and therefore throughout Latin America, one unified and standardized Spanish was spoken. As I
progressed in learning the language, I discovered the great diversity of dialects
that existed in the country, and the profound influence Andean Quechua had
on regional accents as well as on the general lexicon and even the grammat-
ical structure. Little by little I found out that there were other Indigenous
languages, but I didn't yet possess the intellectual instruments I needed to
decipher such an intriguing and provocative panorama. Manuel helped me
as much as he was able, and my father—a practical man—took my siblings,
Rita, and me on explorations of that profound and marginalized country.

At least twice we traveled to the Tingo María jungle, on the Huallaga
River, journeying downriver in astonishment aboard a raft made of balsa
wood trunks and guided by two jungle river men who stopped on lonely
beaches to hunt, fish, and gather wild fruits. There, along the banks of that
river, I discovered people I'd never seen before, unexpected faces, accents I
hadn't heard, and even perhaps whole languages I didn't know.

Tingo María was the region where my father, just arrived from Italy in
the mid 1940s, had tried to become a *chacarero*, a jungle farmer. He and my
Uncle Franco, the sailor, had purchased several hectares of high Amazon forest in the Cordillera Azul (blue range). The land already had some planted
tea brought over at the beginning of the twentieth century by earlier Italian
immigrants.

That Italian tea plantation in Tingo María never really prospered. It didn't
even manage the modest success achieved by those groups of Austrians, Ger-

mans, and White Russians, who lived in Posuzo, Villarica, and Oxapampa, and who subsist today with their little Tyrolean-style houses, fabulous marmalades and honeys, cheeses and breads, and the blue eyes and blond hair that show up from time to time in some of the Amusha (Yánesha) and Campa (Asháninka) children.[5]

My father and uncle's agricultural endeavor failed miserably. The two Studebaker trucks that were supposed to transport material and merchandise between Lima and the Cordillera Azul couldn't withstand the Carretera Central with its immense potholes, rivers of mud, landslides from the hills—the famous Andean *huaicos*—and the foul moods of the Peruvian truck drivers and mechanics who insisted on humanizing industrial products to the point where these eventually accepted their condition and declared themselves sick, tired, and ready for retirement.

Furthermore, someone had convinced my father and Uncle Franco that raising Dutch pigs would be a thriving business. Attorney Varese and sailor Franco embarked on an adventure that ended up being a duel to the death between an Amazonian jaguar—possibly ancient, toothless, and without the strength to hunt—and the piglets that fed the jaguar and his descendants for a couple of years. Somewhere I have a photo of Uncle Franco with a 16-caliber rifle cradled in his arms, sitting on a river rock waiting for a jaguar who was too intelligent to come out in broad daylight to be killed by an Italian sailor.

That attempt to "colonize" the Cordillera Azul jungle failed, but my father confessed that his best years in Peru had been in the Amazon.

Later my Uncle Franco found another passion for adventure on Peru's Pacific coast where, whenever possible, he drove his small Volkswagen across the sandy dunes of Paracas and the Nazca desert.

I had already left Peru when my cousin Marco wrote to tell me my uncle and his car had disappeared for several days. When his children and wife, Elda, a devotee of the miraculous Father Pío, thought only divine intervention could bring him back, the miracle occurred: Franco and his car found their way east once more, by way of the very Catholic Pan-American Highway.

5. Asháninka is the self-denomination while Campa is the name used by other Peruvians. The same occurs with other Indigenous names like Amuesha / Yánesha, Aguaruna / Awajún, among others. In the first mention of the specific Indigenous people we will show both denominations; in the following mentions we will use only the self-denomination.

LONGING FOR THE JUNGLE, Papá took us on those nostalgic and didactic trips that made us fall in love with Peru and with people ignored by those who lived in Lima and were "rediscovered" by the Genovese attorney Luis Varese Guerci-Lena and his offspring.

After several days on a raft, floating on the Huallaga River's slow current, and cool nights camped on solitary beaches, we arrived at Puerto Tocache, a small village with houses on stilts and roofs made of palm leaves, or *shapaja*.

One of my father's old friends welcomed us with smiling hospitality. I think his name was Leoncio del Águila. We stayed a couple of days at his house without electricity, lit only by Coleman oil lamps, and connected to the world by a shortwave radio that continually broadcast international news. Leoncio del Águila and my father talked about international events and culture.

The floor of the hut was piled high with copies of magazines, from *Life* to others from the People's Republic of China and the Soviet Union. Because I knew nothing of Peruvian intellectual life at the time, I don't remember the names of the books, but imagine that in those piles and in those bookcases there must have been works by José Carlos Mariátegui, Luis E. Valcárcel, Julio C. Tello, perhaps a novel by Ciro Alegría or López Albujar's short stories, and the anarchist writings of Manuel González Prada. There may even have been Spanish translations of V.I. Lenin, Karl Marx, and Friedrich Engels, because they circulated freely and cheaply at the time, thanks to the Communist International's post-Stalinist propaganda machine.

Back then my father wasn't exactly a leftist, much less a socialist, but a practicing Catholic with a sense of social justice and compassion symptomatic of his upper-class education. We didn't talk about these things on our journeys, except with Rita who, because of her more working-class background (she was the daughter of a trade unionist who worked at the Genoa port), always insisted on imbuing every conversation about Peru with a social and mystical tone.

From the little village of Tocache, it was at least a two-hour trip along a trail cut through the forest. We had a horse or mule to carry our things. When we arrived at Uchiza, we boarded a twin-engine plane for Tingo María. These trips along the upper Huallaga, by river raft and land, whet my curiosity for the Amazon and its wilderness. I was intrigued by what was hidden in these mountains and by who lived along these rivers. Were they Indians? And where did they come from? What lay beyond each small tributary that flowed into the Huallaga?

Once back in "Lima the horrible," all I wanted to do was take off again, continue exploring this new country that was so different from the lands of my childhood, and get to know more of its peoples and their history. A year after my arrival in Peru, I think I could speak Spanish fluently, read it, and was beginning to write it without too many errors. It would soon be time for me to give serious thought to my studies.

ADDED TO THE POLYPHONY of the country's languages and those we spoke at home, was a musical range that increased and broadened when Gigi and Chiara reached puberty. From Italy, I had brought my passion for modern jazz and the crazy illusion that I might one day learn to play the trumpet like Chet Baker.

My father played a decent classical piano and the accordion when he performed popular tunes from Liguria and Italy. But his real interest was Baroque music and opera. When he got home from work or on weekends, he would play Debussy, Mozart, and occasional operatic arias. In all the living rooms of all the houses we inhabited in Lima, the record player was always available for any type of music we wanted to hear, except for the musical storm provoked by the Beatles that my brother Gigi, with certain tact, added to Papá's repertoire of Puccini and Verdi.

Peruvian creole music and the Afro-Peruvian tones of the coast arrived with Gigi and Chiara and a friend of theirs who played the guitar and rhythm box. I made my own contribution with a mix of jazz on some friend's recorder or rhythm instrument. Finally, during the Velasco Revolution of the first half of the seventies, Andean music erupted in the house, implanting its joyous nostalgia on my consciousness. It is hard for me now to think of the Peru I learned to love during those years, without evoking the Andean pentatonic scale.

It may be my fear of performance, even for family and friends, that got in the way of my learning to play music. I can recall melodies and reproduce them in my mind. I can whistle them, sing them, tap them out on my fingers, and improvise musical themes in the manner of modern jazz. But I could never really learn to read music, much less play it.

Perhaps this a left-brain limitation, the problem of dealing with the familiar. Or perhaps it is due to the overdevelopment of my right hemisphere, which continually commits itself to new experiences: music, words, never-before-seen images. Because I do not recognize them, I have nothing with which to compare them, and keep them carefully until I can place them in the archive I know, the left hemisphere, from which, at the opportune moment—for example, when I might want to learn to play a musical instrument—I can retrieve, assess, analyze, and transform them into rational utilitarian knowledge. C. G. Jung, whom I began reading in Italian back then, said that "all cognition is recognition."

Today, in my later years, I realize that I owe the best and most enjoyable aspects of my intellectual and creative life to the right side of my brain. It has always pushed my mind toward the abyss of the unknown, and to the delight of recognition.

I HAD MY FIRST trumpet teacher in Turin, when I was fifteen. On those cold dark Turinese winter afternoons when I got out of school each day, I would go to a record store exactly two blocks from the apartment building at Via Pietro Micca No 20, where I lived with my maternal grandparents.

At that store, lacking enough money to buy even one little 45 rpm album—those records with a single song on either side—I pretended I was looking for something that didn't exist while shoppers with more money listened to the musical selections of their choice. The young employee must have taken pity on me, because in a matter of weeks we had developed a friendship that prompted him to offer me trumpet lessons. Without a lire to pay for the classes, or a trumpet on which to practice, I can no longer remember how I got ahold of an old instrument and was able to take those classes the young man must have given me free of charge. It might have been my half-sister Giliola, older now and on her own, who helped me out with her modest nurse's salary. A few months later, the young jazz teacher left for the United Sates, and I imagined he was going in search of Dizzy Gillespie or Miles Davis. The truth, which I eventually learned through my sister's friends, is that he had gone to study nuclear physics.

When I traveled to Peru, I left that Italian trumpet at my grandparents' house, and I suspect my mother, years after my betrayal, must have sold it to a musician more talented than her son Stefano, or given it to the Santa Teresa parish for some orphan child.

The Peruvian trumpet appeared in Lima a few years later, as part of my father and his wife Rita's plan to seduce Stefano to stay in Peru. Without being aware of its nature as a bribe, and with the shiny gold instrument in hand, I went twice a week to the simple apartment of an animated musician named Willy Marambio. He was Chilean, but a devotee of Afro-Cuban music with a limited grasp of pedagogy. In time, I resigned myself to stop trying to be a musician. I gave up the trumpet and the classical flute that I'd purchased in a burst of optimism during a week I spent in the United States, and which I keep among my books in its closed case, as inscrutable as it is challenging.

My wife Linda, headstrong as her Nordic culture commands, every so often suggests names of flute teachers and mentions the psycho-philosophic benefits of not giving up.

CHAPTER 6

Of Trains and Ships

🌀

I NEVER LIKED THE TRAIN that ran from Genoa to Turin on those dark Italian winter evenings. An ex-employee of Uncle Carlo's clothing store somberly took Ilaria and me to Turin's Porta Nuova station. I must have been eight and Ilaria ten. I didn't understand why we had to go with this boring man instead of with Papá when we went to see distant and unfamiliar grandparents at an old house like a cold and solemn palace in a city shrouded in fog.

That was the beginning of my feelings of banishment and my sense of loneliness at not living with Papá and Mamma in a place of our own.

On Sunday, January 12th, 1947, Attorney Luigi Varese Guerci-Lena and Miss Rita Scotto Ivaldi left the port city of Genoa on the SS/Andrea Doria and headed to Buenos Aires, Argentina.

Rita, the young secretary/lover, wrote her impressions of the trip in a 1947 appointment book in which each day she included an Italian recipe adapted—according to the introductory explanation—to post-war scarcity. I think it was my brother Cecco, or maybe Gigi, who discovered that travel diary, photocopied it, and many years later gave it to me along with a photograph of my father Luigi and stepmother Rita.

From today's perspective, Rita's notes during that journey's early days display a certain cruelty. It is like looking at the scar Papá's treasonous abandonment left on the memories of our mother Pina and we who were their children.

In those brief notes, one can read the agony of leaving Italy and family members. There are complaints about the lack of privacy on that humble post-war transatlantic steamship, where two lovers could not sleep together and where, above all, one was anguished at not knowing what awaited on the

34

With my sister Ilaria in Genoa when our father left us, Genoa, circa 1947

other side of the ocean. What is heartful in these notes, however, is what is not said: there isn't a single mention of ten-year-old Ilaria, eight-year-old Stefano, or Giliola, the stepdaughter of sixteen.

What for me, ten years later, was a journey of discovery and perhaps even adventure, was a risky exile for Rita, wrapped in a fog of blameless passion.

CHAPTER 7

Via Pietro Micca

꩜

*Pietro Micca, Savoyan bricklayer and soldier who sacrificed himself in 1706 defending
the city of Turin from French invaders by dynamiting its underground access, and died
alongside the French soldiers. A revisionist history claims that Pietro Micca made a
mistake by cutting the fuse too short.*
—(My apochryphal revisionist history of the city of Turin)

M Y MATERNAL GRANDPARENTS' HOUSE in Turin was never
home to me or Ilaria, nor would it ever again be Mamma's.
One could access the apartment on the fourth floor of the 19th
century palace on Pietro Micca by way of an elevator of wood and etched
glass, or an aristocratic staircase rising from the "noble" or second floor to the
fifth-floor loft where, a few weeks after my arrival, I learned the baker lived.
His store was cattycorner from the palace. This was an important discovery
for me as I was the one Nonna Massa asked to go each morning to buy that
day's bread.

The baker, with his long white whiskers and ruddy nose—probably from
all the wine he consumed—treated me with the almost aristocratic respect old
Turinese shopkeepers had for their customers, even if these were children. He
spoke to me in the Turinese dialect—in complicity with my grandparents?—
that I was beginning to understand, although I couldn't respond in kind but
only in my childlike Italian with its Genovese accent.

In time, I think a mutual friendship developed with that baker who became a daily presence in my life. I always knew it was him when I'd hear the
resounding opening and closing of the elevator doors on the fifth floor. I was
especially intrigued by the mysterious connection between that baker and

cockroaches. In Nonna's Piamontes language, she called it the *boia panatera*. I don't know if the more than two million Piamonteses who live in northern Italy and in the Argentinian provinces of Santa Fe and Córdoba, or throughout the rest of Latin America, use this name to describe that insect older than wheat. Nor do I know if Nonna possessed some pre-genome information about the DNA shared by cockroaches and wheat, but the name *boia panatera* remained with me from then on.[6]

By central European standards, the apartment on Pietro Micca was quite large. An entry hall opened into a dining room and kitchen, and then came an ancient toilet room that was long and narrow and terrorized Ilaria with its flushing system which consisted of a high tank and long chain. For months, perhaps years, Ilaria made me pull the chain every time she used that toilet. She thought that if she pulled it, the whole tank would fall from the wall, wounding her fatally. I don't know if Freud would have had something to say about that.

I, on the other hand, developed another neurosis. Aside from systematically wetting my bed every night, I discovered it was easier to go out onto the long balcony that looked over the interior patio and slyly urinate on its stone floor or, occasionally, on more festive winter nights, on the snow that blanketed the patio four stories below. Tattle-telling neighbors put an end to this neurosis, but I was unable to solve the problem of my nocturnal incontinence until I was twelve or thirteen years of age.

Along the left side of the apartment ran the ill-fated balcony with its stone floor and wrought iron railing that began at the entrance, included a small construction called a casotto, and ended outside my grandparents' bedroom. On the right was a long hall, from which several doors of wood and etched glass opened onto three more bedrooms and the bath. Halfway down that hall was a wood stove that Nonna lit each cold winter afternoon and night. On those same evenings, she would read the future by breaking egg-yokes and egg-whites into a glass of water. Nonna Massa interpreted that alchemy early the next morning, when its metamorphosis revealed the space/time relations in our close relative, the hen's fresh egg.

I remember my Grandmother Massa as thin and bony, with crooked legs and an aquiline nose, and as a great cook of Piamontes dishes such as *bagna*

---

6. The root of the word panatera in Piamontese is bread (translator's note).

cauda smothered in garlic and anchovies, polenta in tomato sauce, epic pu-runá, and spring vegetables in dressings of vinegar and herbs. All those dishes were served with red wines.

I think I remember that she was Toscan, born on Isola del Giglio, the small island in the Toscan archipelago that was only a few square miles in size, and had a small number of inhabitants. It had even fewer mountain goats, those animals that, from the time of the Etruscans, had given it its name. My grandmother's father, my maternal great grandfather, had been a machinist on a train, which is why I imagine that as a child Nonna Massa must have emigrated from the island to the continent and from there north to Piamonte, which in those years was a part of Italy's Risorgimento and national unification.[7]

I assume that the *casotto* situated at the beginning of the balcony must have held a toilet in the 19th century back when the building was constructed. It became my favorite hideaway and the castle of my fantasies. It seemed large to me, although it couldn't have measured more than a few square feet. It had an access door on the apartment side, and a window of glazed glass that looked down from the fourth floor.

Once I hid in that *casotto* for an entire day when, in my first year of Jesuit elementary school, they assigned me such an arcane piece of homework that I decided to disappear from the house. No one, not even my mother who came running from the bookstore, thought of looking for me in the *casotto*, where I had taken refuge as I waited for nightfall. My punishment wasn't that severe, but my mother was unable to correctly interpret my anarchical rejection of that "bank employee's education," as Paulo Freire would call it many years later. I developed a deep aversion, which intensified as the years passed, to studying Latin and mathematics, thus sacrificing the valuable time I might have spent reading and fantasizing.

Only one Italian language teacher, Signorina Piccolis in fifth grade, could point me in the direction of writing and creative composition. With a single honest phrase about a text I presented in class, she changed the course of my education and restored the self-confidence that had been stolen from me by rote memorization and curtailment of my fantasy life.

If the *casotto* was my refuge and hideout, the wood stove was favored by Cosí. Cosí (whom my sister Ilaria called Así) was the Siamese cat that lived in

7. Historical period of Italy's unification, between 1848 and 1870.

the kitchen, where we children spent most of our time. Ilaria quickly became the expert at discovering the secrets of that old house that was our new abode. Most important of all was the pantry, where Nonna hid eggs and sugar. Occasionally, Ilaria transformed those treasures into a delicious *zabaglione* covered with merengue made from egg white and devoured with the delight that comes with prohibition.

One lonely and boring afternoon, I discovered another ancient secret when I dared open a large armoire in the hall. In a series of cardboard boxes, I found some battalions of toy soldiers made of painted tin. They represented enigmatic armies and wore unfamiliar uniforms. These belonged to Uncle Gilberto, who must have been a child in the decade of the 1940s when little boys played games commemorating (or celebrating?) World War I. With devotion, my grandparents had saved this material evidence of their son Gilberto's brief life. I think I understood what they meant to them, and never dared play with them.

When we four Vareses arrived as refugees at this house, our grandparents, Uncle Gilberto and Aunt Marcella (Lella), lived there. Gilberto and Lella were my mother Pina's younger brother and sister. In years to come, I understood my grandparents' generosity, and Lella's annoyance; for years, she had been the family princess. Still young, and with a sensual beauty of which she was very aware, Lella must have been a student at the classical high school at the time. She already played the piano and studied German, bodies of knowledge she refined on trips to Germany, from where she once returned with an American soldier and an idea for her university thesis. She wrote a dissertation on the poetry and novels of the Austro-Hungarian Rainer Maria Rilke, which she defended at the School of Philosophy and Letters at the University of Turin. I cannot remember the year.

When I was ten or eleven and in third or fourth grade at a school run by Marist Brothers, puberty hit full force. Two events revealed the mysteries of my sexuality. In one of the school's confessionals, a fat and balding priest ran his sweaty hand over my naked leg without going to the point of "sinning."

Around the same time, I began to look at my Aunt Lella differently from how I had seen her up to then. I think I fell in love with her, and my aunt somehow understood my infatuation; she invited me to move into the bedroom next to hers.

The remorse I felt during those years in which I occupied the bedroom next to Lella's had nothing to do with erotic fantasies but with the knowl-

My last year of high-school in Turin (1955-56): second row, first from the left

edge that the room had belonged to Uncle Gilberto, who died tragically in an alpine accident at the age of sixteen. I remember Gilberto more because of photos I saw than from any real time we spent together at the house on Pietro Micca.

I have a vague image of the terrible night on which a Franciscan parish priest, from Santa Teresa church, came to the house to tell us that Gilberto had fallen from a rocky mountain in the Alps, where he had gone climbing with some friends. I remember almost nothing about Uncle Gilberto's life or death, only that he was a young high school student and expert alpinist who Nonno Luigi hoped to interest in the business of the Druetto bookstore and small publishing house.

Having my own room marked the beginning of my independent musical and intellectual life. During the first four years at my grandparents' house, I had slept in a huge matrimonial bed with Mamma and Ilaria, in the room at the end of the hall across from that of my grandparents. It must have been around 1950 when, at the age of thirteen, Ilaria was sent by Mamma—and I suspect by our grandparents—to a boarding school run by religious sisters in the Piamontese town of Virle. At last Mamma Pina could sleep alone on the big matrimonial bed in the bedroom at the end of the hall.

I managed to acquire a radio and record player, a small bookcase, and an even smaller desk, in the room that had a large window overlooking Pietro Micca street. Little by little, I collected a few 78 rpm records and even fewer 45s, all of them Dixieland jazz. I must admit it was my cousin Paolo who initiated me into my love of modern jazz by playing "My Funny Valentine" by Jerry Mulligan and Chet Baker. I never liked Paolo that much, however, because of his arrogance, aristocratic pretensions, and military vocation (as an officer in the Italian Army, he went so far as to compete in horsemanship in some Olympics or other).

At the age of eleven, my musical taste was set: jazz on the record player and Mozart, Bach, and Chopin on the piano in the next room.

CHAPTER 8

The Intrigues of Love

🜚

L ITTLE BY LITTLE AND perhaps without meaning to, Aunt Lella pulled me into her "illegitimate" web of love. She would appear unexpectedly in my room in the afternoon, and invite me to the movies. I especially remember a comedy with Red Skelton because that afternoon, upon leaving the theater, she introduced me to an elegantly dressed man who seemed very old to me. She said we would soon be going skiing with him.

A few weeks later, Lella took me by train to the region of Trentino, in the opposite direction from the Piamontese Alps. We arrived at a beautiful place called Canazei. There, at a mountain hotel covered in snow, we met up with a group of Lella's young friends and the elegant man with graying hair whom I'd met at the movies. We spent several days and nights at that hotel in the Dolomite Mountains, and for many years I honestly never understood why Lella had been so generous to me.

The scandal revealed itself a few months later when, in a very Italian scene, my mother and grandmother confronted Lella and accused her of trying to ruin the marriage of the great music critic and well-known author, *il Professore* Massimo Mila. Aside from the American soldier who stayed in the next room and the music critic at the Alpine hotel, I never got to know any of my Aunt Lella's other lovers. Maybe she was trying to protect me from feeling jealous of those more fortunate contenders.

I came to know and sympathize with young Tucci, the tall blonde man with tearful eyes and a bourgeois elegance who married Aunt Lella. I lost track of my aunt when I went to Peru, and didn't hear anything more about her or her musical and intellectual activities. Tucci was a well-known doctor, who offered her and her children a comfortable life, but other demons must have resided in Lella's psyche, about whom one never heard, not even the men who accompanied her—or used her—after her divorce from Tucci.

A letter from my sister Giliola, that reached me in Lima, brought the news that following several days in which no one could find her, they discovered Lella in an apartment on the beach at Liguria, asphyxiated by gas from the oven. I never knew if she left a suicide note. Painfully, I remembered that early love a few years ago when, on a visit to Turin, I ran into Lella's oldest son. He was a well-known dentist living comfortably in that city, and with an intelligence and sensibility that reminded me of hers. He wanted to know everything I could tell him about his mother, once so young and vivacious. I couldn't tell him that Lella had been my first love.

CHAPTER 9

From Whence the Left?

𓎡

MY HALF-SISTER GILIOLA WAS the only leftist in my Turin family. She was born in 1931 to my Mamma, who was single at the time, and a father by the last name of Re whose identity was always kept secret, absent from family history.

Giliola was suckled by a wet nurse far from our grandparents' house, and eventually adopted by my father Luigi when he married our mother. Giliola had olive skin, hair as black as her eyes, the fine features of a woman from southern Italy or northern Africa, and a powerful analytic and critical intelligence which, when she was older, stood her in good stead as a political activist, essayist, author, and translator for important publishing houses. Along with her commitment to all the just causes of her generation, she made time to translate a novel by Virginia Woolf, publish an oral history on the worker occupations of a building in Turin, organize several popular and feminist endeavors, raise a revolutionary son—now a professor of contemporary history in Bologna—and pen some pages of great lyricism, *L'infanzia di Olivia*, that unfortunately did not see publication before her death.

I think it was Giliola who introduced me to leftist humanistic thought. In 1954, three years before I left for Peru, when she was still married to a Communist partisan, Giliola took me to meetings of students and activists where, in an atmosphere thick with cigarettes and wine, they analyzed Italy's and the world's political situation.

It was at one of those meetings that I learned about the CIA's military coup against Jacobo Arbenz's government in Guatemala. A young boy of fifteen, I had only a vague idea about Latin America and couldn't have pointed to Guatemala on a map. In just a few hours, Giliola educated me about the role of the CIA, President Eisenhower, and the United Fruit Company in the coup

With my sisters Giliola and Ilaria in Turin, circa 1947

against Arbenz, Guatemala's reformist president who had begun a redistribution of United Fruit Company land to peasants and Indigenous people. The world's ironies surprised me years later, during Peru's Velasco Revolution, when I ended up working with a revolutionary Vice Minister, Dr. Carlos Delgado, who in his youth had been an activist in the Arbenz government.

At those meetings with Giliola and her friends, I also learned about the coup launched by the United States against another reformist administration, that of Iran's Mossadegh in 1953.

I finally began to clear up all those doubts and questions I'd had since the tense days of the summer of 1948, when at the age of nine a playmate and I had moved through the deserted city of Turin that was occupied by soldiers, without understanding the reason for that military occupation by the Italian Republic's Bersaglierri[8] and Carabinieri.[9] My friend, whose name I no longer remember although I can see his cross-eyed face, told me a few days later that there had been a general strike—*uno Sciopero Generale*—protesting the Fascist attempt on the life of Palmiro Togliatti, the Secretary General of the Italian Communist Party. I guess that little by little my infantile mind was

8. Infantry battalion of the Italian Army.
9. National Police of Italy.

forming a polarized vision of society and the world in which we lived: Fascists on one side, Communists on the other, and that the former were to be feared and the latter were trusted friends.

Later, with other playmates in secondary school, we were going on an outing to the Lobatos Club with the Boy Scouts from the parish of Santa Teresa or maybe to some club at Depolavero, where I rather ambiguously reinforced two opposing world views without fully understanding the lack of harmony between them. And once again it was Giliola, with her heated discussions and suggested readings, who managed to open a crack in my mind, a crack I entered years later in Peru when the poverty and suffering that surrounded me became intolerable and I needed explications in order to bear them. I owe Giliola the hope of a humanistic socialism, as well as the joy of a life well lived.

I remember her now when she visited Linda and me at our modest rented house in San Felipe del Agua, at the edge of the Colonia Popular Volcanes, beneath the suffocating heat of the cement roof, which only in "modern" Mexico could alienated architects have conceived of putting on a house in the tropics. Impressed by our monastic poverty, she was surprised by the fruit crates in which we used to store our clothes, at the *cucarachas* who roamed everywhere, and at the supposedly hallucinatory mushrooms from San José on the Pacific that would have been better in that simple and delicious pasta she made us and which I was never able to reproduce.

The last time I saw Giliola at her Turin apartment, as I fought back tears and repressed sobbing, I found a small girl of some two or three years of age, who didn't yet know how to speak and had no memory of her life. Linda, my eternal comrade, glimpsed a brief light of understanding in Giliola's frightened gaze, and believed she knew that the old man who caressed her with love had existed in their shared childhoods.

CHAPTER 10

The Cave of Books

🙨

HAD I GROWN UP with my sisters Giliola and Ilaria in the privileged home of Attorney Luigi Varese Guerci-Lena and his wife Guiseppina Druetto, most likely in Genoa in the period immediately following the war, I am sure I would have attended a prestigious school and entertained professional expectations more in line with the family's bourgeois aspirations.

But I did not. Because of our exile to Turin, Giliola left our grandparents' home very young, and went to work as a nurse at the Gaslini Hospital in Genoa. At the age of eleven, Ilaria was sent to a religious boarding school to become a young Catholic woman, educated for a traditional marriage. Neither did I fulfill Nonno's expectations, tragically interrupted by the death of his only son, my uncle Gilberto. I didn't fulfill his expectations, because without knowing it, I didn't want to.

From the Druetto Bookstore on the Piazza San Carlos, where my mother and grandmother took me whenever I wasn't in school—they wanted to teach me how to be a bookseller—I have the most wonderful memories of time spent in a fantastic world of high narrow tunnels formed by books and bookcases, the smell of paper and ink, brightly colored book covers, black and white illustrations, and immense encyclopedias. The *Encyclopedia Treccani* was made up of dozens of monumental volumes. That world was filled with books I thumbed through and sometimes read, without really understanding them. I fell in love with books, not so I could sell or make money from them, but for the inexplicable opportunity they gave me to isolate myself in my own world, far away from my duties at school and my efforts to conquer what I would later learn was my dyslexia. I was always fascinated by what the next page would bring.

My mother Pina in the bookstore of my grandfather Luigi Druetto,
Turin, circa 1968

And then there were the people who worked at the store: for a while a German named Franz, Oreste, who was called Fattorino because he was a helper,
and a changing roster of women. Among the latter there were a few who were
young. The most stable were the older ones. All of them were supervised by
my mother and Aunt Lidia, the daughter of one of Nonna Massa's sisters and
a Garibaldi guerrilla whose uniform and gun survived years of inclemency in
the hall of her country house.

Nonna Massa, on the other hand, was always seated behind an immense
chrome-plated cash register. She would open the money drawer, with its handle and numbered buttons, producing a joyous and triumphant sound each
time a sale was made.

Nonno, hidden behind a counter formed by shelves full of books and a
desk with all sorts of hidden drawers, almost never showed his face. One
could hear his voice giving orders and explaining where some rare book a
customer wanted might be found. Nonno Luigi and my mother imbued the
Druetto Bookstore with their legendary memories. If I remember correctly,
my Mamma's memory was legendary until her death. I don't know how she

My grandfather Luigi Druetto in his bookstore, Turin, circa 1965

did it, but she remembered authors, titles, publishers, the year in which a book had been published, and even the contents of a vast number of books. Her mental agility and skill were astonishing.

Each time I would accompany her in her trips around Piamonte, first on a little Lambretta motor scooter and later in a Fiat Topolino, going from bookstore to bookstore, taking orders for school texts, I was reminded of her ability to remember every title in her huge catalogue that included a long list of Italian publishers. Her reputation, along with that of the bookstore itself, grew to the point that she was invited to book fairs in Germany and France. From one of those trips she returned in love with an elegant editor from Hachette Publishers, an affair that only lasted a few months.

During those first years of my mother's job as a publishing representative, I didn't really understand the difficult conditions of her commitment to Druetto Bookstore. At the end of each summer and through early fall, Mamma would get on her little Lambretta wearing a heavy raincoat and carrying a suitcase full of book catalogues and a few changes of clothing. She would travel through several regions of Piamonte, going from school to school and bookstore to bookstore, taking textbook orders for all the public elementary and secondary schools.

The market economy benefited from Italy's post-war economic growth, and this favored publishing houses and bookstores selling school texts. Grandfather Druetto quickly understood that in that new market niche lay the future of a business and an industry that, shattered by decades of Fascism and five years of war, would now be able to take advantage of the new democratic state's investment in public education. I remember that my grandfather and mother—despite their conservative political tendencies—were proud of having invested in Nuova Italia, a leftist publisher that was having great success in its production and distribution of school books for the secondary and high schools.

But the cost of Druetto's economic success, especially in the textbook field, could be seen in my Mamma's exhaustion. The few times I accompanied her on those journeys, which for me meant adventure and fun, I could see how tired she was at the end of each day. She would return to a badly-lit hotel room after a modest dinner and glass of red wine. Her clients and provincial booksellers called my Mamma Madamín Druetto, in a sign of respect that let her know they thought of her as a single woman even if she was accompanied by her adolescent son.

The vital biological cycle has some indignant designs when it hides the sense of privation that sustains it. I left my Mamma precisely when she was still traveling from sad hotel to sad hotel, in the Fiat now, through the province of Piamonte on the trail of those buyers of school books.

Gramsci Devoured

🙏

I DIDN'T UNDERSTAND ANYTHING WHEN I opened an Italian copy of a book by Antonio Gramsci in the basement of the Druetto bookstore, nor do I remember who suggested I read that revolutionary. It might have been my sister Giliola or Count Radicati, a partisan who was the younger brother of one of my Mamma Pina's great loves. She hired him to teach me French, not through grammar lessons but by making me to read Voltaire's *Candide, ou l'Optimisme* and similar texts of which I understood almost nothing but learned a lot.

I thought of Gramsci again once I was at the University in Peru, but it was the stray dog, Orégano, adopted by my lover Linda in Chaclacayo, who forced me to do a more serious reading of the Marxist thinker.

It must have been 1973 or 1974, when my mother sent me a very heavy volume of the complete Gramsci in Italian. I made the mistake of leaving the book on top of my desk in the little house on Hilda Street. Linda went off to the Roosevelt School to teach and I to my office at Agrarian Reform. Orégano, who enjoyed a great diet of sweet potatoes and bits of meat and had a very optimistic vision of life, was tormented by those long hours by himself, and inspired to destroy whatever he could. We got home that night to find Gramsci on the floor, dragged a distance from the desk. Some of its pages were in the small interior patio. While I tried to collect the torn-out bits and pieces, Orégano happily celebrated his attack on Italian Marxism, and Linda calmed me by reminding me that "a book is a book is a book."

SOME HISTORIANS HAVE CALLED the Peru of 1956 to 1968—the years when I was at the university—the period of Civil Reform and Democratic Formalism. I arrived in Peru during President Manuel Prado Ugarteche's ad-

Linda, Stefano, and Orégano in Chaclacayo, Peru,
starting our life together, circa 1970-71

My father Luigi in
Chaclacayo, circa 1970

ministration, which followed General Manuel A. Odría's long dictatorship. Manuel Prado promised a democratic aperture and style of political and economic management that was liberal and geared to development.

In fact, on family trips and my own journeys through the Peruvian Andes and Amazon, one noted some changes in the provinces, mostly limited highway construction going into the Andes, especially in the mining areas being exploited by foreign companies, the International Petroleum Company's oil fields in Talara, the copper mines in the southern part of the country, and the network of highways and roads connecting the Pan-American Highway to the large plantations on the coast.

In my juvenile European naiveté, it seemed perfectly normal to me that they were building roads and bridges and a few schools in urban areas. I thought it was any government's minimal obligation. Papá, on the other hand, with more than ten years in the country, believed it to be of a revolutionary magnitude. I came to understand Papá's position after I returned from a study trip to Cuzco's remote mountains.

It must have been during the summer of 1962 or 1963, when a Jesuit comrade from the Catholic University and I were asked by the bishop of Cuzco to do a research and evaluation trip to assess the social situation on some *haciendas* that belonged to the Church in the district of Lares, province of Calca, department of Cuzco. I was studying philosophy and letters at that school.

In Cuzco, Father Yupanqui received the two students from Lima. I seem to remember that the morning after our arrival we traveled by bus or truck to Calca, and from there began a long trip on mule, as disconcerting as it was surreal. We spent almost two weeks traversing the ecclesiastic *hacienda's* vast territory, from its inter-Andean valleys to its humid heights and permanently cloud-covered and rainy eastern edges, spending our nights tortured by fleas that traveled hungrily over the boards that served as roofs, floors, and beds to our tired bodies.

Having stopped smoking in Lima, I began again in earnest. I also commenced my friendly but respectful relationship with the coca leaf. I *chaq'ché* or *piq'ché* coca leaves with lime. I drank cane *cambray*[10] and *chicha de jora*.[11] I ate potatoes with *ají, rocoto,* and the clay-like and earthy *chiacu*[12] that the

10. Fermented sugar cane juice.
11. Fermented corn-maiz juice.

Andean people have eaten for thousands of years to replace the necessary minerals in their bodies and thereby preserve their biochemical equilibrium. But none of these nutritional or medicinal adaptations of the Andean or Indigenous world could calm the rage that seeing the poverty and miserable conditions of the tenant farmers on the *haciendas* we visited produced in my consciousness day after day. Barefoot malnourished children, their bellies filled with parasites, women broken by the weight of their loads and from working from sun up to sun down, and men bent over in servitude, fearful of demanding more humane treatment.

It was my political and ethnological baptism of fire, as well as the discovery—once again, after my youth in Turin—that the contradictions don't end on the frontier that divides right from left; they remain and become more complex within each political block, such that the Quechua-speaking priest, Yupanqui, could feel superior, and empowered by the Holy Spirit, in the exploitation of his fellow Indians, discriminating against them as if they were inferior beings. And all this took place beneath the forewarned gaze of the young Jesuit who, without intending to do so, was reproducing four centuries of a relationship between an educated congregation and supposedly lost souls.

I RETURNED TO LIMA determined to better understand this new country of mine, and its profound and isolated peoples, so distant from the tree-lined avenues of Lima (the City of Kings), with its shops filled with food, shoe stores that sold hundreds of different models but not a single pair of sandals made from truck tires, schools where a foreign language called Castilian was spoken, and hospitals that cured mortal illnesses such as colds and diarrhea.

But the hardest thing for me was having to respond to questions from family and friends recognizing that, without knowing Quechua, I had been unable to speak to anyone during my entire time in the Lares mountains. What kind of fiction were my university studies when I, a studious learner, was unable to speak to more than half my compatriots? What kind of lie was building in my psychological imagination? What pretense of truth could I assume as I wrote about the Lares *runacuna* and their religious and secular problems?

What I saw in Lares and Calca led me to understand my Papá's enthusiasm for the promises made by presidential electoral candidate Fernando Belande

12. Type of clay containing minerals essential to human health. The clay is made into a watery sauce to which *ají/chile* is added.

Terry and the political platform of his party, Acción Popular (Popular Action). What the country needed were highways, bridges, schools, and more land for the landless peasants. This meant the country's expansion to the east, to the Amazon, a no man's land free for the taking, the *terra nullius*[13] of 16th century conquistadors. Belaunde's doctrine was simple and direct: the conquest of Peru by Peruvians. What wasn't so clear was its ontological premise: who was Peruvian?

That question didn't seem to worry the candidate with more intellectual weight than Belaunde, the founder of APRA (Alianza Popular Revolucionaria Americana, or American Popular Revolutionary Alliance), Víctor Raul Haya de la Torre. Under the cloak of "people's revolutionary," conceived during his exile in post-revolutionary Mexico in 1924, now, almost forty years later, he included all the country's classes and ethnicities in a single group. Anti-imperialism, a socialist economy, Indo-Americanism, a radical agrarian reform, international solidarity, and the rights of the Indigenous population were not contemplated in APRA's 1962 platform. After years of exile, clandestine life, and repression from the right, APRA had abandoned the ideas of its founders so it might legally participate in the presidential race. From the 1950s on, this politically opportunistic trade-off cost APRA many of its best members, who migrated to the Marxist left.

During those years, we had the bad luck of having Acción Popular party's headquarters situated precisely across the street from the building on Colmena Derecha. The street's official name was Nicolás de Piérola Avenue. And so Belaunde's constant bombardment with loudspeaker propaganda managed to alienate our whole family—including Papá—from the man's populist rhetoric, without drawing us to APRA's interclass promises.

The Varese family had no flag and ignored the campaign that ended in July of 1962 in a tie between the aging former dictator Odría, Belaunde, an architect with modernist ideas, and the populist Haya de la Torre. A tie doesn't satisfy anyone, and inevitably leads to fraud which, in Peru, can only be resolved by the Armed Forces, meaning its Army/Air Force/Navy triumvirate. As a way of containing the peasant and Indigenous movements, and especially as a precaution against popular uprisings modeled on the Cuban revolution, that triumvirate promised agrarian reform within a year.

13. No-one land.

CHAPTER 12

From Plaza Francia to Miraflores

༉

I THINK IT WAS MY stepmother, Rita, who managed to convince Papá we needed to move away from downtown Lima, from the noisy electric streetcars that were being dismantled and replaced by noisier foul-smelling buses, and an elegant apartment that wasn't big enough for two adolescents and a step-son in his twenties. The Catholic University's School of Philosophy and Letters, where I studied, was on Plaza Francia, just a few blocks from Colmena Derecha and two from the workshop store of Vasco Jewelers, where my father worked each day.

The jewelry store and workshop had a rather elegant façade and boutique character that attracted the women of Lima's new commercial and industrial petit bourgeoisie, which was pushing its old land-owning oligarchy out into the stately neighborhoods of San Isidro and Miraflores.

Behind the store was the workshop, housing the men who made the jewelry: *cholos*, *zambos*, and one or another Quechua-speaking *serrano*. Papá and Rita had taught them all, except for those who set diamonds and other precious stones, who enjoyed immense prestige, better salaries, and Papá's absolute confidence.

Papá, the criminal lawyer, had developed an unexpected artistic ability. He studied the pre-Colombian jewelry of the Mochica peoples on the northern coast and the Inca nobles of Cuzco. And he combined those designs with precious metals, hard semi-precious stones, and pieces of local crafts such as old beads from the colonial era and 18th and 19th century silver. Lima's rising bourgeoisie, like the entire middle class, looked down on its Indigenous and *mestizo* roots, evident in pieces inherited from parents and grandparents. They came to see Don Luigi bearing bags filled with "junk" which Papá and Rita would turn into exotic pieces of uncertain origin and ambiguous history. Vasco Jewelers—

with its inevitable *cholo* craftsmen—became a successful business that had more than three outlets, the most recent of these inaugurated at a fashionable shopping center in the 1970s that exported to Brazil and Venezuela.

Somewhat marginally, and without any passion for the job, I participated in the growth and development of the Vasco empire. Four times a year, I left my studies to fend for themselves and set out for a week, driving the coastal road to the Great North with a pair of suitcases filled with jewelry samples I tried to sell to shops in the provinces. Vasco paid my gas, lodging, and meals, and I got a percentage on each order I received. With what I earned, I made the payments on the car Papá had helped me buy, paid my very low university tuition, and had enough left over for books, records, and an occasional restaurant and movie.

I wasn't seduced by these commercial activities, just as I hadn't been seduced by my Nonna and Nonno's book business. But I loved those trips: the Sechura desert attracted me with the vastness of its sweet-smelling carob trees and palo santos. Piura, Talara, Puerto Pizarro, Chepén, Chiclayo, and Trujillo always seemed exotic and mysterious. I would spend my nights reading for the university and, after repeated trips along that coast, inspired to write a slim book about the life of the Italian naturalist Antonio Raimondi who, at mid-19th century, left resurgent Italy and emigrated to Peru, where he became the most important botanist and geographer of the young South American republic.

The family's move to the two-story house in San Antonio de Miraflores, and the inauguration of Vasco Jeweler's workshop and store at the Todos Shopping Center, symbolized the Varese's late transition into an emerging middle class that was dangerously aligned with the ideals of the modern urban bourgeoisie stimulated by the Fernando Belaunde Terry administration.

My siblings, Luis and Chiara, now lived three blocks from the Pestalozzi Swiss School. My father needed a car to get to the Vasco store in San Isidro. I had my old VW Beetle, the one I used on my jewelry-selling trips and to go to the Catholic University, still located in the big 19th century house on Plaza Francia. Rita, who never learned to drive, increasingly depended on me to take her places. I also often had to care for the family's youngest member, Francisco or Cecco, who was just a child at the time.

OUR INSERTION INTO LIMA'S urban elite culminated some ten years later when Papá, tired of paying rent on the Miraflores house and pressured by

Rita, bought a relatively large piece of land in Chacarilla del Estanque, the new area of urban expansion to the east of the city where the families of Lima's new bourgeoisie were beginning to move. These were mostly professionals and one or another provincial landowner attracted by the city's modernity and fearful of increasing unrest in the countryside.

On that land, my father and Rita built a modern house, large and full of light, with enough room for all his books, piano, paintings accumulated through years of interest in Peruvian art, and examples of popular art from the Andes and the coast. With its large garden, long grape arbor, Molle and Eucalyptus trees, Palmwood gates from the Amazon, and a cornfield irrigated by an ancient rural waterway in front, the Chacarilla house evokes memories of a sort of intellectual peace mixed with the emotional and creative highs and lows of my university years burdened by the political and social events of Peru and the rest of the world.

With the victory of the Cuban Revolution in 1959, the anti-colonial movement dragging Europe and the United States to the brink of its historic self-blame, growing pacifist and Civil Rights movements in the United States, and Latin American Indigenous, peasant, and worker movements on the rise, my university studies had taken a definitive turn toward the social sciences: first history, followed by my decision to enroll in ethnology.

The young students of that time in Lima carried the weight of a generation of notable intellectuals that had transformed the way of thinking about Perú. Almost everyone was, at the distance between the Atlantic Ocean and the American continent, contemporary of my father, Luis Varese Guerci-Lena born in Genoa at the beginning of the twentieth century. I am referring to José Carlos Mariátegui and Huge Pesce—founders of the Peruvian Socialist Party—and to César Vallejo, who Thomas Merton called "the greatest Catholic poet since Dante and, by Catholic, I mean universal." That generation also included Víctor Raul Haya de la Torre, the politician who founded the American Popular Revolutionary Alliance (APRA), Luis Eduardo Valcárcel, who initiated contemporary Andean history, historians Jorge Basadre, Raúl Porras Barrenechea, and José María Arguedas, the great Andean and Quechua-speaking poet, novelist, and anthropologist. This generation of Peruvian intellectuals was joined by foreign colleagues: French physician and ethnologist Jehan Albert Vellard, Italian philosopher and historian Onorio Ferrero, Rumanian-North American ethno-historian John V. Murra, and French sociologist François Bourricaud.

It was these creative thinkers, along with others, who, semi-hidden at the margins of an official history I cannot even remember, educated those of us born in Europe or Peru around 1940. My friends and I owe them everything, known and unknown: the understanding of that complex and mysterious country I wanted to enter with the delicate respect all arcane millennia deserve.

To my teacher Onorio Ferrero, Italian noble, former antifascist partisan, neo-Hegelian thinker and distinguished historian of world religions I owe my openness to the complex spiritual reality of world people cultures. To my mentor the physician and ethnologist Jehan Albert Vellard, French-Algerian *pied noir*, I owe my passion for descriptive ethnology and the discipline of participant observation.

And so began, in the Catholic University's courtyard and in the old buildings of the French Institute of Andean Studies and the Riva Agüero Institute, my passion for the thought and practice of anthropology and history. I was accompanied on this adventure by other Peruvian university professors and classmates who were changing the intellectual and political landscape of the country and of Latin America in those years: Father Gustavo Gutiérrez, founder of the Liberation Theology movement; old historian and diplomat Raúl Porras Barrenchea; linguists and literary critics Luis Jaime Cisneros and José Miguel Oviedo. I must also mention my contemporaries: philosopher Luis Santisteban; Javier Heraud, the poet killed by the police in the Madre de Dios jungle when he was trying to return home from Cuba; philosopher and student of religions Carlos Beas; anthropologist Luis Enrique Tord; historian Luis Millones Santagadea; and economists Luis Bortesi and Eduardo Mazzini, with whom I went camping at the foot of the Andes and who, along the way, may have lost themselves in neoliberal delirium.

But the oldest and most sorely missed friend of my university generation was Luis "Lucho" Pesce, son of Doctor Hugo Pesce Pescetto, who founded the Peruvian Socialist Party along with José Carlos Mariátegui and had a great deal of influence on Ernesto Che Guevara. With Lucho and other friends—I think Luis Millones Santagadea was with us as well—we would study over long nights of coffee and cigarettes that ended in the street at six in the morning with pickup soccer games. Even when he played pickup soccer on a Lima street, Lucho was good looking and elegant like his Andean-Genovese father. He had a brilliant intelligence and intellectual discipline, and his tremendous generosity was effusive. One summer morning he jumped into the ocean at

Herradura Beach to save a drowning child. He died in the attempt and we, his friends, could never again look at Herradura the same way. In a late effort at paying tribute to the socialist lineage of the Pesce family, I popularized the first scientific ethnographic map of the Peruvian Amazon, crediting its publication to the Communist author, Doctor Hugo Pesce, in my book *La sal de los cerros* (Lima, 1968).[14]

In those years, I didn't have a clear understanding of intellectual formation limited exclusively by university study. In a certain sense, I ended up at the university almost by chance, and because of Papá's dogged insistence. There were times when my life aspirations contemplated nothing but wandering, to live and travel on my minimal family subsidy and the even leaner income I earned as a Vasco Jewelry salesman. Before entering the university, I rarely thought that getting a degree was something that would afford me access to a job with higher pay. Perhaps the fact that at seventeen I had readapted to the life of Papá, now economically comfortable in Peru, blinded me to the new social reality into which I inserted myself. I was no longer in Turin, plagued by an Italy of post-war misery, the economic insecurities of Mamma, and of the hand-me-down clothes I often had to wear despite my intimate desire to dress as elegantly as my wealthiest friends. Nor did I have to travel now on cold and aging buses to visit my sister Ilaria at her religious school in Virle, bringing her a couple of apples and some crackers, precious delicacies my mother managed to extract from my grandparents' larder.

My life now was one of American wellbeing, far from Turin and my grandparents' inhospitable home, with what seemed to be the promise of a good bourgeois life surrounded by the Indian, *cholo* and *mestizo* misery of a Peru that, even as I questioned it with all my radical new assumptions, was left intact by my comfortable class-conscious position.

Even today, forty or fifty years later, these contradictions remain unaltered in some remote corner of my being, and I cannot resolve the dialectic of my emotions.

14. Stefano Varese, *La sal de los cerros* (Lima: Universidad Peruana de Ciencias y Tecnología, 1968).

CHAPTER 13

Poets, Filmmakers, and Revolutionaries

🦂

A T THE AGE OF eighteen, my sister Chiara traveled to Cuba as a guest of the Cuban Revolution, along with her friend Luz Marina, daughter of a Peruvian revolutionary. In Peru, Chiara had been a photographer. On the Island, she became a socially-conscious filmmaker. Her training, although extremely rigorous, was not from formal schooling but by way of the movement the new Cuban film industry was inventing step by step and aided by the solidarity of other revolutionary peoples, despite all the hardships caused by the U.S. blockade.

Only in these last few years, in meetings as sporadic as they were intense, have I heard about Chiara's life in Cuba over several decades. Seated before a television screen in her house in Lima, I have looked and looked again at her profoundly Latin American life, from her memories of having been a baby-sitter for Raúl Castro's children to her encounters with Fidel; her friendship with many of the revolutionary Latin American youth who were in Cuba to escape military dictatorships in Brazil, Paraguay, Uruguay, Argentina, Chile, Guatemala, El Salvador, Nicaragua and the mortal blows to all attempts at democratic life in the Americas; as well as her success as a critical documen-tarian and as a member of international film juries.

I saw Chiara once in San Francisco, California, when she was serving on one of those juries, and I caught sight of her in the distance at a Latin Ameri-can film festival in Liguria. Then in Havana, then in Lima and Quito and the Amazonian rainforest. Each time she tells me another little piece of her his-tory that I am unable to take down with the necessary care because the pisco or tequila or rum or red wine, and the riotous friends who surround us, make my stenographer's job impossible.

I know you would rather make documentaries, and that film is your preferred language, but Chiara mamita, now that you have lived for more than half a century, please write something about your life. What happened at Lima's women's prison when they arrested you? Why were you arrested? And our brother Luis, Gigi, did he have anything to do with your arrest? Was he in Lima then? Had he already returned from Nicaragua and the Sandinista Revolution? Content in my comfortable academic exile at Stanford, I only heard about Luis's arrest and his time at Lurigancho with those of the Shining Path and common criminals, but I never heard about your prison experience. With the help of Eduardo Galeano and a group of students and professors in California, we organized a letter of protest against Luis's arrest and solitary confinement by Peru's state security apparatus. But we knew nothing about you. We didn't sign a single letter. And later, your separation from Carlos, your children Pablo and Martín at school, your misery in that "Lima the horrible," your dedication to your mother, Rita's, old age, and your endemic lack of work—no one can make independent films in a Peru ruled by a neo-oligarchy that only funds apologies of neo-liberalism.

Chiarita, you didn't come in time either when Papá was dying. You were in Mexico, near and far from me, and in Cuba far from all of us, and Papá dying alone at Sol de la Molina, a desperate Rita distancing herself from this world of reason, forever chasing unobtainable fantasies. That small diaspora that Papá kindled in all of us took its toll when he died, and we once again confirmed his generosity: you and Francisco, our Cecco, in the critical creativity of a world of liberating film; Luigi, our Gigi, in his Latin American revolutions; and me in my obstinate anthropology of indigeneity: none of us could get there in time to place our hands on the body of his soul.

I AM TEN YEARS older than my brother Gigi, Luis David Varese Scotto. I arrived in Peru at the age of seventeen, when Gigi had just turned seven and was climbing like a monkey all over the heavy drapes of the apartment on Nicolás de Piérola Avenue—known at the time as Colmena Derecha—causing joyous problems for Papá. Or, completely dressed as a cowboy, he would submerge himself in a bathtub full of water, with pistol and all, because he was running from some bandits, I now suspect may have been large landowners or gunmen in the service of some investor.

A few years later, Papá granted Gigi, who was in secondary school by then, his legal independence, emancipating him as he had me a few years earlier. I don't remember the details, but Luis was still quite young when he traveled to Europe to meet the French mystic Lanza del Vasto, and from there went on to the Middle East where he ended up being arrested in Egypt, accused of being an Israeli agent. I don't know how he got out of that predicament, but I know that the name David, and suspect that the surname Varese, may not have helped clarify Gigi's ethnic-national identity in an Egypt that was being assaulted by the state of Israel.

He returned to Peru from this pilgrimage to his roots with two apparently different but complimentary trajectories: his mystic personal search and a social will to reform the world. The first of these, poetic in nature, took him to live for years on the Nicaraguan island of Solentiname with the Christian community founded by the monk and political poet Ernesto Cardenal. His revolutionary journey took him from Solentiname to the Sandinistas' Southern Front, where he almost died beneath mortar fire.

The explosion threw me into the air, completely deaf, a meter off the ground, and I thought I was beginning my ascent to paradise. I saw Mamá, in her constant protective prayer, that mystical-esoteric mix of the Hindu Sai Baba, Father Pío, and the Madonna, and I could hear the anguished screams of my comrades at arms, calling me by my war name. A few months later, I arrived in Managua wearing the Sandinista uniform, along with victorious Sandinistas and internationalists. The photograph I sent doesn't begin to reflect the pride I felt during that time of Sandinista victory, when the "boys" defeated more than four decades of Somoza dictatorship and more than a hundred years of Yankee intervention. Do you remember that I invited Papá and Mamá to Nicaragua to taste that victory and return to Solentiname with Cardenal, and then came to see you in Oaxaca when those plainclothes federal police, armed to the teeth, stopped us in the high Mixteca, made us get out of the VW van you were driving, with its California license plates? They were surprised to discover we weren't "gavachos" but Latin Americans, and let us go without demanding the proverbial bribe.

Stefa, Oaxaca holds a special meaning for me, not only because I recently learned that Mamá and Papá were secretly married at a civil ceremony in the city of Oaxaca, but because my partner Maruja and I began our Mexican exile there, and Manuel, one of my many children, was born at the Virgin of Carmen Clinic with your and Linda's help, and was later baptized at San Felipe del Agua church. The rest of my story is complicated. I know you will tell me to write it as part of Latin America's history. And in time, I will, although I prefer poetry as a way of narrating history from the heart. I am in a hurry to live history rather than write it. You are in a hurry to write it because you've already lived it.

MY BROTHER FRANCISCO, CECCO, is twenty-five years younger than me. In terms of age, I could be his father. He was born when Papá and Rita had moved to the little house in Miraflores. There Cecco grew up, pampered and spoiled by all his older siblings, parents who had aged too much to be able to impose a strict discipline, and *nana* María who provided all manner of loving and playful privileges.

The family's success didn't distract him toward the empty vanity that sterilized the sensibilities of his friends. I remember him raising chickens and doves in the far reaches of the "bourgeois" garden in Chacarilla del Estanque, building all sorts of technical innovations to work the soil, and inventing new spaces for ancient needs. Papá—well-off by then—sent him to Milan to study architecture. I think Cecco had a grand time in Italy. He returned to Peru with no specific professional vocation but in possession of a good education and aesthetic sensibility that he almost immediately put at the service of his new passion for photography and film.

I entered the film world through a sort of false door, Stefano. When I returned from Italy, I got a job as an adventure tour guide. I had the opportunity of accompanying a National Geographic film team to the Andean region of Titicaca, and there the director put a movie camera in my hands and told me to shoot a scene. He liked what he saw and, from then on, I began to consider the possibility of filmmaking as a profession.

I spent a while in Washington as a camera assistant. I went to work in television for several TV channels, did war photography, also for CNN and other stations, and that's how I got into that world. You know, Stefano, in the extended Varese family I have the reputation of being the least political, perhaps because, unlike Gigi, I have never been arrested by the police or by state security. But I can tell you that my opinions and actions may be as subversive or more so than those of my contemporaries who have

My sister Ilaria, circa 1948

taken up arms. Maybe, as you have written somewhere, this is because a critical conscience must be accompanied by a strategic one. I have tried to exercise my social radicalism—always ethical—"cum grano salis"[15] as Papá would say—and so I didn't end up in prison except when I visited Luis after his small tortures. My expatriations, like yours, have taken me around the world as a filmmaker, my eyes open to the beauty and horror that never ceases to amaze me.

Ilaria, my only sibling from the same mother and father, is two years older than I. Still very young, immediately upon graduating in political science from the University of Turin, she married a veterinary biologist who took her for more than a decade to live in Kenya and South Africa. Her two children, born in Africa, witnessed the lengthy arguments and domestic violence that informed their lives of colonial privilege and petit-bourgeois aspirations.

One day, tired of the abuse, she traveled to Italy, found Aldo, an old friend from my childhood who had been her first love, and in an act of female valor none of us thought possible, remained with him, beginning a new life of work and tranquility. For years, she and her new husband ran a small restaurant and later a camping ground for tourists on the Liguria Riviera. She managed her precarious economic situation well, and the two of them channeled it to-

15. "With a grain of salt", with some skepticism.

ward the new European bourgeoisie's pretensions of personal prosperity and political alienation.

Through these years, we are linked to the two of them by thousands of miles, adopted languages and experiences, and an intense and serene affection born in our childhood that has never been altered by our discordant itineraries. Now that they live in southern France, Linda and I visit them there, where I enjoy the sun of Provençal summers and the perfumed wines that help us bear Ilaria and her husband's illusion that, beyond Italian television, there is nothing but chaos and disorder.

> *"Non voglio più gatti,"* I don't want more cats, she tells me. They make me suffer too much when I think of them dying. Enough sorrow, enough children, enough news of African hunger, and the killing of animals . . . *"ma vedi come I cinesi mangiano di tutto,"*[16] the Chinese eat everything, they will eat anything that moves. I am a vegetarian, I don't want to hear about poor animals killed for our pleasure. I don't know how you can have lived in the rainforest and with Mexican peasants who only eat meat!

> No, Ilaria—I respond—meat is very scarce among the poor and Indigenous peoples of Latin America. Yuca, potatoes, corn, beans and, with luck, a bit of rice and some mountain herbs are what those who can get them eat. The rest—the poorest—eat shit. Or wild nettles, like we did when we took refuge in Prato during the war.

> "Ma dai,"[17] intervenes Aldo, her new husband, they don't know how to eat, they are ignorant like the Africans who are invading Italy and don't want to adapt to our customs . . . but prefer to keep on eating monkey meat."

16. "Chinese people eat everything."
17. Come on, man.

CHAPTER 14

Campa Doctorate

🌵

IN 1963, I WAS twenty-four and studying for a doctorate at the Catholic University. My fourteen-year-old brother, Luis, was in middle school. I had just finished my undergraduate degree, also at the Catholic University; my thesis was on the written sources about the Campa, an Indigenous tribe in the Peruvian Amazon.

My analysis of those historiographic sources had inevitably led me to the archives of Jesuits and Franciscans who, from the end of the 16th century, had been responsible for the "Christianization," religious conquest, and secular control of the Indigenous peoples of the upper Amazon.

The Jesuit's archives were under the personal control of the order's historian, Rubén Vargas Ugarte, S.J. The aging historian wouldn't receive me, much less authorize a young student like myself to look at the order's colonial archives. I had a bit more luck with the Franciscans: a humble Italian friar, Father Pelosi, took pity on me and we soon developed a friendship, more out of our shared gastro-cultural and linguistic interests than over theological doctrine. A few months later, he offered to put me up at one of the Franciscan missions in the Amazon in exchange for my promise not to ask to see the archive of the Franciscan convent at Ocopa, in the central mountains. The Franciscans had their own historians, and a strict monopoly over their historiographic sources.

A few years later, the same Father Pelosi, with a generosity for which I never fully thanked him, brought me some typewritten Franciscan documents from the General Archive of the Franciscan Order in Rome. These were copies of texts from the 17th and 18th centuries, and were about Peru's Central Selva. But Father Pelosi's most generous act was giving me access to the two most important and remote missions the Franciscans had been able to establish in Campa territory during the 19th and 20th centuries, more than one hundred years after Juan Santos Atahualpa's Indigenous rebellion: the mission at Puerto Ocopa on the lower Perené River where it flows into the Ene—where the great Tambo River is formed—and the Oventeni mission, in the Gran Pajonal.

As a young urban university student, I would be able to travel into the heart of rebel Campa territory, those parts of the Amazon which, beginning in 1742, had been liberated by the Campa-Antis, Amuesha, Nomatzguena, Machiguenga, Shipibo, Cashibo, Amahuaca, and a dozen or so other Indian ethnicities under the Spanish colonial yoke. After their liberation, they had been battered by the neo-colonialism of the Republic.

One could get to Father Castillo's mission at Puerto Ocopa only by canoe, paddling down the Perené from San Ramón and La Merced, Amazon jungle towns that had been founded by the Franciscans during the colonial era, taken back by the Campa in 1742, and were controlled by the rebels until 1848 when President Ramón Castilla's Republican troops entered with all their fire power and established Peru's neo-colonial dominion.

One could travel from Lima to La Merced by second-class bus, a journey of ten or twelve hours through the central Andes. One could reach the Oventeni mission in the Gran Pajonal only by foot along an Indigenous trail from Puerto Ocopa, or by a Peruvian Air Force twin-engine military plane that flew once a week and was too expensive for my modest budget.

I decided to enter the Gran Pajonal by way of the Campa trail which, from the Franciscan mission at Puerto Ocopa, ascends northeast toward the Gran Pajonal highlands more than 5,000 feet above sea level.

Papá agreed that my brother Luis should accompany me on this first ethnological fieldwork trip, and so did my stepmother Rita, although with much less enthusiasm.

I had to negotiate my decision to write my doctoral thesis on the Campa of the Gran Pajonal with my advisor, Doctor Jehan Albert Vellard who, with his brusque tone and marked French accent, had insisted I stop reading what colonial and Republican Peru and European travelers had written about the Campa.

Señor Varese, stop reading about the Campa Indians. You are too influenced by the writings of others. The few missionaries, travelers, rubber plantation workers, people of the Andes and the coast, who have visited the Selva Central, will not be able to teach you much about the Campa or about the Pajonal region. Go where they live, learn their language, stay with them as long as you can, and come back with books of notes and photos.

The money and the time I have for this research are very limited—I responded to Professor Vellard. I only have the summer months—January, February and March—when I don't have to be at the University or work selling jewelry. Fortunately, I've been able to get ahold of a Nagra tape recorder and Leica camera I bought second-hand from the Swiss archeologist Baher; with these I will be able to take full advantage of the time I have. My younger brother Gigi will be coming with me and will help me resolve practical matters once we are in the Pajonal.

At the beginning of the Sixties, there were no public or private institutions in Peru that supported anthropological or any other type of investigation. Among the students and professors, it didn't even occur to us that anyone in the country might be able to support such work with a donation. By the end of the Sixties, foreign researchers began to arrive, especially from France and the United States. They had resources from their governments and from cultural and scientific foundations, and the luxury of spending several months or even years living in Andean or Amazon villages, carrying out longitudinal studies of impressive depth, collecting plant samples, ethnographic materials, musical and linguistic recordings, and photographs. Poor young students like ourselves confirmed once again—through envy and a certain resentment—that neo-colonialism and imperialism continued to place us at a disadvantage in all areas of life: economic, scientific, and cultural.

My growing anti-imperialist paranoia was consolidated years later, in 1969, when I went to work for Juan Velasco Alvarado's revolutionary government and looked at all the studies of the Amazon region. I realized that the reports by U.S. academics had grown exponentially from 1968 on, in concert with Velasco Alvarado's nationalist revolution.[18] Was it a mere coinci-

18. A glance at the chronology of anthropological studies published back then reveals that only after 1968 did the first academic studies on the Peruvian Amazon begin to appear in print, and they were all by North American researchers: Donald Lathrop's ethno-archeology in 1968; the summary ethnography by the Evangelical missionary John Elick in 1969; John Bodley's social anthropology studies in 1969 and 1970; the comprehensive ethnology by Gerald Weiss in 1969 and 1972; William Denevan's study of human geography in 1971; and Jay Lenhertz's historic study published in 1972.

dence? Or had the causal relationship already been there as pointed out by anthropologist Shelton Davis?[19] I had begun to believe there was truth in those coincidences.

19. A few years earlier, Shelton Davis found a connection between the territorial occupation of Indigenous areas and the reports made by North American evangelical missionaries from the Summer Institute of Linguistics, the Wycliffe Bible Translators, and the U.S. companies exploiting oil. Was it simply coincidental? The Spanish translation of the book by Father Thomas Ohm, *Crítica de Asia sobre el Cristianismo de Occidente*, had appeared in 1950. There, the Dominican priest had said that the missionaries were the "hound dogs of Western imperialism."

CHAPTER 15

Entering the Gran Pajonal

☙

ARMED WITH MY LEICA camera, my Nagra tape recorder, entirely inappropriate clothing stuffed into a backpack that was much too heavy, shoes that didn't keep my feet dry, notebooks, pencils, and the saving companionship of my brother Luis, we steered a Campa canoe we had rented at the Puerto Ocopa mission to the mouth of the Perené.

It must have been January of 1963. Father Castillo, who had been advised by Franciscan radio of our arrival, received us with the taunting skepticism of one who had lived a life of poverty and privation in the name of a religious ideal not shared by the supposed beneficiaries of his sacrifice: the Campa children and young people forcibly removed to the mission; and shared even less by these young urban men who proposed to understand the Indians on a trip of a few months.

We were given a quick and efficient tour of the mission before the sun went down:

The latrine is the shack at the end of that open field just before you get to the yuca plot. You may urinate anywhere outside the palm rooves, because it's good for the earth. The Campa children — all young boys — sleep together in one dormitory. You visitors may sleep on the second-floor loft, in sleeping bags. Here are some candles, but use your flashlights to move about at night. Since you didn't bring mosquito netting, try to keep your feet, necks, and heads well covered, because we have vampire bats who, lacking cattle, like to suck the blood of humans. Even better if they come from Lima. Here are two air rifles; you can entertain yourselves before you sleep by shooting at the rats that run along the ceiling beams: point with your flashlights and aim for their heads.

I allowed my brother Gigi the sport of this nighttime hunt while I wrote my travel notes by the light of my battery lamp. For a moment, I thought about getting out my Nagra tape recorder, giving a few turns to the little handle that charged the battery, and recording an interview with Father Castillo. But my exhaustion and scant ethnographic experience put an end to that idea.

My baptism by water prolonged itself all that night and the next day. The weather that would accompany us for the next three months announced itself right away: rain and more rain, day and night, only interrupted by a very few sunny days, just long enough to dry clothing that had become moldy from the humidity.

SEVERAL TIMES PRIOR TO this, I had spent days or weeks in the village of Flor de Punga, on the lower Ucayali River. I had gone to Huallaga with Papá, traveling by raft on a few occasions. I had traveled to the Cordillera Azul and through the Central Jungle by car. But this was the first time I had walked for days, in driving rain, crossed rivers swollen with water up to my chin, so I might get to a Campa dwelling with a palm roof and pona floor, raised more than a foot off the ground and without walls to protect it from the cold winds coming from the west, from the snow-topped mountains at Cerro de Pasco.

I wasn't prepared for this test of my endurance, and neither was my brother Gigi. But he responded to the challenge better than I did, and he saved my life when, after the first days of hiking up and down over a mud path, long hikes in the cold of the humid forest, tripping over fallen moss-covered tree trunks, we arrived at the first Campa home and I sank to the floor vomiting bile and shivering with cold, although I was sweating as if I had a fever. I didn't know I was dehydrated and about to lose what scant reason I still possessed. Gigi helped me swallow a bit of yuca fermented *chicha* the men of the house and the Campa guides who accompanied us offered me.

That first day of hiking up into the Gran Pajonal had begun early, when Father Castillo introduced the Campa guides who would take us as far as Oventeni. They were two young men dressed in pants and undershirts, and they carried bulky bags of woven cotton hanging left to right across their shoulders. Later I would discover that this was all they had with them: achiote paste, a palm comb, and the cushma or tunic they would don once we got to the Gran Pajonal. They carried their machetes and, if I remember correctly, one of them also had a 12-gauge shotgun and the other a bow and arrows.

Back in Lima, one of my friends had offered me a 38-caliber revolver—it might have been Lucho Bortesi or Eduardo Mazzini. The revolver was silver-plated and impressive, and in an adventurous moment I'd accepted it. But I never used it; couldn't even get it to work the one time I took it out into the forest. It had been an utterly stupid precaution for someone ignorant of the Amazon and unable to recognize the real dangers in these landscapes, or aim correctly at a menacing snake.

THE INITIAL TEST, OR cultural initiation, took place on the first day, and I wasn't even aware of it until I had spent several months with the Campa. It happened halfway along that day's hike, when our guides asked Luis and me to walk ahead of them and cut through the brush. I thought it might be some sort of ritual I should explore in a moment of rest—which never arrived for me on that day of exhaustion and dehydration. Months later, I would learn that certain places are considered hieratic. These are places visited by sha-mans, where dead *shirpiari* appear, transformed into jaguars.

I remember little about that night we spent at the Campa dwelling on our way to the Gran Pajonal. My brother Gigi, after ministering as well as he could to my health, fell into a deep sleep until dawn. I, on the other hand, spent the night alternating between trembling cold and sweating fevers, my dreams and hallucinations waking the Campa family who had shown us their hospitality. I was afraid I wouldn't be able to make good on my own commit-ment to live for months among the Campa and learn from them how to be an anthropologist.

I wasn't aware that the bits of conversations, laughter, and smell of roast-ing yuca and forest meat I woke to on and off was the Campa's cultural way of sleeping, and wasn't my altered perception caused by dehydration. They had to get up every now and then to reignite the fire that dozed in its human rhythm. That fire not only provided heat and light, but also defended them against possible animal infcursions by keeping the dogs curled up around it attentive in their vigil. The final waking at dawn, when Venus can still be seen in the firmament, is not a return from the oneiric depths, but the end of a se-ries of brief strolls through the dream world that can be clearly remembered and predict the events of the following day, of life itself.

ON THE MORNING OF the second day I felt better and ready to begin the march to the Pajonal. The weather had cleared, and beneath those forest branches the air remained fresh for several hours. Then, without warning, the dark landscape opened up onto an immense and sunny plain covered by giant grasses three feet high. There, among those grasses—the Pajonal—a line of Campa men, women, and children appeared. They were all wearing *cushmas*, and their faces were painted with red achiote and black huito, their dark hair hanging to their shoulders. All the men and boys carried either bows and arrows, hunting or Winchester repeating rifles, and machetes. An older woman carried a basket made of thick leaves on her head, with what appeared to be a burning fire within. Later I would learn it was really a heart of palm that works as a living wick. At the time I, the ignorant young ethnographer, didn't understand a thing. I thought I knew. I thought the name these people went by was Campa; that this was what they called themselves. I shared the ignorance of centuries of Spaniards and Peruvians who had never engaged in respectful dialogue with the Indigenous peoples.

Our two guides made us understand that we must wait by the side of the path while they began what I would later learn was the ritual or ceremony of encounter and exchange of spiritual and material goods that defines the relationship between different Campa lineages.

Later I was able to better understand the complexity of this aspect of Campa-Asháninka culture. *Ayumparii* is the term the Campa use to describe the reciprocal exchange of gifts and objects of value. After months of living with Asháninka families, I learned to decipher the profound ethical and social function of this institution that makes possible the social and cultural cohesion of thousands of families spread over a vast territory and reachable only by days of walking or fording rivers. Back then, I didn't realize there were Asháninka people in Brazil, more than 500 miles from the Gran Pajonal, and that those distant "relatives" visit and participate in feasts, hunting or fishing expeditions, or the exchange of goods that make them mutual *ayumparii*.

Not long after our meeting with that first group of Asháninka—who according to our guides turned out to be an extended family on a trip to another village—a smaller group appeared along the same path on the Pajonal. Once again: long hair, ochre-colored tunics, achiote red and huito black facial paint, arrows and bows and rifles filled the human landscape. And once again, the young ethnologist from the city didn't understand what was happening. Frightened by exaggeratedly high-pitched tones of voice, bare feet stomping forcefully on the ground, the spitting and agitation of bows and arrows, my brother and I kept our distance from what appeared to us to be a pitched battle headed toward violence.

The shouting match goes on for a while until, as if on cue, it suddenly stops and a calm dialogue takes its place. The men remove their bags—their *saratos* or *táato*—and hand them to their counterparts who do the same with theirs. Then each man, with his interlocutor's bag over his shoulder and chest, begins going through it, carefully examining its contents. When he finds an object of interest—a palm comb, a length of bamboo filled with achiote, a wooden stamp for painting the body, a mirror, knife, rifle cartridge or fish-hook—the Asháninka man takes it in his hand and returns the bag to its owner, who does the same. The exchange of gifts ends, and communion has been established. The sacred reciprocity is confirmed, and the other has become nosháninka, "my people, my brother." Now it's time to chew a handful of coca leaves to definitively seal their shared humanity.

At that moment when I entered the Gran Pajonal in January of 1963, without knowing or consciously proposing it, I was respectfully accepting the challenge of understanding the profound and complex cosmological and ethical weave of the Asháninka society of the Peruvian Amazon.

IN APRIL I RETURNED to the gray autumn of Lima with more questions than answers about the Campa-Asháninka and the Gran Pajonal. Nonetheless, I did confirm that the missionaries of the 17th and 18th centuries had been right when they said that the Indigenous trails went from the depths of the Amazon to Cerro de la Sal, situated near Metraro and Eneno in Asháninka territory.

These roads, traveled by Indigenous peoples who live in the vast region of forests and rivers extending hundreds of miles to the north, east, and south of the Gran Pajonal, form a network of cultural relationships and exchange that places the Asháninka people at the center of centuries of Indian resistance to Spanish and Peruvian attempts at occupation and submission.

I found signs of this resistance in each Asháninka community in the Pajonal. In the women's house, near the fire, I always saw a small pitchfork planted firmly in the ground. Hanging from it was a piece of rock salt, of a reddish color, like that of their tunics, wrapped in a piece of cotton cloth or in banana leaves. This salt was from the Cerro de la Sal, and had been brought by *ayumparii* travelers in a centuries-long or millennial act of reciprocity that extended beyond the ethnic Asháninka territory to the river basins of the Ucayali, Ene, Urubamba, Pinchis, and Palcazú rivers, and to the mouths of the Curanja and Upper Purús that flow east through the lands of the Asháninka who had been expelled to the state of Acre, in Brazil, during the rubber era, in the late 19th and early 20th centuries.

For thousands of years, this salt from the jungle mountains must have been the symbol, as well as concrete trading good providing linkage to the many Indigenous nationalities—the Asháninka, Yánesha, Nomatziguenga, Machiguenga, Piro, Shipibo, Cunibo, and dozens more—of the Peruvian Amazon's northwestern region.

The salt from Cerro de la Sal—*Tzivínki*—would also cement my relationship with the profound history of the Asháninka people.

CHAPTER 16

Pashuka, Incestuous Coca, and Asháninka Eros

✵

I REMEMBER PASHUKA'S ABSENT, ALMOST nostalgic, gaze, and her expert hands preparing yuca and fish, and combing her daughter Irerene's long hair, looking insistently for pesky lice as she sang songs evocative of ancient poems and long histories. It was February 1967, near the Unini River.

Long ago, the little bird called Tzia was human. He spent his time tormenting his mother, Mamántziki, wanting to sleep with her and begging her to hand over the coca she kept in her vagina. The story goes that the Sun—Oriátziri—had asked his wife Mamántziki to protect the coca and not give it to anyone. Finally, Tzia overpowered his mother, Mamántziki, raping her and making off with the coca. When Oriátziri came home and asked Mamántziki for water to drink, Mamántziki became desperate and began to vomit coca leaves. Oriátziri understood what had happened, because he saw the coca leaves stuck to Tzia's penis. Furious, Oriátziri burned his son Tzia, threw his wife out of the house, and climbed into the sky, never again to return to earth.

Pashuka's children, Juancito and Irerene, and her husband Rolando, later explained to me the incestuous origin of the coca leaf, laughing at my cautious inquiry about the narrative. Once again, young Juancito was pushing the limits of my timid urban modesty with erotic provocations shared joyously by the rest of the family and ratified by the songs that Pashuka continued to sing for us:

The heron is like me, white and beautiful
Beautiful is the heron of the Ucayali River

You will wait for me in my hut, in Hantani
Come, come. I will carry my fire while you alone will wait for me
Look at me, I am drunk from masato beer
Let's go swimming together in the Ucayali

In all the months of the years I spent in the Gran Pajonal and on the shores of the rivers that surround and cross it, I always felt drawn to the erotic tension that exists in the relationships I established with Asháninka men and women. Visual voluptuousness and sensuality of smell are both rooted in the mysteries of their origins. The sound of flutes in the solitude of the forest, heard along somber trails, knowing they might be played by a lonely woman wanting to shelter a man, followed by the warm rattle of little carved bones hanging from the hand woven baby carrier across the shoulder and breast of a nursing mother, prohibited and unattainable now even in her constant flirtation. Or the penetrating smell of red achiote spread across the cheekbones and cheeks that accompanied a vision of black huito, the lines of which crossed the face, attracting the gaze and sense of smell that seduced them to necks and shoulders adorned with scented seeds. And then the voices and songs, always telling of passions, nostalgias, past and future dreams: concerns I failed to understand in their symbolic density of animals, birds, plants, and landscapes that were mysterious to me.

I am playing with him in Hantani
I have followed him to his hut
Pipópki, pipópki (come, come)
I have thrown his shell now
And we will always see one another
You will wait for me in my beautiful place
And we will always see one another
I will bring my fire and you alone will be waiting
Look at me. Can't you see I am drunk on fermented yuca?
Let us swim together

From indiscreet observer, in time I became the one being observed and an involuntary participant in the string of local stories braided into the audacity of the fermented yuca drink. The ethnographer became the subject studied by the young Asháninkas Kokolito or Pashuka who, in their songs, invited him to reconsider his return to Lima:

You see the Asháninka as they are
But you will be crying,
your tears are already falling
The wiracocha is crying.
He will cry when he goes home
Come, come
Look at me, look at me
Let us go soon to your place, your house
I will go with you, do not wait for anyone else
With us will go my katári and the chowantzi
There in your place you will look, you will search
And not see me
Because you will be with your little shell

One afternoon, seated on the wooden floor of the *káapa*,[20] the men and guests' house, with Juanito, Irerene, and Pashuka, in a single instant I was forced to let go of my petit-bourgeois modesty and face the challenge of understanding and externalizing my sexuality in front of a young adolescent girl, her mother, and older brother. Without fully understanding the symbolic weight of the word *totzíro*—shell—I began to say I would soon be returning to Lima to rejoin my *nototzíroti*. Pashuka and Irerene asked, with all the ease inherent to the Asháninka marriage and relationship system, if I had ever given *totzíro* to my brother.

"No—I responded with little anthropological sensibility—because it isn't our custom."

"Will your wife have given *totzíro* to others?"

"That would upset me very much," I insisted, wrapped in my Euro-Christian morality.

"Pikóye itóziro asháninka?"

And they all laughed happily at Pashuka's question if I wanted to have sex with an Asháninka man or woman.

At that moment I realized, in astonishment, that the comment young Juancito had made several days earlier - *"Pitzi teroche*—Let's make love"-might have been more than a joke. Is Juancito a "berdache" or "two-spirited

20. Longhouse where unmarried adult men and male visitors may stay for days and nights.

man" like those the scandalized Anglo-American Puritans found among the Indians of the North American plains? Is he bisexual? Or is he simply a young man who has gone through the puberty ceremony, received his penis cord and new Asháninka name, and awaits his first woman lover while exploring and practicing his new sexuality? It may simply be a cultural case, like that of the adolescent boys, Nambikwara, who Claude Lévi-Strauss photographed in the Mato Grosso making love in front of everyone—members of his community and foreign visitors—on the clear sands of highland Brazil. *Tristes Tropiques,* that I read back then, came to my aid: my petit-bourgeois and socialist morality was put on notice by the great French anthropologist's cultural gaze.

Why do I bring up the Indigenous incest story precisely now, as I try to evoke my eroticism of nearly fifty years before? Is Tzia my alter-ego, my absurd allegory, my blameless avoidance when faced with the unbearable weight that has been stuck in my throat for decades?

CHAPTER 17

Moisés and the Asháni nka Cosmology

※

OWARD THE END OF 1969, in the Chorrillos neighborhood to the
south of Lima, I got to know an Asháninka—or perhaps he was Nomatziguenga—, an ex-soldier who was then a construction worker.
We had a short intense friendship, finally devastated by our opposing political
positions. That brief friendship, nevertheless, allowed us to get to know each
other's life stories and cultural itineraries.

Moisés Gamarra was from the Central Jungle, born and raised in San
Ramón de Pangoa, in the region of Mazamari-Satipo. He had been "recruited" into the Peruvian Army, trained and taught some reading and writing, and eventually banished from his forest to the miserable urban coast.

I was only able to learn bits and pieces of his childhood and military experience, but his knowledge of the language, culture, and Asháninka cosmology (or Nomatziguena cosmology?) was notable, above all because Moisés
was constantly comparing and criticizing the urban creole society of a Peru
in which he lived in abject poverty. Moisés disagreed with me about the supposed good intentions of the Revolutionary Armed Forces government and
President Velasco Alvarado. For him, Peru's military revolution was but another face of the same oppressive and exploitative system that had ruled the
country for centuries. For me, the Velasco revolution put a crack in Peruvian
colonialism and we had to take advantage of that.

We would get together at night in Miraflores, in a small badly-lit office of
the Raúl Porras Barrenechea Institute at the University of San Marcos, and
there I would go over the field notes I'd brought from the Gran Pajonal and,
with Moisés's help, transcribe my recordings of songs and interviews.

When we began to work on one of the creation myths Pashuka had told me, Moisés made comments that revealed a deep knowledge of Asháninka cosmology. With his invaluable help, we transcribed a more detailed version of the cosmogonic myth of the Gran Pajonal Asháninka, that years later we published together with a lengthy analysis in the French journal *Annales*.[21]

Moisés Gamarra's name figures as the article's principle co-author, but I was never able to tell him that, or give him copies of the published piece. By then, Moisés and I had broken off our friendship and gone our separate ways. In some leaflets that appeared on the Ene River around 1974, Moisés accused me of being an agent of the Velasco "dictatorship" and of being linked to the CIA. I never knew if Shining Path cells were already forming in the forest around Ayacucho at that time; from the 1980s on, the area was occupied by members of that organization. I don't want to believe Moisés could have been so indoctrinated by Shining Path ideology and practice. In just a few years, that ideology and practice showed itself to be as distant as can be imagined from Asháninka and Andean cosmology, and from the utopia they envisioned. The Asháninka communities and villages along the Ene, Tambo, Perené, and Pichis-Palczu rivers, and even those farther away in the interior of the Gran Pajonal, suffered losses of thousands of lives at the hands of the Shining Path, the Tupac Amaru guerrilla, and the Peruvian Army and Police.

For years, I have asked myself how peoples imbued with world visions that integrate the material and sacred, the ethical and aesthetic, and who honor, in the history of the world and of the universe, the idea that no biological or physical being, on earth or in the heavens, tangible or mysterious, ranks above any other, can betray their roots by allowing themselves to be seduced by a Biblical discourse of insipid parables and formulae involving vulgar prophecy and banal symbolism. The Fourth or Fifth Sword?[22] In the Andes and in the Amazon, there have been no swords since the 17th century.

To what remote and arcane symbols, buried in what popular subconscious, do these formulae and liturgy of the word appeal? In what moment of the millennial history of the Andes or Amazon were dogs hanged from posts or

21. Moisés Gamarra and Stefano Varese, "Deux versions cosmogoniques campa: esquisse analytique," *Annales*, Vol. 31, N. 3 (1976): 469-480.

22. Shining Path's leader Abimael Guzmán presented himself as the "fourth sword" of Marxism-Leninism-Maoism, the first three being, of course, Marx, Lenin, and Mao.

trees?[23] Whoever decapitated and dismembered human bodies, and why, and who buried them later in a shameful pile of defeated hopes? Or were those macabre rituals anonymous efforts to rekindle the memory of the Peruvian Conquest, its terror and the Indian exegesis of Inkari, the divine hero dismembered and buried by the Conquest in the hope that he would return in the form of a renovated Indian Peru?

THE COLD AND RAINY afternoons in the Gran Pajonal lend themselves to telling stories. On one of those afternoons, seated on the *Kaápa* platform, I listened as Pashuka told me about Moon-*Káshiri* who earlier, much earlier, had been *Tzirámpari*, a human being.

> See, he has his amatéríntsi, the crown on his head, like the Asháninka. He wears his crown when night appears in the sky. Then he goes to the Ucayali River to fish, and you don't see him anymore. There he does his work of fishing and collecting fish, but not only fish, also dead Asháninka. Those who killed themselves, those who died of influenza or measles, those killed by arrows, babies who die a few days after they are born. Other Asháninka he does not pick up, he let them walk through the world . . . but he gives all of them (those he picks up and those he leaves) to his wives: Mamántziki and Inankáuti. Only Inankáuti accepts the dead. Mamántziki doesn't want to know anything about the dead, she doesn't like them, she doesn't want to see them. Mamántzki is alive, she doesn't die, she is like us. Inankáuti, on the other hand, is dead and she receives the dead who are like children and raises them all together. She nurses them and when they are big they get together and have their own families.

Pashuka continues to tell me how in earlier times, in the beginning, Kásiri-Moon was an *añuje,*[24] *sháwo*, and ate yuca:

> One day Kásiri-Sháwo tells Mamántziki's father: "Follow me, we will go to my house to collect fish." When the fish are finished I, Kásiri, will come

23. Shining Path militants announced the beginning of their revolutionary war by hanging dogs in public view in Lima as a symbol of what would happen to people joining the government army and police forces rather than participating in the "Revolution."

24. The *añuje* or *agutí* is a rodent of the tropical rainforest whose principal nourishment comes from seeds; the biological species is *Dasyprocta puntata*.

to your house to visit you and harvest yuca, and I will say: "Náare tátzimi
náani kaniri, I have come to take yuca." The next day all Mamántziki's family goes to Kásiri's house, up there, toward the sky, on a great path, straight
and clean. They stay there for a while and when the visit is over they leave
Kásiri's house, but Mamántziki cannot find the way back. She gets lost and
cannot return and there she stays. But Mamántziki is alive and that is why
she does not want to receive the dead.

Two years later, in Lima, Moisés tells me that Moon's real name is Manchákori and that his relationship with the young adolescent girl whose name
might be Mamántziki is much more complex. Moisés says that the whole family of a young girl who had her first menstruation had gone to the mountains to
look for earth to eat. The young girl is left in the small hut that the Asháninka
build for girls when they menstruate for the first time. There the girl busies herself spinning cotton and patiently waiting for the bleeding to stop.

The young girl heard a noise near the hut and, without thinking, spit out
a little of the plant she was chewing to regulate her cycle.
    "You have committed an error, why have you spit me out," Moon-
Manchákori asked her. "From now on, when I am up there in the sky, you
will see blemishes on my face."

Other Asháninka say that the blemishes are from when Moon slept with
the young girl, the girl amorously caressed her face with her hands that were
black from the fire's ashes, and marked her for eternity.

    "Don't your parents have anything besides earth to eat? Look, from now
on the people will have food."
    And Manchákori caused all the fruits of the forest to appear.
    "When your parents return, you are going to say that those fruits are
there in the forests. When they want to eat them, they must gather them
in order, without taking all of them, without mixing them, without undo-
ing what I have just made."
    When the parents returned, they listened to Manchákori's and the
young girl's story and hurried to the jungle to gather the fruit. They did so
carelessly, falling over one another, eating until they were satiated and ru-
ining the order of the plot that Moon had so carefully planted in the forest.
When Moon-Manchákori returned, the Asháninka were frightened and
began running in all directions. Those who fell to the ground were trans-

formed into insects like Katzikori, the ant we eat now. Those who climbed into the trees were transformed into sloths, and others ended up being forest animals. It is because of what happened back then that all the fruits of the forest are tossed about and grow randomly.

The only people who remained human beings were the mother and her young daughter. After a while, the daughter realized she was pregnant. When she was about to give birth, Moon-Manchákori said to the young woman:

"You are going to grab onto that tree so you won't feel pain or burn yourself."

She was pointing to the *Tziritosi* (Tucunay) tree, but the young girl grabbed the Oropel.[25] The Asháninka say that is why they know when the dry season begins, because of the Tziritosi flowers, and they know that when the flowers dry up the rains will come. When the child was born, it wasn't human like we are, but a bit of ember that burned its mother completely. Sun-Katzirinkáitiri was born with a very long tail, like a star. That was its umbilical cord. Moon-Machákori cut it into pieces, saying:

"This is white, this is black, this is good, this is bad, and this last little piece is Asháninka."

In time, there will only be a few Asháninkas left. And right away he blew and dispersed the whites, the blacks, and the Asháninkas so they would all have their lands and places in the world. Later Moon-Manchákori called the young woman's father and Maonte appeared.

"Come, hurry: take this hot ember far from here and bury it so it can awaken later. If it burns too hot, don't pour water on it, only earth, but only where it burns you."

While Maonte was carrying him, Sun-Katzirinkáitiri kept growing and burned too much. Maonte poured water on him so he could continue to carry him and finally bury him far away. Then he returned to where Luna-Manchákori was.

25. The Oropel, with its bright red flowers, is a native tree now used by the mestizo settlers to mark the boundaries of their land. It is a tree of the *Magnolides* family, of the *Erythrina spp* species. I have not been able to determine the species of the *Tziritosi*.

"Did you pour water on him?"

"No, I certainly did not."

"Well, we will see."

In a while it got light and the darkness disappeared and the sun was born in the east. But when the sun was born, the fog also appeared. And then Moon-Manchákori told Maonte:

"You poured water on him, and from now on there will be fog. You lied and there will be rains. There would never have been rains if the mists hadn't collected water. But your mistake was not to have poured the water everywhere and from now on there will be a lot of rain in some places and very little in others."

At dawn, when the sun came up, Maonte said:

"I have made a mistake."

And seated in the hut he watched Sun from sunup to sundown, every day. And that is why his back is black. Moon-Manchákori asked Maonte:

"Are you sad?"

And at that moment Maonte turned into a night bird who, because he lied about his error, does not sing except on nights of a full moon.

"Well—said Moon-Manchákori—now you have someone to give you light during the day. You need someone to give you light at night . . . " it was too dark because there were no stars in the sky. Before going up into the sky, Moon-Manchákori left Maonte's youngest son, Tasorintzi, in her place. And Moon began to rise in the sky and got bigger and bigger until we could see the blemishes on her face."

IN THE GRAN PAJONAL, Pashuka, Lidia, other women, and Sebastián and Coronado had told me that many beings, who were humans at the beginning of time, were also turned into animals by Oriátziri when, irritated by the robbery of the coca leaf, he rose into the sky and wanted to take his people with him.

Onkiro, the mouse, said he had a toothache and couldn't go into the sky with Oriátziri. But he was lying. The truth is, his mouth was full of grains of corn and his wife had stuffed her mouth with pumpkin seeds. They slashed and burn their field-chacra so they could plant the seeds, but the smoke rose to the sky and upset Pawá who turned Onkiro into a mouse with only two teeth at the front of its mouth. And from then on, Onkiro eats corn, pumpkin and yuca from the Asháninka's fields because he thinks they belong to him.

With Coronado in the Gran Pajonal, circa 1962-63

It took me a while to understand that for the Asháninka the loss of their divine condition and of the sacred statute humanity/animality/hearthly integrated in a single unitary cosmos is always the result of errors. It is the error of Tzia, incestuous and profane, that causes Inoki, Sun-Oriátziri's, ascension into the sky. The errors committed by the first Asháninka provoked the loss of their primordial human condition and turned them into animals/humans/plants that now and forever populate the universe. Our Earth-Kipátzi, who once linked Sky-Inoki with the world of Clouds-Mekóri, and Subterranean-Kivinti is now Kamaventi-the Land of Death, because we are no longer immortal like we were in the beginning, in the Poerani—The Before—with which all Asháninka stories begin.

It took me even longer to acquire a clear image of Asháninka cosmology. Many years later, in 1975, I read and was able to compare my understanding of the Asháninka world with that which the anthropology of those years had produced.

Between 1963 and 1964, I went from the Gran Pajonal to the confluence of the Perené and Ene rivers, and from there set out with two Asháninka in a motorized canoe down the Tambo River. On the first evening, we arrived at a little Indigenous hamlet on the left bank. When we turned off our outboard motor, the first thing we heard were the notes of one of J. S. Bach's Brandenburg concertos.

A thin young man received us with the dignity of someone who has lived many months in isolation from his own culture and in the liminal space of another that is just beginning to be revealed. Gerald Weiss was a doctoral student in anthropology at the University of Michigan. I understood his mistrust because I myself had felt it several times when some stranger came too near my field residence in the Gran Pajonal. Furthermore, Gerald Weiss had gone through the devastating experience of having lost all his field notes, recordings, photos, plant samples, and some of his equipment on a river trip down to Atalaya and Pucallpa. Our encounter, if I remember correctly, was brief: a couple of days of circumspect conversation about our respective studies of Asháninka society. I understood that Weiss had accumulated an extraordinary empirical knowledge of the Asháninka who live along the river. I secretly admired his linguistic ability, his easiness conversing in the Campa language—which is what we called the Arawak language of the Asháninka back then—and I had to restrain the envy I felt of the technology Weiss had access to in the depths of the Amazon rainforest.

In my precarious condition of an underdeveloped leftist Peruvian student, I rationalized my own doctoral project's insufficiencies in terms of the crude academic "dependency theory" and the sociological hypothesis of "unequal development." Nonetheless, my meeting with this genteel and brilliant "agent of Yankee cultural imperialism" pushed me to try to learn a lot more about the Asháninka of the Pajonal, about whom Weiss himself confessed to knowing very little.

When Gerald Weiss published his doctoral dissertation in 1975, I had already finished and published mine, which would later become a book, *La sal de los cerros* (Lima, 1968). When I read his dissertation, I could see great commonalities with my own, but also profound ethnological and theoretical differences.

Something similar occurred with the dissertation by another U.S. anthropologist, John Bodley, who would publish his texts on the socioeconomic adaptations of the Campa-Asháninka in 1970. I had a closer friendship with John Bodley than with Gerald Weiss, perhaps because of the social commitment that Bodley always had to the Indigenous peoples of the Amazon as well as to those throughout the wider world. Gerald Weiss had followed a more strictly academic path, which I somehow interpreted as being farther from the Asháninka's concrete needs.

Yet I had to revise my feelings about Gerald Weiss's supposed distance, when I read the lines he wrote and published in 2005 on the visits he had made to Asháninka communities in 1977 and 1980. Weiss paid tribute to Asháninka resistance to the oppression against them by all Peruvian stripes and political and economic creeds, and recognized that the fundamental goodness of the Asháninka people has been responsible for their survival, and for their stubborn adherence to their own cultural values

CHAPTER 18

Kirinko, Wiracocha, Chori, and the *Kamári*

҉

THE CAMPA-ASHÁNINKA COSMOLOGY — ITS VISION and perception of the world — only partially and begrudgingly recognized the existence of evil. I captured the essential tenet of this Campa vision and practice back in the Sixties, mostly thanks to spoken narrations I was able to understand with difficulty, and to the analysis I tried to make of them with the help of Juancito and other talented and patient young people.

Spoken narrations take place between two people in the presence of others. They may be demands for debts in reciprocal exchange (what I called the reciprocal system of *ayúmpari* in my book). They may also be cosmological and ethical reaffirmations expressed metaphorically in hunting and fishing anecdotes or on journeys for the purpose of exchange. Or they may obviate the need for metaphor, in order to repeat chunks of cosmogony narratives that reaffirm the immanent nature of things.

Nevertheless, I confess that I did not arrive at this understanding alone. I needed some time to read what other interpreters had to say about Campa-Asháninka culture and, above all, my own notes and the ongoing conversations I was able to have with Asháninka and other Indigenous peoples from other places. All this aided me in penetrating these moral exegeses.

When I wrote *La sal de los cerros*, I'd acknowledged that the Asháninka's central cosmological and philosophical principle, one I dared declare "gnostic," established the fact that error produces loss and that loss is the absence of goodness and beauty. Evil — *kamári* — exists, and manifests itself in entities that are negative and harmful; what in our Mediterranean Judeo-Christian-Islamic ideology we might call demonic. When it appears, it causes terrible damage to people; however, it can be repaired by the intervention of "Our People, Our Brothers," Nosháninka-Noshéninka, intangible spiritual beings that populate the universe at all cosmic levels. And above all by the saving intervention of the *shiripiári*, the shaman, healer of the world, an exceptional individual who is capable of a "lifelong marriage" to tobacco, to the powerful spirit and substance of the most sacred of Asháninka plants.

With tobacco-shéri and other sacred Teacher Plants—ayahuasca-kamarámpi, horóva[26] leaves, lily of the valley-nato, and Datura saáro—the *shiripiári* sets about to repair human error and restore the equilibrium that has momentarily been lost. The spirits of the sacred plants are what cure the world, and the *shiripiári* is the intermediary between the goodness of the plants, the goodness of the intangible Asháninka who populate the universe, the goodness of other sacred beings who materialized in the beginning of time, and humans who often commit errors, lose their way, make mistakes, and cause the world and themselves to become ill because of their carelessness.

Evil-*kamári* is the negation of life. There is no explanation for the existence of evil. The Asháninka only know that *kamári* exists, that it manifests itself with special violence through illness of the body and spirit, and that the *wirachocas* (Peruvian creoles), some highland *chori-mestizos*, and the *kirinko* (ligh-skinned foreigners) are particularly susceptible to being carriers and spreaders of *kamári*. The stories they tell always confirm this, from the Spaniards of colonial times and missionaries who accompanied them to the Viceroyalty militia who went to fight the rebellion of Juan Santos Atahualpa in 1742 and military forces that in 1965 who were sent to exterminate the guerrilla fighters of the Movement of the Revolutionary Left (MIR). With their indiscriminate bombings, summary executions, and state terrorism, the only thing these outsiders have brought is *kamári*.

The *kirinko*—gringos—began to appear long before the U.S. military advisors who installed themselves at Mazamari to defeat the guerilla fighters. There were *kirinko*—tall and blonde, men and women—living in the Indigenous hamlets, learning the Indian languages so they could write the same stories or stories like those Jesuits, Franciscans, and Dominicans had been preaching for so long.

Now missionaries from the Summer Institute of Linguistics, those strange men and mysterious single women—why aren't they home taking care of their

---

26. "Chacruna" in Amazonian Spanish (*Psychotria viiridis*). The leaves of chacruna are used in the preparation of ayahuasca, without chacruna the drink would not have psychotropic effect.

children?—add other rules to the Catholics'. Now the Asháninka are no longer supposed to drink the fermented yuca juice that confuses the senses, they should stop eating fish without scales, abandon the use of sacred plants: shiri, kamarámpi, koka, sááro and all other curative and spiritual herbs—ivénki-piripiri that regulates pregnancy, mends hearts broken by amorous misfortune, defends against the murderous bullets of the military, police, and bosses, and can even help bring back fleeing lovers. These are very large sacrifices for a nation of good people who shouldn't have to pay for the misdeeds of invaders they don't know and ancestors from the unknown Middle East.

While I was in the Gran Pajonal, especially at the Franciscan mission of Oventeni, next door lived two evangelical missionaries from the Summer Institute of Linguistics. I thus witnessed, with particular intensity, the struggle between two versions of vulgar and ignorant Christianity. That struggle was now aimed at Asháninka children and adolescents in exchange for a few pieces of candy and future celestial bliss. But I wasn't able to go deeper in my understanding of this massive hijacking of adolescent boys and girls practiced by the Franciscan missions at Oventeni and Puerto Ocopa, and to a certain degree approved of by the evangelicals.

Both these two sectarian and dogmatic versions of an authoritarian and fundamentally racist patriarchal culture benefitted from their work of destroying the Campa-Asháninka culture by later retrieving the human spoils that accrued to the *kamári* world of the *wiracochas* and *kirinko*. The Indigenous people worked as domestic servants, abject peons, cheap labor or "informants" and evangelical pastors. The sordid cycle of coloniality is accomplished by destroying the emotional and intellectual native world through humiliation and the imposition of a meaningless parody in which the good *kamétza* spirituality has been displaced by the misery of an unleashed *kamári* that is now beyond the *shiripi*ári's domain.

CHAPTER 19

Poshano, the Shiripiári, in California

𝕳

I N CALIFORNIA'S NORTH CENTRAL valley, the month of March signals the end of winter and impetuous arrival of a spring that is both brief
and intense before it gives way, in May, to the extreme dry heat of summer. This dry heat inhabits the lives of plants, animals, and humans all the
way into early November. It isn't until after the Day of the Dead, All Saints,
and Halloween, that the children—stuffed with sweets and festivity—resign
themselves to dress for winter and wait impatiently for the next cycle of sun
and heat.

For the Indigenous peoples in the United States, spring and fall mark the
time of the world's renovation, ceremonies of dance, music, and celebration
of words that insure the universe will continue for another year. The eternal
cycle of life and death, regeneration and transition, is observed in this way by
modern urban Christians of uncertain faith and by Indigenous Californians,
survivors of a genocide that began more than a century and a half ago.

I might have been inspired by my repeated meetings and conversations
with California's Indigenous people and the Mexican-Americans in my university classes, or by the friendships I managed to develop with my Indian
colleagues at the University of California—Davis, but the truth is that in
March of 2006, when I was writing a new introduction to the fourth edition
of *La sal de los cerros*, all those sensations and memories of cosmic cycles and
celebrations of life in its finite sense once again came flooding into my mind.
A sensory perception beyond the purely material, in those infinite spaces of
quantic essence, the feeling that an endless number of ontological mysteries
must continue to exist, dominated my consciousness once more as it had in
the Gran Pajonal.

As I was engaged in the concrete work of writing, I thought again of Poshano, the *shiripiári* who, after forty years had surely turned into a protective (and threatening) jaguar of the Asháninka and, why not, of that *wirachocha* who had visited him at Chenkári way back in 1967. I had described some of these mystical and mysterious sensations a few years earlier, in 1992, in a text about the anti-Colombian commemoration of five centuries of the ill-named meeting of two worlds.

For the third time, I write about my meeting with Poshano in 1967. I do so with the deliberate intention of contrasting my experiences of the peoples of the Amazon, the Andes, and Mesoamerica with those of my twenty years living near Indigenous peoples in the United States, and especially California, even if these past twenty years have been limited to the confines of the academy in a department of Indigenous Studies.

When I found Poshano, the shiripiári who lived in the wooded hills of Chenkari, beyond the Kishimashdwo grasslands, I never imagined that this skinny and diminutive man, with his dark and penetrating gaze, would provoke a radical shift in my vision of the Campa-Asháninka, and in my research project itself. He was a passionate teacher. For months, I had been asking members of the family with whom I was living on the banks of the little Chitani River to take me to meet this famous shiripiári who had threatened missionaries, military men, and settlers with all manner of mystical hostile acts. His reputation had reached the Campa settlements far beyond the territories under Franciscan control and those controlled by the evangelicals from the Summer Institute of Linguistics. It had triggered my imagination and lent a certain unrest to my residence at Chitani. My intuition told me I had to meet and speak with Poshamo in order to cast some light on several aspects of my research that remained vague and obscure. I was right. Poshano became my third professor and accidental guide.

In the entries of my 1967 field diary for February 25, 26, and 27, I wrote the following:

It is almost impossible to describe the impression Poshamo has made on me. It is possible that what I imagined beforehand influenced how positive it was. I had imagined an arrogant individual, an introvert, perhaps pretentious . . . Whoever said that shamans must be neurotic, mentally unstable, or at the very least epileptics? Poshamo inspires a sense of security

Poshano, the Shiripiári, in Chencari, Gran Pajonal, circa 1963-64

and peace. I feel like I am in the presence of a psychologist. The old man is dirty, with long tangled hair that hides incipient balding. Around his head, just above his eyebrows, he wears a chuchuhuasca band. He walks tall, with sure steps that seem weightless, almost as if his bare feet aren't touching the ground. And he wears a permanent smile, as if he doesn't take himself too seriously. Yet he is neither vain, nor superficial, and demonstrates this the moment we begin to talk and I ask him questions. What continues to amaze me is his extreme simplicity . . . his deep, ironic and warm eyes . . . his cordiality . . . He answers all my questions: there are no mysteries he must protect, nothing I want to know seems to upset him . . . What astonishes me about this wise man is how open he is, and his clarity. He seems to know a great deal about what exists outside the natural physical world. During my recording of his sacred songs, Poshano asks me: "After I die, will these songs remain?" It frightens me to think I might not have time to learn from him . . . there is something in all this that is so profound and mysterious I cannot imagine how my studies will help me. How can I learn something about this reality? . . . When we begin to walk toward his field behind the intómoe[27] to collect the sacred plants he uses to heal and travel

27. The house of women.

through the universe, he whispers in my ear: "I leap into the sky. And I always come back"

Coronado, Omaga, and I leave Poshano's house early in the morning.

"Posamo will accompany us on our return trip," Omaga tells me.

After the first trail, descending Chenkari hill, we stopped at a purma to rest. A woodpecker approached and confidently perched on the stump of the fallen tree upon which I was resting. Omaga told me that bird was Poshano. Twice more during our return trip we saw the woodpecker. After those three times, I never again saw a woodpecker the whole time I stayed in the Gran Pajonal, but I never again saw Poshano either.[28]

Once in Indigenous California, I no longer had such occult experiences. I fear I must attribute their absence to the insidious secularization and materialism that have impregnated the Indian world in the United States, dominated as it is by a capitalist economy, the absolute commoditization of everything that exists in the universe, the reduction of every cultural expression to vulgar materialism and, finally, to the Indigenous people's resigned surrender to market capitalism's hegemony and its system of political control.

Perhaps the anti-imperialism I had brought with me to California from Latin America contaminated my judgment to the extent that for years I continued to view in the Indigenous peoples of the North the most successful outcome of colonialism and imperialism. And that attitude of mine closed the fissures through which the mystic experiences of these latitudes might have filtered. Perhaps, without thinking about it too much, I had succumbed to the seductive current of consumerist materialism that silences the spirit and excites a sense of ownership.

Or perhaps it was the unfortunate event that my son André experienced at the age of ten when, filled with excitement, he ran down to receive the ritual gifts being offered during a Pow Wow, and a man with a long ponytail rudely stopped him and sent him back up to the bleachers where the non-Indians sat: "The gifts are only for the Indian children."

That admonition, somewhere between solemn and haughty, was given in the name of an essentially racist and vengeful Indian nationalism, that takes it upon itself to include and exclude, dispense or deny generosity in accordance

---

28. *La sal de los cerros. Resistencia y utopía en la amazonía peruana* (Lima: Fondo Editorial del Congreso del Perú, 2006), liv-lv.

with who requests it, Indian or white. It doesn't matter that these false, racialized and racist, sociocultural categories are exclusive, socially divisive, and emanate from the very alienation of imperial colonialism.

After a while, I put the incident behind me and could talk to my colleague Jack Forbes, that Indian with the long ponytail who, for my son André, represented his first "welcome" to the world of Indians in the United States. My children, Vanessa and André, had experienced the generosity of the Zapotecs of Oaxaca, and had always felt welcome in their homes and at their *fiestas*. Linda never forgot the insult and often reminded me that it was a metaphor for the profound degree of internalized colonialism that runs through Indigenous society in the country to the North.

I don't believe that mysticism has been entirely banished from Indigenous life in the United States. Rather, it resides in a few isolated and reduced personal spaces in which the sacred and spiritual, not material and mercantile, manage the miracle of an almost clandestine survival. Engraved in my memory are figures such as Dave Risling, a Hupa, and Sarah Hutchinson, a Cherokee, both generous and hospitable people who taught me that the sacred survives, even in the university, cathedral of materialist rationalism.

Poshano would not feel at home in this arid world. What reason would he have to visit us, if reciprocal equilibrium has been forgotten and commodities, with their seductive power of emotional fraud and fleeting bliss, have taken its place? Or is that last jaguar they killed in Arizona a few years ago, almost within reach of the Mexican border, the metaphor for the imperial assassination of the cosmic transmutation that resists annihilation in the Amazon country of the Asháninka?

CHAPTER 20

The "Chino" of Hilda Street

❧

CHACLACAYO'S HILDA STREET RAN from the Central Highway just a few hundred feet into the foothills of the mountains. Bordered by lush cypress trees and two irrigation canals of ambiguous cleanliness, the small dusty street had become our refuge. We'd managed to rent a little house with a single bedroom and miniscule garden, where the two of us and our dog, Orégano, barely fit. We'd found Orégano starving and near death across the way from one of the village stores. There, on Hilda Street, beneath an almost Andean sun and on the few afternoons I managed to steal from my work at the Ministry of Agriculture and Linda from teaching at the Roosevelt School, she and I tried to cleanse ourselves of Lima's sinister drizzle and resulting anemia.

On one of those afternoons, perhaps in 1971, "Chino" Velasco and his wife appeared, walking arm in arm past our house like a couple coming from Sunday mass. Orégano was the most surprised by our meeting. By then he'd received the honorary title of "Black Waters Retriever" due to his stubborn propensity for running and throwing himself into those irrigation canals each time we made the mistake of letting him out onto the street.

Little impressed by Orégano's overreaction, Division General, Chief of the Revolutionary Armed Forces and President of Peru, Juan Velasco Alvarado, came to the doorway and began to talk to Linda and me as if we were neighbors.

At that point, my political/law enforcement paranoia was such that it was ever-present in my daily life. My now consolidated amorous affair with a North American gringa of suspicious origin had circulated like wildfire through the halls of Agrarian Reform and SINAMOS—the National System of Social Mobilization—where I worked as a social anthropologist in

98

Linda in Chaclacayo, circa 1970

the service of the Peruvian Revolution. I don't really remember if my superior, the principal ideologue of the military revolution, anthropologist Carlos Delgado—indirectly, and along with "Cholo" Vázquez, the person who drew me into the revolutionary process—perhaps due to valid national security precautions or perhaps due to hormonal jealousy, was the one who had leaked the news that Linda had appeared in the Peruvian Amazon precisely when I and others had begun to organize judicial-territorial reform for the Indigenous populations. Or the erotic-political hypothesis might have been cooked up by someone inspired by an ex-lover who, aside from accusing me of abandoning her bed, added the more serious accusation of abandonment of revolutionary principles, and spread the word that I had been seduced by imperialism. Because of all this, I was surprised when "Chino" Velasco asked me:

"What do you think of Doctor Carlos Delgado?"

"Truthfully, Mr. President, I believe Carlos Delgado is a great ideologue who has been able to combine the best anti-imperialist indo-American tradition of APRA with socialist ideals of social justice."

And, under the impression I was being interrogated, I continued to offer an analysis of the professional friendship that linked me not only to the anthropologist Delgado but to all the other social scientists who had committed themselves to the Revolution of the Armed Forces.

Meanwhile, under the pretext of getting Orégano inside, Linda emerged from the house with a jar of elderberry marmalade she'd made with fruit we'd harvested with our own hands a few weeks before in the Jauja Valley. By then, a uniformed aide was reminding General Velasco that he had more important commitments than marmalade and neighbors. I think I concluded my conversation with President Velasco Alvarado with a diplomatic ethnographic opinion about the nutritional value of Peruvian Sambucus, the millennial universal beliefs regarding the great power against evil spirits possessed by that tree ("Remember, Mr. President, one should never cut a sauco without performing a small ceremony asking the tree's forgiveness"). I finally went back in the house, protected by Linda, who added in her incipient Spanish that we had gotten the sáuco by climbing on an adobe wall that shielded some pigs from the Central Highway of the highlands.

Linda and I never learned how that Peruvian Sambucus marmalade had gone over in Velasco's presidential dining room. We'd only made one jar and had used the rest of the fruit we'd picked to make a fermented wine we carefully bottled, dated, and stored in a small leather trunk, promising ourselves we would open the bottle when our first child was born. When, years later, we were forced to leave the country in a hurry, in the post-revolutionary confusion we lost, among many other things, that bottle of sáuco liquor. I cannot remember what we drank to celebrate the birth of our daughter Vanessa in the Mexican city of Oaxaca in 1975. Maybe just beer.

AT THE BEGINNING — IN 1970 — I had gone to work on the Peruvian Revolution's Agrarian Reform not so much because I agreed with the ideology embodied in the so-called Inca Plan, but rather out of a pragmatic desire to put some of my timid anthropological knowledge to the test. For me, the Revolution of the Armed Forces, with its populist and social justice rhetoric, provided the opportunity to test some social and cultural ideas and practices among the Indigenous ethnicities of the Amazon, which the Peruvian oligarchy or even the bourgeoisie would never have considered, much less accepted.

The Peru of my youth, the Peru of the 1950s and 1960s that I had known as an young immigrant, was a country that was fundamentally colonialist and racist, dominated by no more than a hundred creole families of large landowners and exporters of raw materials. These families were completely submissive to the United States. They had no ideals of their own, were devoid of cultural intelligence, and stubbornly alienated from their own Indigenous and *mestizo* nation.

From my early Spanish lessons—taught thanks to the hard work and discipline of Calcagno, the young Chilean student of the Jesuits and son of the tenor who sang Italian opera—I had been determined to read the Peruvian Republic's critical texts. Calcagno introduced me to Ricardo Palma and, dismayed at my linguistic hesitancy, presented me with the wisdom of comic strips such as *Little Lulu* and the Chilean *Condorito* (Little Condor). To their delight, I shared both with my younger brother Luis and my little sister, Chiara. My father, on the other hand, always optimistic when it came to my linguistic ability, gave me books by Ciro Alegría: first *La serpiente de oro*, and later *El mundo es ancho y ajeno*. Finally, he had me read the works of Enrique López Albujar and, bringing me back once more to his favorite writer and friend, works by Dino Buzzati, author of *Il deserto dei Tartari* [29] and other books of European history written in Italian. Papá was an avid reader of Roman history, the French Revolution, and Napoleon.

And so, with a Spanish burdened by Italian and an Italian that was resentfully Spanish, I discovered on my own the existence of a scientific traveler from Milan's "Risorgimento" period, a man who became a lover of Peru—her landscapes, her biology, and her people. A few years later, in 1965, I would write a little book for secondary school students called *Antonio Raimondi*. It appeared in the series "Men of Peru" produced by the Editorial Universitaria publishing house. It was my reading of Antonio Raimondi's *El Perú* at the National Library—at the time there were no copies to be found in Lima's few bookstores—that enabled me to discover, in his meticulous and loving descriptions, what my Papá Luigi had shown me with a similar passion when I arrived from Italy ten years earlier: the Sechura desert, mountains of the Callejón de Huaylas, the Mantaro Valley, the Valley of Tarma, the rainforests of the Huallaga River, the Cordillera Azul, and coastal sands between Puerto Pizarro and Tacna.

What Antonio Raimondi hadn't told me about Peru were its inhabitant's sorrows, the ancient, obstinate, secular miseries of its people. Whereas it was Papá's Catholic compassion and his bourgeois, almost aristocratic, back-

29. The Desert of the Tartars.

ground that gave him a somewhat distant sympathy for human suffering, and the ability to interpret it with deference and respect for his family's youngest generation. Only a few years after I arrived from Italy and traveled around Peru, I would find in the classrooms of the Catholic University on Plaza Francia the other readings that would point me toward a critical vision of my newfound country. I have been having a somewhat indiscreet affair with that critical vision ever since.

The Center for Research on the Amazon Jungle was housed in an old mansion in Miraflores that had belonged to the historian Raúl Porras Barrenechea. The National University of San Marcos inherited the house. It was provisionally restored, and now functioned as a research institute under the auspices of the Dean of Philosophy and Letters, Jorge Puccinelli. There, on the second floor, in a series of rooms with huge windows reached by a steep staircase directly from the street, they sent me in 1967 as the new director of the Center.

Years later, consumed by memory, I wondered if there hadn't been some symbolic meaning in the fact that those rooms may have been the servants' quarters, the place where marginalized and dark-skinned Andean women and men lived, silent witnesses to their own subordination by a creole bourgeoisie, necessary actors in the development of a country that did not belong to them. There was no furniture, only high and heavy adobe walls that could have benefited from a bit of interior decoration and academic elegance.

With a timid respect, I hung the Campa-Asháninka arrows and bows I had brought from my trips to the Gran Pajonal. A bit to one side, I suspended the *cushsma* or Asháninka tunic dyed in brown and red achiote, the bag-*táato*, its precious contents of achiote contained inside a length of cane secured with a corncob plug, the comb with its palm teeth that was so important to the aesthetics of the long-haired men of the Pajonal, a chunk of mineral salt from Cerro de la Sal, and the sacred coca leaves and gourd of lime to calm anxieties, restore strength, and please the gods. I seem to remember that I bought the table, chair, and bookcase at the Surquillo market, only a block from the Institute. Armed with these symbols of anthropological authority, I went to work, filled with doubts in my new role as a "specialist" on Peru's Amazon rainforest.

At the Center, I started publishing a magazine I modestly called a bulletin, and baptized it with the Asháninka name *Kiario*. *Kiario* was *Keá'riro*, "Truth." I wanted it to reach Spanish-language readers who weren't versed

In Yanesha territory (Peru's central upper jungle) helping to raise the "axis of the world" after the assault and desecration by missionaries and colonists, circa 1971

in the phonetic refinements of the Indigenous language. The choice of metaphor could not hide the young arrogance of my academic endeavor. The bulletin promised to revolutionize the anthropology of the Amazon and introduce its readers to Asháninka poetry and song and the struggles of the Amuesha (now Yanesha) in defense of their lands and sacred places against the Franciscan missionaries in concert with outside settlers. It lasted but a single issue. The text was by a young U.S. Peace Corps member, Richard Chase Smith who, first calling himself Dick and later Ricardo, became a dear friend. He earned his doctorate in anthropology from Cornell and went to live in Peru, where in time he became a courageous defender of the rights of the Indigenous peoples of the Amazon, Peru, and Latin America.

I never knew if my appointment as director of the Center for Research on the Amazon Jungle had been due to my own academic merits as a young assistant professor at the University of San Marcos or because of the friendship the Dean of Philosophy and Letters, Jorge Puccinelli, had with my father and his respect for my father's fame as a criminal lawyer and specialist in the Roman Law he brought with him from Italy. Puccinelli always insisted that my father should alternate his jewelry business with a university professorship, to which my father responded that he'd left the law behind on the day the ship (the Andrea Doria?) set sail from Genoa in 1947 with him and his future wife Rita aboard.

What I realized right away, though, was the prestige this academic position brought. The petty jealousies of San Marcos's department of anthropology and the low esteem in which its director, Doctor José Matos Mar, held me — for him my interest in the Amazon rainforest was a meaningless passtime — had been difficult. My new position also mitigated two problems in my academic trainining: my doctoral degree was earned at Peru's Catholic University (an unpardonable sin for leftist San Marcos), and my intellectual connections to the head of my committee, the French doctor and professor Jehan Albert Vellard. The latter was too Catholic and conservative, too "pied noir" about Algeria, and too good an empiric ethnographer little given to the philosophical-cultural speculations of his old fellow traveler in the jungles of Brazil, Claude Lévi-Strauss.

Or perhaps my association with the poet Emilio Adolfo Westphalen stood for something. Some months earlier, Westphalen had agreed to publish my denunciation of "The New Conquest of the Jungle" in the cultural magazine, *Amaru*.[30] My text focused on a scandalous event that took place on the Yaquerana River, near the Brazilian border, in which, on direct orders from then president of the Republic, Fernando Belaunde Terry, the Peruvian Air Force had dropped incendiary bombs on the Mayoruna (now Matsés) villages to clear the way for national and international logging. I was gaining intellectual prestige through a system of moral entanglements in which the story of a massacre counts more than the massacre itself.

It must have been at dusk one day in September or October of 1969 when Mario Vásquez came to see me at the Center. I knew little about the anthropologist Vásquez, only that he had been named to an important position at the Ministry of Agriculture, and that his intellectual trajectory had begun a few years earlier when Allan Holmberg, of Cornell University, had recruited him as a research assistant on an applied anthropology project at the ex-*hacienda* Vicos in the Callejón de Huaylas, and then taken him on as a doctoral student. Mario was from the area, he spoke Quechua, and had everything needed to understand the social and cultural problems of the Andean Indigenous peoples. I felt honored, and at the same time a bit frightened by his visit. He was a man of few words. Like someone from the Andes, he used the dense and detailed Quechua language with its pitiless vagaries. The gist of the conversation must have gone something like this:

"You have written about the Campa, you've lived with them. Do you really understand what they want, what they need? Are you willing to come to work with us at the Ministry of Agriculture in the program of Agrarian

30. Stefano Varese, "La nueva conquista de la selva," *Amaru*, No. 3, Lima (July-September, 1967).

Reform, to look for a project of alternative development for the tribal peoples of the Amazon jungle?"

Suddenly, the moral weight of what I had written hit me like an Andean landslide. What I knew about the Campa-Asháninka was contained in an incomplete ethnography and their own long history of a people in resistance against centuries of colonialism. I knew this from sources written during colonial times and before then from those penned during the Christian Conquest, as well as Republican documents and texts and later contemporary materials. But above all I knew it on an emotional level, through what may have been "a philosophical intuition" à la Henri Bergson, about which the young philosophy professor Alfonso Cobián had spoken. Not many years after he was my teacher at the Catholic University, Cobián died of pneumonia at the University of Louvain in Belgium. He had put me in touch with the idea that intuition recognizes the linguistic symbol's limits of rehearsal (or the idea it represents), or understands it for what it is: an effort to represent substance and its properties without being able to arrive at its essence. Henri Bergson and skinny, stooped Alfonso defined that intuition as the simple and indivisible experience of being drawn to something—through which the observer enters its innermost being, the most intimate realm of another's human experience—to attach oneself to what is most unique and ineffable.

The Asháninkas Pascual, Coronado, Pashuka, Irerene, and the old *shiripiári* and wise therapeutic shaman Poshano had aided those acts of my emotional intelligence, my intuitive exercise. And especially Juancito-Omaga, the young man of cutting and erotic irony, a great translator and interpreter of his culture, today an old and wise political leader. But it may also be that I received some knowledge from my frightening initiation into the power of liquid tobacco—the sacred Asháninka substance that shouldn't be taken lightly—endured during two days of atrocious intoxication when the whole universe spun inexpressibly, allowing me to glimpse the Campa-Asháninka's most closely guarded intimacy.

And now "Cholo" Vásquez was asking me to reduce these experiences to a few pages on development, formulated in legislative terms, for the protection of all the jungle tribal communities.

This Mario Vásquez, so physically slight and modest, made a good impression on me. He didn't seem like someone seeking a political position, nor was he "an emerging *mestizo*" of the new Peruvian sociology. I asked myself what the great social scientists in the country thought of him: Pepe Matos Mar, "Prince" Aníbal Quijano—as José María Arguedas called him—, my young friends and colleagues Luis Lumbreras and Rodrigo Montoya? And what would my father and his wife Rita and my brother Luis—Gigi—make of this offer? My working for the military, revolutionary or not, might be a bitter pill to swallow for an antimilitary family with democratic dreams.

What most worried me at that moment was San Marcos University. If I accepted the job at Agrarian Reform, I would have to abdicate my assistant professorship at the University, and lose the few years of seniority I'd been able to accrue, abandon a stable career, and let go of what I loved most: research, with its trips to the jungle and all the rest. It was a dilemma! And just when I had arrived at the Center for Research on the Amazon Jungle. And then there was the not insignificant issue of salary. Mario hadn't said much, except that it would be a "position of trust"—I think that's the term he used—and that therefore he couldn't assure permanency. Who knew how long this revolution would last?

With my salary at San Marcos, a few extra courses at the La Molina Agrarian University—where José María Arguedas had gotten me work some time before—and my periodic trips to the northern coast as a traveling salesman for Vasco Jewelers, I had managed a decent income that had enabled me to buy a Peugeot. Well, I used the car mainly when I went north and when I went camping with friends—with Lucho Bortesi who was already working at Agrarian Reform, with Eduardo Manzini, with Carlos Beas, the great philosopher and historian of religious thought, with "yogi" Fernando Tordoya who other good people of Lima believed was Hindu rather than from the highlands because he taught classes of Hata Yoga, and with my brother Gigi. The truth was, I didn't know what the hell to do.

THE OFFICE SEEMED LIKE some scene from a neo-realist black and white Italian film, with the impoverished and dusty dignity that came from years of careful lack of care, and from the deaf hopes of heroic flights of inhabitants fed up with absurd and useless affairs of state. Its walls were nothing but thin wooden screens topped by opaque glass cut into graceful rounded forms at the top as if to give a "feminine" touch to rigid and disciplined authority. There wasn't a single place to hang a poster. On the high wall that ran to the false ceiling, I was only able to put the map of Peru I had brought with me from the Center. I placed my desk facing it. No exotic Asháninka arrows or baskets. There was another desk across from mine, at which a lawyer by the name of Landeo was already sitting, smiling.

"Pleased to meet you, Anthropologist. I am Doctor Landeo, attorney at your service. On Doctor Mario Vásquez's orders, we will be working together to draft a law for the Amazon Indian tribes."

"Indian tribes" seemed more archaic than disrespectful to me, because he might well have said "savage tribes," the most common expression in Lima at the time. Like all creole lawyers (or was he *mestizo*?), Dr. Landeo wore a decorous and somber suit and tie that in the Peru of those years barely concealed the hardships of his class and profession.

Beyond the screens was a sea of tables, each supporting a monumental black typewriter. Seated at those typewriters were men and a few women who couldn't have been much older than I. They were all engaged in activities about which I had no idea. In time, those workers, whoever they were, continued to be inscrutable. Only two of them lost their anonymity for me: Mr. Gil, who provided me with white paper, carbon sheets, and pencils, and a young man of Chinese descent who introduced himself as "the sociologist Sergio Chang."

In Peru, it was the beginning of times of difficult optimism for some and anguished fear for others. The Revolution of October 3, 1968 had expropriated and nationalized the U.S. company Standard Oil, occupying its installations at Talara with tanks and soldiers. An Agrarian Reform Law had been promulgated, and began with the expropriation of large landholdings on the coast and their transformation into cooperatives co-managed by peasants, workers, technicians, and State inspectors. The United States was threatening the country with reprisals, isolation, and demands of reimbursement for the oil expropriations and North American interests in land and mines. Cutting off military assistance and arms sales from the U.S. was celebrated by all the leftists in the country, and bemoaned by the oligarchy as evidence that Peru's entire revolutionary military had turned communist. It was true that Velasco Alvarado had gone to the Soviet Union to buy war planes and tanks denied him by the United States.

At home, my father and Rita supported the Revolution, Papá against all possible precaution given his role as co-owner of a small jewelry business. He argued with his associate and brother-in-law, Uncle Memi, that it was high time someone in government proposed these social justice reforms, the lack of which had allowed a few to become rich at the expense of the majority.

The threat of expropriating the factories and putting them in the hands of their workers never materialized, but remained something that could happen at any moment and was feared by their owners, until the Revolution promulgated an Industrial Reform law that established a new set of rules for small and medium businesses.

Political tensions soon overtook my family in Lima. Uncle Memi and his wife Elda, who were (I think) minor partners in the jewelry business, lined up on one side, in timid alliance with Uncle Franco, who was more interested in sports fishing along the coast and his adventure trips to the interior of the country, and less interested in his little jewelry workshop with its four employees, and so didn't perceive substantial threats to his lifestyle from this "communist" military and their radical ideas. On the other side were the Vareses, with old Luigi at the head accompanied by Rita and followed by Stefano, who by this time was in total support of the military, Luis—Gigi—, in his early flirting with the Revolution, sister Chiara, who was still at Pestalozzi High School, taking pictures and fascinated with the idea of going to Cuba to study film—something that would happen a couple of years later— and Francisco—Checo in Spanish and Cecco in Italian. For the moment, the latter was interested in raising chickens and doves in the farthest reaches of the garden and learning carpentry from the Andean teachings and erudition of one of María's sons. With her unmistakable profile and golden skin, María, the aging nanny who cared for Papá's whole family had also provided the jewelry workshop with the experienced and generous offspring of Lima's highlands inhabitants.

The Revolution was welcomed at the house in Chacarilla. The molle trees (Schinus molle), well cared for by Papá and the old Japanese gardener (who, on his weekly visits, never used metal tools but only those made of wood and bamboo because "Don Luis, plants don't like being touched by metal"), the narrow Italian grape arbor that ran along the brick wall to the end of the garden, the geraniums that hung over the swimming pool from their low rock wall, and the roses and other flowers that adorned the front and sides of the house, reinforced a vague sense of stability and serenity announced by the slow millennial passage of life in its biological mystery.

The house stood untouched far from the noise of the city and protected from the street by a gate made of palm wood (Batrix ciliata) brought especially from the rainforest, a cornfield across the way, and an irrigation ditch of Arab origin like those from time immemorial that survived Spain's Moorish expulsion and centuries of Spanish colonialism in the arid Americas. All of it would disappear a few years later, destroyed by urban underdevelopment.

Papá insisted upon listening to classical music and opera, especially Puccini whose arias he would perform on the piano while, at family parties he played old Genovese songs on his accordion: "Que l'aggie ou que nou l'aggie mi ghe la vegiu da . . . "[31] or the student songs with their delicious words, whose hidden meanings my younger siblings had finally come to understand in recent years: "Chi grida di quá, chi grida di lá, chi batte la faccia (o figa) per terra, e questo l'é'inn, e questo le l'inno de guerra . . . ".[32] Little by little, the Beatles could be heard on the high-fidelity record player in the living room, and eventually also became part of Papá's piano repertoire.

There was no denying, though, that the Varese-Scotto family's social relationships with its surroundings were changing drastically. Father Harold Griffith, who for years arrived punctually each Thursday in his little Morris automobile to have lunch at the house, began to distance himself from Papá and Rita. Finally, he stopped speaking to us altogether. A member of Lima's oligarchy, the priest had become acquainted with Papá through the Aspíllaga family, owners of the Cayaltí *hacienda* on the northern coast and longtime clients of the jewelry store.

The rupture with the Aspíllagas, with whom Papá and Rita had established a friendship, was much more abrupt and traumatic. It occurred after my participation as a member of an Agrarian Reform team on a visit to evaluate their *hacienda* to establish its value for expropriation. I had visited Cayaltí as a young man, enjoyed the Aspíllagas' lordly hospitality, ridden their Paso horses, napped in rooms of aristocratic elegance, waited on by servants, cooks, chauffeurs, laborers, and even police. And now, as a member of the revolutionary administration and "class traitor," I had come back to visit the hacienda and its big old empty house, hurriedly abandoned ty the Aspíllaga family and timidly and respectfully occupied by some of the workers.

Those same workers who, years before when I passed by on horseback, had put their hats to their breasts in a sign of submission, now engaged with us in complicated conversations about the management of "their hacienda"

31. Translation from Genovese: "If it has it or does not have it, I want to give it . . ."

32. Translation from Italian: "Who is shouting here, who is shouting there, who hit the face (or ass) on the ground . . . and this is the hymn, and this is the war hymn . . . "

that had become an Agricultural Production Cooperative (CAP). Our Italian friends, as well, at their *hacienda* in Chepén, and all the small and medium business owners my father knew, some of them Italian or of other nationalities, the rest creole, distanced themselves from him. They saw him as betraying capitalism's finest principles.

On my weekly visits to the house at Chacarilla, occasionally with Linda but more often alone so as not to disrupt the family's bourgeois morality too much, my father held forth with political analyses where his life in Fascist Italy during the war served as a comparative framework through which to speak of socialism, Catholicism, capitalist enterprise, and the profit principles he considered indispensable so as not to fall into the abuses his neo-Thomist formation considered morally wrong.

My daily life was now divided between my work as chief of the Division of Native Communities of the Jungle at the Ministry of Agriculture on Salaverry Avenue, the sunny little house on Hilda Street in Chaclacayo, and my weekly visits to my father's house. Linda and I left home in the morning as the sun was just coming up behind the Andes, and after a half hour of fast driving immersed ourselves in Lima's dense and melancholy fog, stopping first at the Roosevelt School to drop Linda off at her teaching job and then continuing to Salaverry Avenue.

I made this trip each morning invaded by a stubborn sense of self-blame for having convinced her to leave her country, family, friends, and her loves and memories, in exchange for a dubious social utopia and brute nationalist hostility on the part of my father, Rita, and many of my friends and colleagues. Her extraordinary beauty—green eyes and amazing way of looking at things, her tall body that evoked Irish and Indian origins, and her turned up nose framed by flowing hair that I took in my hands and smelled as if it was made of waves from the sun—wasn't sufficient. Neither was her passion for everything Latin American, her penniless visits to the impoverished peoples of Colombia, Ecuador, Peru and the Amazon country, among the Machiguenga and Ashnáninka peoples, collecting plants, making drawings of hidden worlds, searching for herself in agreements and disagreements. None of this was enough to break through the blindness of those times on the part of Peruvians who harbored a confused insecurity toward governments, cultures, politics, languages, and ideologies, and who predicated their nationality as if it was a voluntary option rather than the result of historical accidents.

Following a few weeks of work with Attorney Landeo, going over the country's scant legislation written into the Constitution, and the civil and criminal codes regarding Indigenous peoples, I began studying the population censuses in their pathetic imperfection and abundant although useless information collected by evangelical missionaries and Catholics who, for decades and centuries, had traveled through the Amazon jungle looking for souls to convert to Christian doctrines of capitalist modernity. Fortunately, I had the advantage of already having read the greater part of this mountainous and boring material, and the colonial and contemporary literature about the Amazon that had helped me write my doctoral dissertation.

Armed with that baggage, optimistically and a bit idealistically, I set about to devise a program of ethnographic investigation of several ethnic communities in the jungle, the results of which might serve as underpinnings to a general plan of development for the hamlets and villages of the Indigenous peoples of the Peruvian Amazon. At least thirty years would have been needed to carry out this type of fantasy.

After getting the sociologist Chang on board, I convinced Mario Vásquez to let me hire my ex-student Jorge Osterling and a small group of university interns to make a preliminary survey of the Aguaruna (today Awajún) communities along the Upper Marañón River. The work plan I presented to our bureaucratic superiors was intended to analyze the zone of the northern Amazon close to Ecuador—a country traditionally in tension and conflict with Peru over border disputes—where the military had established a model of demographic occupation and colonization with marginal Andean and coastal peasants and other poor people to whom they had given family plots of land in the ancestral territory of the Awajún people.

Military Colonization of the Upper Marañón, as the plan was called, had functioned badly for several years, thanks to the irresponsible ideas of now defeated President Belaunde Terry—a proud direct descendent of the Spanish Conquest—who had argued that "the Peruvians must conquer Peru." That plan had been based on a violent policy of occupation of the Indigenous territories of the Amazon by landless peasants, themselves displaced from Andean and coastal communities by the ongoing privatization of their farmlands at the hands of large creole landowners.

These territorial policies were laced with racial, ethnic, and class prejudices, and an arrogant ignorance that began in colonial that, in the crude imaginary of the oligarchic élite, still envisioned Peru as a minority of white creoles controlling the destinies of millions of Indigenous peoples, their ancestral lands, and a distorted history of their past, turned into a simplistic parody for the apology and benefit of the white Euro-Hispanic minority. What this elitist ideology was denying in the most sinister way was the autonomous future of millions of Peru's original inhabitants.

Before going off to visit the Upper Marañón, I went to see Papá. I remember his ironic comments regarding the ideas of a military colonization that proposed to favor the Aguarunas' cultural assimilation by establishing family parcels of "civilized" settlers along with parcels for Indigenous families. In this case, an absurd racist hierarchy judged that poor Andean peasants could be "bearers of civilization to savages from the jungle."

"Suggest to those military civil servants of the colonization program that they should alternate parcels of Communists, Apristas and Christian Democrats, to see if they can implement democratic harmony once and for all," Papá said. The brief survey revealed, in empirical data as well as in numbers, what we already knew yet had to be demonstrated irrefutably to the civil servants and military men of the Agrarian Reform. Contrary to popular belief, and to what those civil servants thought of the "primitive Aguaruna Indians"—that they lived the precarious existence of nomadic hunters and fishermen barely able to survive in the natural world amidst internal conflict and crime of all sorts—we could argue that all the communities we visited enjoyed an economic subsistence that was more than healthy. It was based on immensely productive agricultural practices that allowed them to sell their surplus to the settlers and military camps, and above all with highly sophisticated control and management of their territory in social as well as ecological terms. With the sale of their surplus, the Awajún purchased the industrial products they needed: rifles and ammunition, machetes, outboard motors, transistor radios, recorders, batteries, cloth, and pots and pans.

The ethnobotanist Brent Berlin, of the University of California—Berkeley, with whom I had established a professional relationship, could be found at that time in the region of the Marañón and Santiago rivers. In my bureaucratic report, I used some of the preliminary information Berlin had collected during his months of fieldwork on the Marañón. In his analysis, he found that on a normal plot an Aguaruna family cultivated up to fifty varieties of yuca (manioc, Manihot esculenta), dozens of varieties of beans, corn, bananas, peanuts (cacahuates, Arachis hypogaea), sweet potatoes (Ipomea batata), peppers (chiles, Capsicum) and a multitude of other agricultural products endemic to the humid tropics.

The Aguarunas used the same productive and consumer structure as did most of the farming peoples of the South American Amazon and, with special relevance to my experience, I encountered once again an exuberant production of carbohydrates and vegetable and animal proteins that resulted in a diet of high nutritional value—as long as refined sugar, canned goods, and white flour didn't interfere or dominate. As in the case of the country's Central Jungle, where I had done my ethnographic work from the early 1960s on, the Indigenous communities of the Amazon—that had achieved a certain level of cultural, political, and economic autonomy in the face of the expansion of Peruvian society—showed a great capacity for demographic continuity and cultural survival through their practice of subsistence economy. In the hamlets of the Auajún, Wampi, Asháninka (the Kéesihatzi of the Gran Pajonal) or Matsés of the Yaquerana River, one hardly ever saw children with bloated bellies, skeletal legs, and empty stares.

This was in sharp contrast to the coastal communities of migrant Andean and Amazon peoples, "assimilated to modernity and to the capitalist economy." How to translate this obvious message to civil servants and politicians trained in the ideology of modernity, progress, and neo-Social Darwinism, immersed in the ideas of a nationalist imaginary whose model is always to be found in the North or on the other side of the Atlantic? How to interrupt the archaic Eurocentric monologue and facilitate a dialogue involving multiple cultural truths, heterodoxies, and unexpected and subversive rationalities? How to recognize my own humanity in someone different from myself, whose words I do not understand, whose music seems like noise to me, whose reason upsets me, whose emotions alarm me?

I returned to Lima with my students, books of notes, pages and pages of questionnaires, and hundreds of unanswered questions. I produced an administrative report with a pompous title: "Research Survey of Six Aguaruna Communities of the Upper Marañón." I presented it to Mario Vásquez and the other administrators at the Ministry of Agriculture, and immediately began to work with my colleague Sergio Chang on the study and subsequent general report on the native communities of Peru's Amazon rainforest. That study saw the light in 1972, in a modest mimeographed edition entitled "The Native Societies of the Rainforest: Preliminary Socioeconomic Diagnosis of Peru's Rural Area," and was published under the auspices of the General Direction of Rural Organizations, of the National System of Social Mobilization (SINAMOS).

As happens with a great many social scientists when we enter the Academy, this study served me on other occasions as a source for the elaboration of articles and lectures about the situation of the Indigenous peoples of the Peruvian Amazon. The most important use I made of some of these materials was in writing up the study that I took to the first meeting of the Barbados Group in 1971. My essay, titled "Inter-Ethnic Relations in the Selva of Peru," appeared with a dozen other articles on the situation of the Indigenous peoples of the humid tropics of several Latin American countries, in an English-language book published in Geneva in 1972 under the auspices of the University of Berne and the World Council of Churches.

The Spanish version of this book had a more heroic history. Published by Terra Nova in Montevideo, all copies were immediately confiscated by the Uruguayan military dictatorship and burned under suspicion of containing subversive information and a socialist analysis. During the entire period of Latin America's Fascist dictatorships, I think most of the social scientists, intellectuals, and Indigenous activists who participated in subsequent meetings (II and III) of the Barbados Group were careful not to include that first Spanish edition of our "subversive" texts on our curriculum vitae.

The only thing subversive (today it would be called "terrorist") those works contained was the denunciation of the inhuman conditions in which most of Latin America's Indian populations lived, particularly those Indigenous peoples in the tropical lowlands who endured ongoing colonization by steel and fire at the hands of national governments and multinational corporations. What was sadly absurd in those pages of Latin American anthropology, was that while some members of Barbados Groups I, II and III had to remain anonymous and travel incognito to the meetings, others returned from political exile to those same meetings, and still others chose banishment and exile in order to survive those years of repression and State terror.

In my naïve foray into the analysis of the social situation of the Indian communities of the Amazon, I had predicted little of this, first as an anthropology student and later under the presumed protection of an official government institution, even if that institution was revolutionary. From 1964 to 1965—I no longer remember the date—when I was in the Gran Pajonal with the Campa-Asháninka—I was interrogated although not exactly detained by two members of Peru's Investigative Police (PIP) about my activities in the region. I had traveled from the Lower Tzitani River to the Franciscan Mission at Oventeni to pick up provisions and rest for a few days at the very modest "boarding house" belonging to Don Pancho and Doña Rosa, *mestizos* from the Jauja mountains who had lived for some time in the Gran Pajonal and hired Campa-Asháninka labor to work in their fields, labor they paid poorly in kind.

Back then, Oventeni occasionally received military DC3s left over from World War II and Cesna air taxis of even more dubious safety, loaded down with little pigs, hens, bags of food, and Andean and *mestizo* small farmers. The arrival of a twin-engine plane was always a festive occasion for Campa boys and girls, the priest, the Mission's nuns, and the few *mestizo* inhabitants of the hamlet, the *chori* as the Ashnáninka called them, or *cholos* in good Peruvian Spanish. I too got excited at these rare occurrences, and ran — sweating — to the small airfield as soon as I heard the plane's engines flying over the valley. One always hoped for something new from those flights: new faces, objects, or longed-for foods, beer that was fresh, if not cold, to replace the warm bottles stored in the warehouse at Don Pancho's boarding house. Like everyone else in the hamlet, he had no electricity.

I remember two people emerging from that DC3 bearing the three colors of the Peruvian flag and the initials of the FAP (Peruvian Air Force), as well as merchandise that the Asháninka of the Gran Pajonal for centuries interpreted as gifts from the god Pachamaite that had been intercepted and stolen by the white *wiracochas* and the *chori* to prolong their dependency and suffering. The two travelers wore green police uniforms and carried small packages and somewhat antiquated machineguns that reminded me of the "mitra Sten" I had seen in my childhood on the *partigiani* of Prato Sopra la Croce in the Ligurian Alps.

A few hours later we all end up in Rosa's kitchen, drinking coffee strained through a cloth and trying to warm ourselves from the rain that falls insistently every afternoon in Oventeni. The PIP policeman who seems to be in charge is a pale *cholo* with a sad air and little substance. The other is a mixed-blood from the coast with curly hair and a rapid, broken way of talking, interspersed with repeated "p's" that confirm his syntactic doubts and scant familiarity with the type of formal dialogue his superior is trying to establish.

The next morning, over a breakfast of eggs, rice, and fried bananas, I tell the policemen I must return before nightfall to Coronado's and Pashuca's "camp." They don't seem too impressed by my work, and insist instead that I accompany them downriver along the Tzitani so they can explore the area and do some fishing. I grumpily accept their invitation and an hour later the three of us are sloshing through the Upper Tzitani with its clear cold water and few fish.

The official talks to me about Che Guevara, the Cuban Revolution, the Soviet Union, and ex-Aprista Luis de la Puente Uceda who, according to him, wanted to overthrow democratically elected president Fernando Belaunde Terry in a Communist-inspired armed and violent revolution. Between his questions and my vagaries, the official now and then shoots a blast of machinegun fire into the forest, with the hope, perhaps, of killing some Communist hidden there. Childhood memories return and I can hear the partisans' Sten machineguns that, when I lived in Italy, hunted Nazi Fascists rather than Communists.

In October of 1965 (before or after my encounter with those two policemen in the Gran Pajonal?) a column from the Movement of the Revolutionary Left (MIR) is intercepted by the Army in the Central Jungle, and the guerrilla leader Luis de la Puente Uceda is killed. A few months later, in January of 1966, Guillermo Lobatón of the Tupac Amaru guerrilla column is executed in the jungle of Junín. A movement, organized a few years earlier by groups of Quechua peasants under the leadership of Hugo Blanco, and preceded and accompanied by innumerable centuries-long struggles by Indigenous communities for the recuperation of their lands, turned those military defeats into victories and raised the country's social consciousness.

In 1965, Héctor Béjar, founder and leader of the National Liberation Army (ELN), is arrested in the central rainforest and imprisoned until 1970, when General Juan Velasco Alvarado liberates him and invites him to join the Revolution of the Armed Forces.[33] The memories of some of the colonels and generals of the Peruvian Army who participated in the repression of those years reveal the embryonic idea that in that unequal war it wasn't a matter of a regular army fighting Communist delinquents, but of an army of mercenaries protecting the privileges of an elite oligarchy against young idealists and thousands of Indigenous peasants armed with clubs and machetes.

33. I must have been relatively close to Héctor Béjar when he was captured in the Central Jungle and I was doing fieldwork in the Gran Pajonal. Later, between 1970 and 1974, Béjar was one of my bosses at SINAMOS during the Velasco Revolution. Many years later, our paths coincided again in friendship when we both received the Medalla Haydée Santamaría awarded by Cuba's Council of State in April 2017.

The two PIP remained at Oventeni for a couple of days and, if I remember correctly, then went on horseback to visit Shumahuani "hacienda," a small agricultural enterprise abandoned by highland settlers and reoccupied by an Asháninka lineage under the authority of an important blind chief (he'd lost one eye in a fight somewhere), and managed by his four wives and dozens of children, daughters- and sons-in-law, and grandchildren. There were rumors that guerrilla fighters had been seen in those parts. I returned to the hamlet on the Lower Tzitani to continue my work with Pashuka's family, and forgot about the event.

More than twelve years later, the encounter with the two PIP interrogating me in Oventeni about my possible ties to Communist guerrillas came back to me in the form of an airmail envelope with red and white borders and Peruvian stamps that arrived at Eucaluptus Street in the little village of San Felipe del Agua, on the outskirts of Oaxaca, Mexico. From its first paragraph, the letter, written in timid blue calligraphy, recalled that meeting in Oventeni and the successive dramatic events in the life of post-Velasco Peru, not the least of which were the police strike, repression, dissolution of the Investigative Police (PIP), massive layoffs, and intensified endemic poverty of all Peruvians.

It didn't take me long to identify the letter writer. If was decidedly not the *cholo* official, who surely had been able to save himself from purges and layoffs, but the mixed-blood from the coast with his curly hair and creole humor. He wanted me to help him emigrate to Mexico. He too was a throwaway remnant of a social project gone bad, asking for help from an exile equally unsure of his own place in the world.

DURING THE BRIEF VELASCO period, the words of the day were consciousness, mobilization, and popular participation. By 1969-70, the ideas of Paulo Freire, contained in his book *Pedagogy of the Oppressed* (1968), were common currency among activists. We had all been nourished, in one way or another, by reading Frantz Fanon and Jean Paul Sartre's prologues to his two books, *Black Skin, White Masks* of 1952 and *The Wretched of the Earth* of 1961, and of course by all the Marxist-Leninist literature published in the Soviet Union and the People's Republic of China, available for a few *soles* on Colmena Derecha, between Plaza San Martín and the big old house which was the University of San Marcos. It was possible that a few young poets—especially Javier Heraud, who was killed in 1963, naked and without a weapon, floating on the Madre de Dios River—had access to some anti-colonialist texts by the poet Aimé Césaire, not yet translated into Spanish (*Discourse sur le colonialism*, 1953).

A generation of poets emerged during those years, mostly on the coast, all born between 1940 and 1950, and they gave the country some of its richest and most passionate literary pages. For my part, up to my neck in the politics of Amazonian ethnicity, I had no time to search out the poets, except for my young friend and colleague in revolution and socialism, Tulio Mora who, at just twenty years of age, promised to become one of Peru's best poets and a journalist of great social and political vision.

Tulio Mora and I worked on SINAMOS's magazine of culture and politics, edited by the historian Hugo Neira, and we traveled to the jungle to write articles and essays, to interview another great poet and writer from the Amazon, César Calvo, and hoping to drink ayahuasca with the father of the Iquitos painter Yando Ríos, a healer and partaker of ayahuasca who was famous throughout the Amazon. The filmmaker Carlos Ferrand came with us to photograph and make a 16-mm black and white film of the scenes that would later come together in *Visión de la selva*, a documentary I had proposed in support of the Indigenous communities of the Amazon.

All of us who worked for the Velasco cultural revolution engaged in several administrative and creative disciplines simultaneously. We saw this as breaking down the old bureaucratic structures we wanted to do away with. SINAMOS had a vague mandate, somewhat generic and not all that specific, of inventing new forms of popular and "democratic" participation that would take the place of the antiquated party model. We saw this new model as authorizing us to explore innovative roads, unusual strategies, and consciousness raising and mobilization techniques that might lead to greater people's involvement in the reforms the revolutionary government was initiating from above.

CHAPTER 21

Interlude with Margaret

✾

O N ONE OF THOSE trips to the Lower Amazon, I accompanied and served as guide to a young North American. Darcy Ribeiro was head of the Center for Popular Participation appointed by the United Nations' International Labor Office (OIT), and I was his national counterpart designated by SINAMOS. It was Ribeiro who, with his habitual seductive authority, convinced me to accompany this good-looking *gringa*, poet, journalist, and longtime friend of the Cuban Revolution, so she could explore the Amazon country outside the city of Iquitos.

It must have been around the year 1973 or 1974. I didn't like the idea of having to be a kind of tourist guide for a U.S. citizen I didn't know, who in a few days hoped to acquire a vision of the Amazonian rainforest and its people. For reasons I can no longer recall, until the moment we boarded the Fawcett Airlines plane for its flight from Lima to Iquitos, I thought I was accompanying some tourist who, because of her feminine attributes, had caught Darcy Ribeiro's facile eye. Nevertheless, I had to do a double-take when faced with the solid sensibility of Margaret Randall. She ingratiated herself with her panic of mushrooms, socialist outbursts, and generous sympathy for the Peruvian Revolution.

Her mushroom phobia wasn't simple. We agreed that I would walk ahead of her on the trails through the rainforest and tell her whenever I saw a mushroom innocently growing on a fallen tree trunk or somewhere in the shadowy vegetation. The unsuspecting mushroom caused such terror in Margaret that she might lose consciousness. Upon our return from Iquitos, Linda and I had Margaret and her Brazilian partner (or was he Bulgarian?) for a couple of days at our little house in Chiclayo.

I didn't see Margaret Randall again for many years, until after her time in Cuba and Nicaragua, exile, and return to the United States. I reconnected with her in Havana amidst the warmth of other poets, novelists, Latin American writers, and the hospitality of Casa de las Américas. The two of us, gray-haired now, had freed ourselves of the mushrooms in our journeys through ideals, passions, and the joy of still being alive.

CHAPTER 22

The Revolution's Limitation

🙊

THE CONTRADICTIONS AND LIMITATIONS of the Velasco Revolution became evident soon enough. It seemed to us that the revolutionary generals hadn't foreseen the fact that the people's needs were going to require much more rapid and radical advances than they were prepared to establish.

When the government expropriated the national newspapers and gave them to worker, peasant, and professional organizations; when it made Quechua a national language on an equal footing with Spanish and introduced it as a written language in the official register; and when, under these directives from above, Quechua-speaking Andeans and the country's other Indigenous peoples began to feel that perhaps they could stop being foreigners in their own land, the mobilization and popular participation the generals had wanted to control and restrict went beyond their ability to do so.

More and more, the reforms seemed insufficient, and more and more the old privations and sufferings produced an eagerness for total solutions: all the land for those who work it, all the factories for the workers, all the mines for the miners, all the sea with its anchovies and bass for the fishermen, all our languages for all our students in all our schools.

In my reduced radius of action with the Indigenous communities of the Amazon, various native congresses also took place more frequently and radicalized their demands. Now they didn't simply want a rapid implementation of the project of law, which the leadership clearly understood must lead to the recuperation of historic territory lost over centuries of colonialism and national oppression. Territory, water, forests, mines, symbolically sacred places, animals, plants, and the ethnic community's full jurisdiction over the totality of its surroundings must now be within the scope of the autonomous development of the Indigenous peoples of the Amazon.

I think I remember that the end of my radicalizing initiatives arrived following some of my trips to consult with the Indigenous organizations. It might have been after the consultation mission to the Lower Amazon jungle, that trip on which Margaret Randall accompanied me, or perhaps it was the scant dissemination we were able to give the Indigenous communities in the pages of the Center for Popular Participation's magazine, or the documentary *Visión de la Selva*, that provoked the suspicions of someone in State Security.

The net result of our audacity led to members of the Investigative Police (PIP) raiding Carlos Ferrand's small film laboratory, requisitioning all his filmic and photographic material, and leaving his office semi-destroyed. I understood the message clearly. The worst damage I suffered wasn't so much having to come to terms with the Peruvian Revolution, but with the loss of all my Super-8 films, photographs, and sound recordings gathered on a luminous journey I'd made with Linda a short time before to the Mayorunas-Matsés of the Yaquerana River.

It must have been in July or August of 1970 when the Director of the Summer Institute of Linguistics (ILV) at Yarinacocha invited me to visit the Mayoruna Indians, contacted only two years earlier by two evangelical missionaries, Harriet Fields (Sister Luisa) and Hattie Kneeland (Sister Enriqueta). These were the same Indigenous people about whom I had written my denunciation of atrocities committed against them by the Peruvian Air Force between 1964 and 1968, during Fernando Belaunde Terry's administration.

Linda and I were only the eleventh and twelfth non-Indians who visited them after the first peaceful contact by the ILV. The Matsés—called by their Quechua name Mayoruna (people of the river) by the *mestizos* of the Amazon—had been in armed conflict with the people of the Lower Ucayali and the Amazon for years, especially around Requena, over the perceived bad habit the Matsés had of kidnapping women along the river bank and taking them to their villages.

Since the early 1960s, the people of Requena had organized punitive armed expeditions into Matsés territory, without ever finding an Indigenous woman, only their empty villages and plots. The expedition systematically burned both.

In 1964, President Belaunde Terry's government had engaged the support of several combat helicopters sent from Panama by the U.S. Southern

With Linda in Matsés territory
(Mayoruna, Yaquerana River), circa 1971

Command to assist the Peruvian Air Force in bombing with Napalm and machine-gunning the Matsés' hamlets. A few years later, Linda and I flew in a little ILV plane from the base at Yarinacocha in Pucallpa to the hamlet's tiny airstrip.

We stayed a few days with Sister Luisa and the clan of Matsés that lives in Peru; the other three clans were living in Brazil, on the other side of the "imaginary" border. My brief experience was extraordinarily illuminating. The only person who spoke some Spanish was an elderly grandmother of *mestizo* origin, who in her youth had been kidnapped by the Matsés. I was able to tape and film a long interview with her in which she described her life, happy enough in the hamlet, being served fresh meat and fish each day brought by young hunters from the forest. To my questions about whether she missed her *mestizo* people, she responded that even as a child she had been forced to work from dawn until dusk just to have enough to eat, and that here, on the contrary, she was served every day by members of the clan.

With an edge of humor, she told Linda and me that the Matsés had been able to avoid major damage from the bombings by taking refuge in the forest,

Linda talking to an old Matsés man
(Mayoruna, Yaquerana River), circa 1971

letting the bombs destroy only the village and their huts. She said, however, that they had to plant small fields, dispersed and hidden in the forest, so they wouldn't receive the wrath of the bombs. They'd also had to adapt their large clan house, the *maloca*, to the nomadism imposed by the Peruvians. And their dogs, so important to all Amazon hunters, had to be trained not to bark when the Peruvian *mestizos* came close on their punitive raids.

One afternoon, the men of my age invited me to go into the forest with them. Fascinated in one of those strokes of luck that only happens to an eth-

The *maloca* or Asháninka long house, Gran Pajonal, circa 1963

nologist once in a great while, I was able attend the initiation rite of young Matsés men.

Masks of their ancestral spirits appeared to these young men and, amidst frightening songs and screams, the mysteries of their culture were revealed in a ritual of sacred terror that would only end that same night when, upon discovering that the masks were really the adults of the clan, everyone—young, adults, and old, running and dressed up as spirits—would rush to the *maloca*, where they would destroy all the women's ceramic pots.

The life cycle would begin again through the ritual destruction of the previous cycle and the manufacturing of new female pots for the period to come. Amidst barely concealed laughter, several days later the grandmother told me the older women know that the men are behind the masks, high on their hallucinatory substances and drunk with their powers of persuasion.

An essential part of the masculine rite consists in provoking hallucinations by injecting themselves directly into the capillary arteries in their arms and burning them with the secretion of the giant Bufo toad (Bufo marinus). It is in this hallucinatory ritual that the men periodically reencounter a power that is eroded through the daily life of the women in the home. The male hunters and basket makers find this power in the fibers and animals of the mountain, and in the strength of resistance they exercise cyclically and symbolically when they destroy the artifacts of domestic culture to be found in the ceramic pots in the women's *maloca*.

Almost at the end of our stay, and in my pale urban nudity, I tried to go into the forest and along the river, far from Sister Luisa's puritanical gaze, not only to attempt—uselessly—to imitate the statuesque beauty of the Amazonian men, but to reaffirm myself in my right to difference, even if it bordered on ugliness. And it must have been this same need for reaffirmation that motivated some young Matsés men, perhaps with Linda's subtle urging, to allow me to cover my torso and arms with the clan symbols painted with *huito* (Genipa Americana), a fruit of aesthetic powers and magical therapeutics, whose transparent sap, applied in complex and invisible designs by the expert hands of little Matsés girls, emerged little by little with the sun's light.

We returned to Lima with our bags filled with photographs, films, recordings, and notes, and my body covered in clan symbols the meaning of which I did not know. In a few days, the *huito* faded slowly from the surface of my skin. I felt a deep and undefined nostalgia and sense of irreparable loss, for a face of humanity I knew was threatened with extinction. I was left with no material from that experience: the PIP took it upon themselves to destroy everything in an act that foreshadowed what would be taken from the Matsés. Linda and I only retain a few photos in black and white, in which you can see a naked old Matsés man trying on Linda's glasses with a huge smile of discovery on his face, and another in which some prepubescent girls are painting my body with *huito*.

I THINK IT WAS around the beginning of 1972 that the revolutionary government took the initiative of creating the Center for the Study of Popular Participation as a joint dependency of SINAMOS and the United Nations' International Labor Office (OIT/ILO). And it must have been Carlos Delgado who invited the anthropologist Darcy Ribeiro—exiled by the Brazilian dictatorship, first to Uruguay and then to Venezuela and Chile—to assume the Center's direction for the UN. Carlos Delgado and Darcy Ribeiro offered me the direction of the Peruvian section. In a burst of modesty, from which I almost immediately repented, I refused the offer, leaving the job to someone who turned out to be a mediocre bureaucrat. I did accept a position as Darcy Ribeiro's scientific counterpart.

And so, I ended up as the Center's Director of Research, installed in a cozy office on the second floor of a neo-Victorian style house with large windows that looked out on one of Lima's parks, the name of which I no longer remember. My position as Director of the Division of Native Communities of the Jungle, at the Ministry of Agriculture, went to my friend and colleague Alberto Chirif.

I accepted the transfer with the commitment that I would continue to work on legislation for the Indigenous peoples of the Amazon, maintaining an intense level of collaboration and consultation with the Division of Native Communities. It was in this hospitable office, surrounded by some of my books, where I retreated to cry with rage midday on September 11, 1973, when we heard on the radio that Salvador Allende had been assassinated by the Chilean military and that the dream of a democratic Latin American socialism had been dealt a death blow.[34]

Because of his power to convoke, and the prestige of the Peruvian Revolution—in truth somewhat ambiguous—Darcy Ribeiro brought some of the most important social scientists in Latin America and Europe to the Center. They were there for varying lengths of time, from a few days in which they might give a lecture or organize a seminar or workshop to several months in which they participated in more lengthy research projects.

The axis of the Center's research-action program could be summed up in the formula put forth by the great Argentine physicist and mathematician Oscar Varsasky,[35] who, from his exile in Venezuela, had proposed the possibility of planning and carrying out socialist development—something he called the National Project—using numeric simulation and computational models capable of handling the immense number of variables that must be considered when implementing national policies.

Varsasky brought with him two mathematicians and systems analysts, also

34. Later we discovered that, according to an official investigation by the Chilean government, Salvador Allende had committed suicide inside La Moneda Palace as it was being bombed, in order not to fall into the hands of those who had staged the coup.

35. Varsasky had proposed, from his exile in Venezuela, to plan and execute a socialist development that he called National Project based on numerical simulation and computational models that would be able to manage all the numerous variables that intervene in the elaboration of national policies.

On the roof of the Center for the Study of Popular
Participation/ ILO/SINAMOS, Lima, circa 1974

in exile, and one Brazilian cybernetic mathematician, Carlos Senna de Figueiredo, who had been exiled in Allende's Chile since 1970. Senna de Figueiredo
had worked with Stafford Beer, the creator of "operational research and management cybernetics" and director of Cybersyn, the national computerized
system for the real-time management of Chile's socialist economy. Oscar Varsasky, Stafford Beer, and Carlos Senna de Figueiredo had for some time been
involved in intense discussions about the enormous potential of applying
cybernetic techniques to all types of human organization and institutions
that require immediate shared decision-making based on precise and detailed
information.

   Stafford Beer's and Oscar Varsasky's theory holds that all individuals involved in an institution or organization can and should have a say in it, not

only at the leadership level but at all levels. For this reason, each of the organization's members, and everyone who to a greater or lesser degree communicates and interacts with the organization, must contribute to its management. This type of co-governance, or self-governance, as it relates to national sectorial policies, can be designed through "cybernetic management," conceived of and carried out for Chile's national projects by Beer's Cybersyn, using Oscar Varsasky's "numeric experimentation."

Stafford Beer's visionary project in Salvador Allende's socialist Chile had its own operational headquarters, where 500 telexes were linked to a central computational system that permanently and in real time received and exhibited information on the national economy. It aspired to establish a more participatory society, one that was less centralized and bureaucratic or, as Varsasky, in his hypothesis, proclaimed, one that " . . . tried to find the abacus that would allow us to calculate and activate our dreams, our utopia."

Cybersyn and the utopia of a participatory and democratic socialism were destroyed along with all the other achievements and thousands of lives by the military coup of September 11, 1973. Carlos Senna de Figueiredo had arrived at the Center just a few months earlier. I think Stafford Beer worked as a consultant for the Venezuelan and Mexican governments before his almost monastic retirement to Wales.

For me—along with Oscar Varsasky, Carlos Senna de Figueiredo, Jorge Itzcovitch, Benjamín Zacharías, the Roman unionist Roberto Magni, and Darcy Ribeiro—it meant rethinking the "abacus" of the dreams of the Indigenous peoples of the Peruvian Amazon.

Two ideological and political challenges constantly presented themselves, and their rhetorical demands made my and our work more difficult: on the one hand, there were the constant provocations of most of the developmental economists at the National Planning Institute (INP) who, in the light of their liberal university training—rarely Keynesian—systematically questioned our unorthodox hypotheses and our distance from the scientific "rigor" of the social sciences (bourgeois social sciences, we would say).

Other accusations came from the political left and from anthropological purism, and these did trouble my conscience. The great Marxist historian, Eric Hobsbawm, had published an article in *The New York Times* in which he defended the Velasco revolution even though he recognized that it was not a "true" socialist revolution. My friend Ricardo "Dick" Smith responded to Hobsbawm in a letter to the editor, arguing that Velasco's revolution was

hurting the autonomous hopes of Peru's Indigenous peoples through its un-
fulfilled promises, obstructionism, and the demagogic manipulation of their
demands. This criticism—severe and somewhat unfair—by my friend Ricardo hurt a lot, and brought me to a moral standstill in my enthusiasm for
the process.

Just as my leaving the University of San Marcos had provoked some profound ethical questioning and all sorts of doubts about the wisdom of that
decision, this intervention by my friend Smith pushed me to rethink the social scientist's role and academic's usefulness in the context of a nation in
crisis.

The Weberian aspect of the matter wasn't important to me. I was more
interested in maintaining a coherent position in line with C. Wright Mills
and his *The Sociological Imagination* and *The Power Elite*. Was it better for
the Indigenous peoples of the Amazon for one to keep oneself apart from the
process, in a position of critical independence or, on the other hand, should
one sink one's hands in the dirty mud of politics and mix of ideas, only a little
cleaner than those idealists of a revolution accused of being "petit bourgeois
and populist" to which I was devoting myself with everything I had? What
might one do from the outside that one couldn't do from within? What possible analytical and informational contributions could I make, that would be
of use to the Indigenous communities? And how to implement them, how
to transmit them so the people themselves would make them theirs? Or was
Goethe right when, centuries earlier, he said that "the pessimist resigns himself to remaining a spectator"?

An initial response to these questions came from the Indigenous communities themselves, and from anthropologist friends, in the form of a pretty severe critique of the notion of "native community" we had introduced into the
revolutionary government's official political language. The argument made
by Indigenous and non-Indigenous critics alike—and which they continue
to put forth four decades later, even as I write—is that strictly speaking in
the Peruvian Amazon there is no such thing as an Indigenous community.
Rather, there are groups of people of low demographic density and extraordinarily disperse settlements.

Along the rivers, in the zones between them, and in the steep Andean valleys of the forested Eastern Andes, Indigenous people settle in small disperse
hamlets at a prudent distance from each other in the forest, giving them space
to cyclically rotate their cultivated fields. Only due to the "concentrations"

of Indians during the colonial period, to the rubber and lumber exploitation of more recent times, and to the actions of the missionaries, have some people come together in larger villages of several dozen families. All this knowledge, which I had already accumulated, written about in various studies, and shared with several academic colleagues as part of my ethno-ecological work, required an intellectual leap to reduce it to a simple sociocultural formula, one bureaucrats and politicians could understand and low-level local people manage. The latter, after all, were those whose job it was to implement territorial policy.

The term "native" was a device if not, frankly, a ruse I invented with Attorney Landeo to sidestep the hegemony of the term "peasant," which was favored by the military and was completely inappropriate in the Amazon, and even questionable for the Andes. "Native," as a value-neutral noun or adjective, and with a slightly Anglophone flavor, was used as a substitute for old discriminatory terms such as tribes, Indians, savages, or jungle people.

What, then, was this ghostly Native Community that appeared in the official documents produced by the government and the revolution? They gave the name Native Community to the office at the Ministry of Agriculture responsible for the Indigenous peoples of the Amazon, and it appeared in the title of the legal project aimed at those same Indian peoples. It even began to be adopted by some Indigenous peoples of the Amazon. The truth was, it was a sociological invention like so many categories of taxonomy that populate the analytical texts and encyclopedias in the contemporary social and natural sciences.

I basically referred to the traditional use of categories such as "community" and "society", introduced at the beginning of the twentieth century by the German sociologist Ferdinand Tonnies: *Gemeinshaft*, the community, identified and mutually recognized as an entity of solidarity (families, hamlets, kinship systems), and *Gesellshaft*, the society which, in contrast, is based on principles of convenience and instrumentality by individuals. While community is used when speaking of non-industrial rural societies, society expresses the individualist and impersonal social relationships mediated by money and capitalist culture. In a human geography such as the one that exists in the Peruvian Amazon, in which Indigenous people, river dwellers, and *mestizo* settlers mostly practice a subsistence economy weakly linked to the capitalist market, the community tends to grow based on the kinship system and "neighbors" who from time to time appear at varying geographic distances.

For the Indigenous peoples of the Amazon, the community is primarily a social entity, historically constructed as a network of blood and political relationships that exist as discreet groups of a few nuclear or extended families in a large territory they consider as belonging to the group. The relationships between those people in the same linguistic/dialect group tend to be friendly but always tense and competitive, often mediated by fights, attacks, and deaths, or renovated rituals of alliance. Matrimonial links, or links created by political kinship and horizontal relations of three ascendant generations, can become a community.

One individual Campa-Asháninka adult, for example, refers to his or her community by the term no-sháninka (my people). Their people may be spread out along a river over several miles or in the grasslands and forests, but those distances aren't important in terms of their feeling connected to their people, a connection they are careful to maintain through expeditions of "commerce" or trade and exchange of goods, participation in dances and *masateadas*, and hunting and fishing trips. In a sociocultural context of this sort, how does one translate the notion of "Indigenous community," in all the manifestations one finds in the Amazon, to a category that can be understood by mentalities trained in the traditions of European and Western sociology?

It was in this stage of the process of sociological imagination that Oscar Varsasky's ideas and theories and Darcy Ribeiro's ethnographic experience came to my aid. I proposed to the Center's team that it elaborate a mathematical model, or one based on "numeric simulation," that would allow us to assign number values to all the variables that might intervene in the definition of the Native Community of the Amazon, and in determining a minimal and ideal way to recognize and deed lands, territories, and natural resources for the stability and demographic, economic, and ecological development of the Native Communities of the Amazon. I hoped to be able to devise a relatively simple numeric formula based on reliable qualitative data that we, along with mobilized and trained Indigenous people, could use, so that the Division of Native Communities, the Agrarian Reform division, SINAMOS, and all regional and local agencies of the Ministry of Agriculture that intervened in the application of the proposed Law of Native Communities could, in the most expeditious way, assign titles to communal lands and to the ethnic territories.

Time was short. I think it was already 1973 or 1974. The empirical data we had was scant, if not frankly absurd. The National Planning Institute, which had tremendous prestige as an entity of social research, knew little if anything about the Indigenous peoples of the Amazon rainforest. The National Office for the Evaluation of Natural Resources (ONERN), which had published dozens of studies of evaluations and biological inventories, hadn't paid attention to issues such as native populations and their resources. The national census, from the most recent decade, was grotesque in its inadequacy. There was nothing to do but resort to the old trick of assembling bits and pieces of information gathered from Catholic and Evangelical missionaries, taking care not to offend any of the orders or sects and seducing ecclesiastic authorities and the Summer Institute of Linguistics (ILV) by arguing for the humanism of our research.

By this time my relations with the Franciscans had totally deteriorated. My old acquaintance, Father Pelosi, so generous with me during the years of my work with the Campa of the Gran Pajonal, and very knowledgeable about the Franciscan order's mission territory, had broken all contact, disillusioned by my critical writings about the missionaries. The Dominicans and Jesuits exerted a pretty severe control of their sources of information, except in the case of the Dominicans' missionary bulletins and the Jesuits' official history under the authoritarian control of Father Rubén Vargas Ugarte, S.J.

No priests from other orders, such as the Maryknoll, worked in the Amazon, except for a few Canadian priests from Quebec who were quite progressive and had missions among the Quechua peoples along the Lower Napo. Secular priests, almost all of them adherents of the dissident Liberation Theology set forth by Father Gustavo Gutiérrez, had no archives of any importance for our project, except for the basic critical vision of Catholicism that Father Gutiérrez had been preaching in his writings and classes. Gutiérrez, who some years earlier at the Catholic University, had been partially responsible for my having been systematically educated in a Latin American interpretation of Marxism, was also partially responsible for my Franciscan excommunication and Father Harold Griffith's disapproval.

Finally, five hundred years of intimate and frenzied coexistence between Catholic missionaries and the Indigenous peoples of the Amazon resulted in endless and tedious theological tirades and the baptism of long lists of "infidels," which only filled the missionary coffers without clarifying anything about the reality of the Amazon. As for the evangelicals, especially those from the ILV and New Tribes, their formal and beaming responses to our official requests was that they had no information except for their partial progress in teaching literacy and assembling phonetic systems for some of the Indigenous languages, making it possible for them to translate and disseminate the "Word of God among the savages." It was with this fragmentary information and our own ethnographic assumptions and comparisons, obtained from secondary sources, that we at the Center threw ourselves into designing a simulation model for the dissemination of territories to the "Native Communities" of the Peruvian Amazon.

At the beginning of 1974, Darcy Ribeiro invited the Polish-French economist Ignacy Sachs to the Center so he could give some workshops on what he called eco-social economy. I owe Sachs a few ideas, as brilliant as they were apparently simple, on the Amazon peoples' possible forms of economic development and ecologically sustainable production. Sachs introduced a notion that was both moderate and obvious: instead of defining and giving land to the Indigenous peoples and to the biosphere, we should limit and reserve land for development, such that each "pole" or development center in the Amazon would be clearly circumscribed, contained, and communicate with all others via an established network, preferably by river. This idea flew in the face of the common practice of designating reservations for the Indigenous peoples' "lack of development" and leaving all other land open to all types of ecological destruction and economic lack of control.

In France, Ignacy Sachs had already taught one Peruvian student, and his opinions began to carry weight at the National Planning Institute where an architect of great intelligence and social sensibility—I remember him only as *El Negro* Collantes—was training study teams for the Amazon region. Everything seemed to be coming together to support my and our plans for designing the conceptual instrumentation we needed to be able to put forth and apply the legal and political reforms that would recognize, deed, and develop a culture of land reform appropriate for the ethnic/communal territories of the Amazon.

The program seemed workable, above all, because resistance to change and conservative political opposition in the Amazon were fragmented and lacking in organization. In the Indigenous zones, there were few large landowner interests that would be affected, only the profound ideological obstacles and ethnic-racial discrimination that all Indigenous peoples of Peru had been suffering for centuries at the hands of coastal and Andean settlers who were as poor, if not poorer, than they.

From a political point of view, perhaps the most problematic economic interests were those on the part of the lumber companies and corporations

engaged in oil exploration and expropriation, when these were in the Indigenous territories. I believed that the program of restoring the Indigenous peoples to their lands and giving them legal jurisdiction was within reach, especially because of the heroic work that Alberto Chirif and his group were
doing at SINAMOS and the Ministry of Agriculture.

And yet, things were not going to be as easy as I predicted from the illusory
certainty of my research laboratory at the Center. During the gray months
of Lima's winter in 1974, we began to hear rumors—which we thought un-
founded at first—about internal disagreements in Velasco's cabinet. Abrupt
ministerial changes were followed by the premature retirement of several officials of the Armed Forces whom we considered to be among the most progressive. In their place, we saw the increased visibility of some high-ranking
Air Force and Navy officers. These were the two branches of the Peruvian
Armed Forces that had most forcefully resisted Velasco's reforms.

Several months earlier, my own experience had told me we could not trust
the Navy. Put forth by SINAMOS, the proposal of nationalizing the Summer Institute of Linguistics' installations and operations at its headquarters at
Yarinacocha, Pucallpa, was taken from SINAMOS' control by high-ranking
Navy intelligence officers who decided to expropriate the American missionary installations and use them for Peru's Military Intelligence. All of us young
idealists involved in the project had to put immediate brakes on our enthusiasm and tell more than a few Indigenous leaders we wouldn't be able to fight
on that weak flank just then.

I think I remember that it was the Awajún leader Evaristo Nugkuag—himself a deserter from the ILV—whom we contacted right away and told not to
organize Indigenous mobilizations around that issue. Better to put up with a
little shoddy biblical imperialism at the hands of evangelical fundamentalists
from the United States than nationalist neo-colonialism at the hands of the
military. Luckily, the proposal on the part of the Indigenous peoples of the
Amazon and on the part of the ILV's evangelical missionaries who, for the most
part, were honest and in their own way caring, and who professed an unwav-
ering faith in the coincidence of Near Eastern Judeo-Christian cosmology
with capitalist individualism and the market economy spirit that Max Weber
had described more than a hundred years before, didn't go forward.

I am always surprised by the turns our lives take. In 2008, at a tiny and
very expensive apartment in Paris, I was writing these pages when a Peruvian
expatriate friend called to tell me that Mr. Juan Maldonado, a Shipibo leader

and mayor from the Ucayali, would be giving a lecture on the social and cultural situation of his people and province. Linda and I hurried over to the Maison de l'Amerique Latine on Boulevard Saint Germaine. We got there after the talk had begun. Juan Maldonado spoke in Spanish, and a small elegant woman with long black hair who looked to be Vietnamese or Filipino translated his talk into impeccable French. After it was over, I approached Mr. Maldonado and his translator to ask a few questions, and discovered, to my astonishment and with nostalgia, that the woman was Edith Estam Nugkuag, my old friend Evaristo Nugkuag's niece. Awajún herself, she had done her professional studies and established herself in northern France, where she founded and promoted an association of Awajún women artists, artisans, and activists involved in the international movement for Indigenous autonomy.

THE LAST TIME I saw President Juan Velasco Alvarado I was still working at the office of the Native Communities Division on Salaverry Avenue and Linda was teaching the lower grades at the Roosevelt School. It was early, around seven on a cold morning, and Chaclacayo's Andean sun had not yet dissipated Lima's fog. I remember as if it was yesterday how upset I was when I turned the key in the Peugeot and heard the sad dry sound of its dead battery.

"Goddamn shitty car!"

"Hurry up, Linda, we're going to have to push the car. It won't start. Grab your things, close the front door, and don't forget to leave the back door open so Orégano can go out to the patio."

From the house on Hilda Street to the Central Highway there was less than a block, and fortunately downhill. We'd only gone a few yards, in second gear, key in the ignition, me jumping in and out of the driver's seat and Linda pushing the car from behind, when two imposing American cars passed. I immediately recognized Velasco's official vehicle by its little flags and other characteristics. One of the president's aides, a Navy officer, got out, stood before me, and with a military-style salute said something like:

"The President wants to know if you need our help with your car."

I think I responded something to the effect that my wife and I could deal with it. The aide returned to Velasco's car, and a few seconds later came back and told Linda and me that the President insisted the police patrol give us a push to help start the Peugeot. And that's what happened. Luckily, our little car rose to the occasion and, before we got to the Central Highway, reacted favorably to presidential intervention. I don't know if it's my imagination or the weak and selective register of memory, but I think the President's car sounded its horn in a couple of brief signs of approval that the mission had been a success.

I never wanted to see symbolism in this simple act of citizenship and good neighborliness. But now, more than forty years later, I find in it a metaphor for Juan Velasco Alvarado's openness and humanity. He was a settler from Catacaos, a poor Indian community of sand and hunger on the Sechura desert, who had been able to overcome all the limits imposed by a society built on injustice to retrieve in Peru's depths a people's greatest wisdom and generosity.

CHAPTER 23

From Ethnographer to Activist

᪔

I'VE ASKED MYSELF MANY times how I went from being an academic anthropologist—an ethnographer in fact—to an activist. If I had to put a date to my emotional and intellectual leap into activism, it would be 1971.

In these retrospective reflections I realize that as an individual I come out of a collective process that brings together in time and space the diverse wills of peoples and communities I knew or with whom I never interacted except in ideas and sentiments. It was on the island of Barbados where, along with a dozen or so other Latin American anthropologists, I'd been invited by the University of Bern and the World Council of Churches based in Switzerland to the meeting called Barbados Reunion I. Our goal was to analyze the situation of oppression and human rights of the Indigenous peoples of the South American lowlands. We were all relatively young social scientists except, perhaps, for the Brazilian Darcy Ribeiro and the Mexican Guillermo Bonfil Batalla, both of whom had histories as ministers of State, persecuted political exiles, and directors of important social institutions. The rest of us were all in our thirties. We had practiced anthropology in the jungles and mountains of Paraguay, Brazil, Peru, Ecuador, Colombia, and Venezuela, sometimes in repressive political conditions that threatened our personal safety. That was the "lost decade," when neo-Fascism, supported as always by the United States, raised its Hydra head throughout the Southern Cone and in much of the rest of Latin America.

The Barbados I meeting produced fundamental documents for the rebirth of the movement of liberation and decolonization of Latin America's Indigenous peoples: the Barbados I Declaration—a few pages of denunciation and a call to action—and a collection of reports by the participants which was published simultaneously in English and Spanish under the respective titles of *The Situation of the Indians in South America: Contributions to the Study of Inter-ethnic Conflict in the Non-Andean Regions of South America* (Geneva, 1972) and *La situación del indígena en América del Sur* (Montevideo, 1972).[36] The *Declaración*[37] was immediately translated into English, Portuguese, and French, and a few months and years later into several Indigenous languages by the Latin American Indigenous organizations themselves. The two editions of the book had different destinies: the English version barely circulated in European academic circles and had practically no repercussion within the US academy, immersed as it was in its proverbial imperial insularity; the Spanish version, as I mentioned before, had the ambiguous privilege of being confiscated and burned by Uruguay's military dictatorship. This showed us how dangerous and threatening the simple publication of some anthropological texts denouncing the situation of exploitation and oppression of Indigenous peoples ignored in the depths of the forests and mountains of Latin America was to the continent's military dictatorships.

Those were the years of intensification of the "new imperial conquest" of the last Indigenous frontiers, just as Darcy Ribeiro had analyzed a bit earlier in the case of Brazil[38] and I myself had denounced in 1967 in Peru in "La nueva conquista de la selva" published in *Revista Amaru* in Lima.[39]

In those first texts written in the mid-1960s, I still oscillated between a strictly anthropological lexicon—"anthropology of urgency" or "the anthropological problem of the Indigenous territories"—and the first signs of an ethical and political commitment that began distancing me from the supposed empirical objectivity of my discipline. In 1968, under the title "An-

---

36. Walter Dostal, ed., *The Situation of the Indians in South America: Contributions to the Study of Inter-ethnic Conflict in the Non-Andean Regions of South America* (Geneva: World Council of Churches, 1972) y Georg Grunberg and Pedro Agostinho da Silva, eds., *La situación del indígena en América del Sur: Aportes al estudio de la fricción inter-étnica de los indios no-andinos* (Montevideo: Biblioteca Científica, 1972).

37. *Declaración de Barbados*, IWGIA Document No. 1 (Copenhagen: International Work Group for Indigenous Affairs, 1971).

38. Darcy Ribeiro, *Os indios e a civilizaçao* (Rio de Janeiro: Civilizaçao Brasileira, 1970).

39. Varese, "La nueva conquista de la selva."

thropología, política y neutralidad" (Anthropology, Politics and Neutrality), published in *Amaru*,[40] I questioned the bourgeois notion of "scientific objectivity" appealing to the Marxist critique I had learned rather randomly in my Italian youth. Finally, my work with the Revolutionary Government of the Armed Forces and my farewell to the classrooms of the National University of San Marcos and the Peruvian academic world paved the way for my committing myself fully to the thought and practice of activist anthropology. During the five years in which I worked for the Revolutionary Government I was able to travel to some of the Indigenous regions and territories of the Amazon that were most threatened by colonist settlers and lumber, agricultural, and petroleum companies.

As I already mentioned in previous pages, in 1970 my wife Linda and I were able to travel to one of the Matsés-Mayoruna communities that had survived the bombings of the Peruvian Air Forces. An aging grandmother who spoke rudimentary Spanish narrated what had happened a few years before and made it possible for us to understand the dimension of the large-scale genocide committed by President Belaunde Terry's "democratic administration."[41]

Years before, at the 38th International Congress of Americanists that took place in the German cities of Stuttgart and Münich in 1968, a group of European and American anthropologists convened by the Norwegian anthropologist Helge Kleivan debated the role our discipline should play with regard to the situations of neocolonial oppression of the Indigenous peoples. What today seems an issue put to rest, at those moments in academic anthropology, especially in the North, seemed almost an insoluble challenge. I remember that during the discussion in one of the Congress's rooms where Helge Kleivan was explaining his project of putting together working groups to observe and denounce cases of overt oppression or ethnocide of Indigenous populations, some of those present got up in irritation declaring that such was

40. Stefano Varese, "Antropología, política y neutralidad," *Amaru*, No. 7, Lima (July-September 1968).

41. Of all the film of the forest that Carlos and I had worked on, I was miraculously able to save the short documentary *Visión de la Selva* (Vision of the Forest) in which scenes of the Amazon can be seen interspersed with long interviews with the journalist and writer on the Amazon Roger Rumrrill—at the time a consultant to the Revolution's Minister of Agriculture—explaining the plans and challenges that the Velasco revolution confronted in the Amazon.

not anthropology's role. "That is for politicians and governments," they said. Among those who abandoned the hall I recognized the Harvard University anthropologist Professor David Maybury-Lewis, followed by a group of his students and colleagues.

Helge Kleivan's initiative advanced rapidly and in just a few months the International Work Group of Indigenous Affairs (IWGIA) took shape in Denmark where its main chapter was located. It began to publish reports, analyses, and legal documents in an attempt to mobilize public opinion in Europe, the Americas, and later the entire Third World, about the reality of native populations across the globe. For a very brief period Kleivan named me International Secretary for Latin America, perhaps for a lack of anyone who could commit him or herself more seriously to that work.[42] I was fully occupied with carrying out the revolutionary plans for the Indigenous peoples of the Amazon and really had little time to involve myself in the "reform" of academic anthropology in the northern hemisphere.[43]

In 1972 David Maybury-Lewis founded his own non-governmental organization of aid to the Indigenous peoples and nationalities of the world, Cultural Survival, which, along with IWGIA, has done an extraordinary job of supporting native peoples. Professor David Maybury-Lewis had the intellectual generosity to acknowledge his initial error in Stuttgart and graciously invited me to be part of Cultural Survival's Board of Directors for several years. This in spite of our ideological differences which have never been fully debated.

42. Stefano Varese, *The Forest Indians in the Present Political Situation of Peru* (Copenhagen: IWGIA, Document No. 8, 1972).

43. For readers interested in this micro-history of Latin American anthropology I suggest Stefano Varese, Guillermo Delgado, and Rodolfo Meyer, "Indigenous Anthropologies. Beyond Barbados," in Deborah Poole, ed., *A Companion to Latin American Anthropology* (Malden, MA: Blackwell Publishing, 2008). Also, Stefano Varese, *Witness to Sovereignty. Essays on the Indian Movement in Latin America* (Copenhagen: IWGIA, 2006).

CHAPTER 24

European Interlude

༄

I DON'T KNOW TO WHICH benefic spirit of the Kichwa people of Lamas and the forests of San Martín and the upper Mayo River I owe the gift of having met Bernard Lelong, a man of cosmic sensibility, practitioner of Sufism, explorer of Indigenous spaces, and collector of curative plants. Bernard and I became friends during long conversations in the bars of Lima and at forest inns, always accompanied by the sweet dates Bernard insisted I eat before beginning each conversation.

Between 1969 and 1970 Linda and I decided to travel to Europe in a trip that would put me in touch with my Italian past, a search for her Irish ancestors, and finally to visit my mother Pina and introduce her to the woman who would become my wife.

With the little car my mother lent us we were able to do a bit of sightseeing, motivated by my nostalgia and Linda's astonishment when confronted with the continent of her ancestors. Finally, assuming considerable risk, we took that little car through the Mont Blanc tunnel to Switzerland, France, and on to Paris. We arrived the next morning just in time to meet my friend Bernard Lelong at the end of Rue de Vaugirard, near the dilapidated Grand Hotel de France where we stayed for a week of feverish activities organized by Bernard.

My European tour as an anthropology activist began there, at a café in the Latin Quarter. It allowed me to know, or at least identify, some of the most important Latin Americanist intellectuals of the time. It was thanks to Bernard Lelong and those to whom he generously introduced me, that I was able to publish articles in *Les Temps Modernes*,[44] the magazine founded by Jean

---

44. Stefano Varese, "Considérations d'anthropologie utopique," *Les Temps Modernes*, No. 316, Paris (November 1972); and "Au sujet du colonialism ecologique," *Les Temps Modernes*, No. 321, Paris (April 1973).

Paul Sartre and sometime later a long essay of a more academic nature in the classic journal of history founded by Marc Bloch and Lucien Febvre in 1929 and later adopted by the Fernand Braudel school, *Annales*.[45]

I must say that on that tour that began in a café in the Latin Quarter with my friend Bernard guiding me in hasty walks to cafés, bookstores, and Paris apartments of difficult access and uncertain elevators, I came to know the sociologist Jean Duvignaud; the anthropologist France-Marie Renard Cassevitz, who years later would publish important texts on the Machiguenga people of the Peruvian forest; Phillippe Descola, who between 1978 and 1979 undertook his magnificent studies of the Shuar people of the Ecuadorian forest; the young Jean Copans, who in 1975 would publish an essay of mine in his book *Anthropologie et impérialisme*;[46] the mathematician Robert Jaulin, author of *La paix Blanche*,[47] the book that denounced the genocide of the Bari peoples of Colombia; François Morin, an anthropologist with whom I would reconnect a few years later in Peru; and Jean-Patrick Razon, who headed the French section of Survival International and who for years devoted his energies to the Indigenous cause.

I cannot recall the precise sequence of that vertiginous trip through Europe in the somewhat hazy memory in which my passion for Linda blends with the excitement of having found along the way a community of activist intellectuals forged in the anti-colonialist path. I think we returned to Turin, gave the car back to my mother, and continued on by train to Denmark where my friend Helge Kleivan received us. Kleivan, director of IWGIA, and his young colleagues and former students, the anthropologists Peter Aaby and Søren Hvalkof, had produced an alarming condemnation of the fundamentalist Christian missionaries of the Summer Institute of Linguistics: *Is God an American?*[48]

45. Varese and Gamarra, op. cit.

46. Stefano Varese, "Les communautes tribales de la foret dans la nouvelle politique peruvienne" in Jean Copan, ed., *Anthropologie et impérialism*, Coll. Biblioteque d'Anthropologie, Dir. M. Godelier (Paris: F. Maspero, 1975).

47. Robert Jaulin, *La paix blanche. Introduction á l'ethnocide* (Oarus: Seyukm 1970).

48. Peter Aaby and Søren Hvalkof, *Is God an American? An Anthropological Perspective on the Missionary Work of the Summer Institute of Linguistics.* (Copenhagen: International Work Group for Indigenous Affairs-IWGIA; London: Survival International, 1981).

A couple of years after that meeting in Copenhagen with Peter and Søren, now back in Lima, I found myself in the delicate position of having to intervene in the possible expulsion of the ILV missionaries from Peru. In the Division of Native Communities of the Forest, on the eve of signing the expulsion decree, we learned that the Navy was about to take over the entire infrastructure of the U.S. base at Yarinacocha and install its center of operations for the whole Peruvian Amazon there. At that moment in the Revolution the most conservative branch of the Joint Command of the Armed Forces—almost Fascist in nature—was precisely the Naval Intelligence Service. It wasn't hard to choose between allowing the Christian fundamentalist missionaries to continue ploughing the surface of the Amazon civilization and delivering the native communities into the devious political-cultural and racist hands of creole officials of the Lima elite. A less damaging of the two agreements was ratified between the Government and the ILV, and finally all the U.S. missionaries stayed in Peru and continued preaching their domesticated and conservative gospel even as they provided strategic information to the government and corporations of the United States, as they had been doing for years in every country in the world where they'd managed to insert themselves.

In Copenhagen, Linda and I stayed for a few days at Peter Aaby's commune where everyone shared clothes, all cleaning and cooking duties, the young children were cared for by all when their parents were busy, and a large table in the basement of the two-story house was always well-provisioned with marijuana that the members of the commune smoked with a sense of calm and without apparent enthusiasm. There we met some Kurdish political refugees from Turkey—or were they from Iraq? We danced at parties that were anything but Nordic, and endlessly discussed the fate of Nixon and the war in Vietnam. No one seemed to have the slightest doubt that Yankee imperialism would soon collapse beneath the weight of the horrors it was perpetrating: in Southeast Asia, in Latin America, and in the open veins of the United States itself.[49]

On that journey of solidarity and social activism from Paris to Scandinavia, we identified with our new friends because of the generational links of having been born between 1940 and 1950, the ideological connections

49. Eduardo Galeano, *Las venas abiertas de América Latina* [The Open Veins of Latin America] (México: Siglo Veintiuno, 1971).

with a socialist left, and a common recent history. We had all been sensitized by the 1968 student and workers rebellion in Paris, we had all—directly or indirectly—been marked by the massacre at Tlatelolco Plaza in Mexico that same year, we had all reached maturity under the influence of the Cuban Revolution, and we all identified with the Vietnamese people in their war of national liberation and with the black citizens of the United States in their struggle for civil rights.[50] The American Indian Movement, founded in Minneapolis in 1968, was already a part of our collective memory. A couple of years later, in June 1972, the moral scandal of President Nixon's administration and the corruption of imperialism and its Latin American satellites confirmed for us that what we'd long intuited had become the normal state of affairs, accepted by all the quasi-democracies and every sort of dictatorship.

Our trip through Scandinavia continued with a series of conferences sponsored by IWGIA at the universities of Aarhus, Stockholm, Oslo, and finally Bergen, from where we left for Newcastle, England. It was an epic journey through the North Atlantic, during which I vomited the last morsel of a marvelous banquet of herrings and sardines in brine, and huge quantities of beer I ingested as the ship made its way through the calm waters of the Norwegian *fjords*. My Genovese navigator's ancestors were unable to come to my aid. On the other hand, Linda's Irish ancestors did a marvelous job and Linda saved me from the humiliation of descending shakily from the ship instead of confidently on the elegant Nordic arm of my lifetime companion.

50. Martin Luther King was assassinated in 1968. As I review and copy-edit this section of the English translation of my book, I find it outrageous that today, in June 2020, more than 50 years after the Civil Rights movement and the African American civil uprising for equal rights, the whole U.S. and large portions of the global community are still protesting in the streets against police and militarized police unrestrained violence against Black, Latinx, brown-skinned, Native American/Indigenous, and poor disenfranchised peoples. I wonder if the children of the children of my children will still have to witness these horrendous crimes because of the color of their skin or their social class position.

CHAPTER 25

A Leap into the Future by Way of the Past

🜨

I T WOULD TAKE ME almost five decades of world travel and life in Peru, Mexico, Central America, and California to fully internalize my brief experience of European and Scandinavian democratic socialism and compare it with my lengthy experiences of other democratic models, quasi-democracies, and post-democratic capitalism. Between the 1970s and 1990s I also visited socialist Yugoslavia and Poland and the People's Republic of China. Five decades of ever more frequent questions about the moral abyss that has surrounded us with its seductive and illusory materialism and its forever delayed hopes.

It is hard to assign a date to the dawning of consciousness, to those moments in which a sudden synthesis of the accumulation of thought and feeling becomes a solid revelation. These are the epiphanies of our secular life.

In the most recent years, living in the United States, I have witnessed with horror thousands of massacres and killings of innocent victims, of girls and boys in primary school, of infants in kindergarten, of teachers, and of simple passersby who found themselves in the wrong place at the wrong time; or thousands of blacks and those of other ethnicities wantonly murdered by police indoctrinated in a panicked terror of "the other, different and unknown." Living the scandalous reality of a capitalist democracy in which citizens are armed to the teeth with more than 300 million high caliber guns, where automatic weapons designed for wars of extermination can be purchased in minutes by young people 18 years old who aren't yet of legal drinking age, where the most basic ethical notions aren't available to the minds of most people, where the answer to murderous violence is more murderous violence, I too had to face the dilemma of accepting the absurd and this moral deviance as normal, as neutral expressions of life in a capitalist democracy.

I retain my belief in social justice, my search for a "moral economy" and an ecological and cultural ethic such as that proposed by the Kichwa people of the Amazon and by the Andean Quechuas and Aymaras under their philosophical rubric of *Sumak Kawsay* and *Sumak Kamaña*, life in harmony with the cosmos. And it was as a young immigrant that I added to my constant return to the profound sources of Indo-American wisdom the democratic socialism I had reencountered in France and Scandinavia in 1968 and 1970 and the readings of U.S. socialists C. Wright Mills, Howard Zinn, Noam Chomsky, and Edward Said that I was fortunate enough to find on my torturous road to California. I also read leftist journals such as Monthly Review, NACLA Report on the Americas, and Latin American Perspectives.

During a brief stay at the University of California—Berkeley, where I taught some anthropology courses upon our return from Europe, Linda wanted me to visit San Jose State University and especially introduce me to her ex professor of psychology and advisor Dr. David Newman.

In an astonishing stroke of luck, that weekend the German philosopher Herbert Marcuse had arrived at the University of California—Santa Cruz. He had been in the United States for a number of years at that point, as a refugee from the Nazis and a professor at the University of California—San Diego. At that moment the black leader Angela Davis was standing trial in a federal criminal court accused of being a Communist militant involved in "subversive acts." Angela Davis's defense committee was coordinated by the young Communist Bettina Aptheker, an activist in the Berkeley Free Speech Movement and young assistant to her father's friend, the black intellectual leader W.E.B. DuBois, now an intimate friend of Davis. I didn't know anything about Angela Davis, Bettina Aptheker, or the U.S. Communist Party. Of Herbert Marcuse I knew only that the Frankfurt School considered him the initiator of the New Left, so popular with university students. The Italian translation of his book that my mother would send me hadn't yet reached my hands.[51]

I was flustered when I arrived from Berkeley by car at David Newman's home in San Jose. My confusion and social insecurity mounted when I entered that room filled with famous people I didn't know. I thought I would recognize Angela Davis from photographs I'd seen in newspapers and maga-

51. Herbert Marcuse, *Eros e Civiltá* [Eros and Civilization] (Torino: Luigi Einaudi Editore, 1974).

zines, and Marcuse because I had skimmed books and articles that included photographs of his graying head. My astonishment grew enormously when Bettina Aptheker, Herbert Marcuse, and Angela Davis wanted to know more about the Peruvian Revolution that David Newman mentioned when he introduced me. There, in the heart of California, in what would soon be the world center of electronic capitalism, I found once more the "internationalism" of the left that in my naiveté I had attributed only to Latin America and the Third World.

In 1990 I arrived at the University of California—Davis to begin teaching in the Department of Indigenous Studies. I was fortunate to be welcomed by a great humanist intellectual, Arnold Bauer, who in our first weeks invited Linda and me to his home on the outskirts of the city to enjoy a glass of Dos Patos, wine he produced himself. Our conversation was as warm as it was creative. Bauer was a wonderful storyteller who knew how to extract the subtlest and most colorful threads from the skein of the history of the United States and Latin America. From him I learned to take a new look at my somewhat juvenile prejudices about the poverty and lack of depth of the U.S. socialist movement. He always reminded me that the American social movement's lack of memory is a recent phenomenon, that until the 1980s intellectuals such as Michael Harrington, founding member of the Democratic Socialists of America, fulfilled a fundamental function in keeping socialist ideals on the platform of the Democratic Party.

For Arnie, only in the past two decades the country's complex anarchist, socialist, syndicalist, and pacifist past had faded beneath the media's avalanche of neo-liberal ideology. "Stefano—he'd say in his excellent Spanish practiced for years in Mexico and Chile—you have to understand that our university students haven't had any contact with the classics of socialist literature. They have no idea who Karl Marx was, or what historic materialism is, and even less that this country has its own rich socialist tradition. Ask in any of your graduate courses if anyone knows who the Chicago martyrs were, or the anarchists Sacco and Vanzetti. U.S. social history has been sanitized, censured, and replaced with an official history that is nothing more than an apology of late stage capitalism."

Arnold Bauer had been in Nicaragua and Cuba and was able to compare notes with the Chile of Allende and Pinochet and Mexico's post-revolutionary PRI and the Zapatistas. His sense of humor, which was very Latin American, distanced him somewhat from his academic colleagues who lacked his irony or Mexican puns. I owe Arnold Bauer, with his German and farm roots in Kansas and his cosmopolitan vision, my being able to approach the deep history of U.S. social movements with respect. But I owe him much more. I owe him the deep affection he gave Linda and me, the love he made me feel for the agricultural plains of California's Central Valley, its suffocating heat and chilling winds, the calls of the geese as they flew to and from Canada, and the wise crows that gaze at me now from the exuberant painting by his wife and widow Danielle Greenberg de Bauer that hangs above my desk.

CHAPTER 26

The Spiderweb

𝕉

A FEW YEARS BACK, MY brother Luis published a collection of poems he titled *La telaraña de Dios* (God's Spiderweb). The great Brazilian poet Amadeu Thiago de Melo—friend of Pablo Neruda—liked the book a lot. He translated it into Portuguese and published it in Brazil. And so the exiled Peruvian poet Luis Varese, a fugitive in many lands, is better known in Brazil than in his native Peru, where the archives of the Secret Police are full of false accusations of revolutionary feats that would put Leon Trotsky to shame, but the bookstores don't carry his poetry or essays.

I like the spiderweb metaphor because, like the Amazon metaphor of the hammock, it reminds us that the multitude of knots that link our memories are coincidences, synchronies, contacts, and renewed contacts, the ebb and flow of what is near and what is far, junctures and separations that together make up the weave that holds all the thousands of beings that touched us or had something to do with our passage through time. Naturally at my age the spiderweb and hammock are denser, but they also contain some holes for which I hope I will be forgiven.

1979 can be considered a parting of the waters in the history of Latin American Indigenous movements, initiating as it did two decades of Indigenous activism on the world stage. After years of opposition and armed struggle against the dictator Anastasio Somoza, the Sandinista National Liberation Front of Nicaragua (FSLN) had managed to liberate the whole country and extend its revolutionary socialist program to the Atlantic Coast inhabited by Miskito, Sumo, and Rama Indigenous communities as well as Garífuna black creoles.

The history of relations between these native peoples of the Atlantic Coast and the Spanish-speaking *mestizos* of the rest of Nicaragua was marked from colonial times by open racism and a nationalist sense of superiority on the part of the *mestizo* peoples of the Pacific Coast and central part of the country. For the next ten years the Sandinistas were involved in a violent war with the Indigenous population and creole blacks of the Atlantic Coast, especially with the Miskitos who were supported militarily by the government of the United States in its continuous efforts to impede the establishment of social democracies with a popular base. At the same time, the Maya in Guatemala and the farmers and Indigenous peoples of El Salvador and Honduras endured genocidal wars in the name of "neo-liberal democracy," with full backing and arms from the United States, and in the case of Guatemala, with the collaboration of the state of Israel. All Indigenous and *mestizo* Central America was in flames.

Towards the end of 1985, when the administration of President Ronald Reagan was fully involved in the Iran-Contra scandal, known in the United States as Irangate or Contragate, I was named—along with Martin Diskin, Thomas Bossert, and Salomón Nahmad to be a member of the Latin American Studies Association-LASA's commission to investigate the human rights situation on the Atlantic Coast of Nicaragua.[52] The mission had the dual goals of observing and eventually making public the situation of the human rights of the Indigenous, black creole and *mestizo* peoples of the Atlantic Coast, and at the same time calling attention to and condemning, especially in the United States, the serious abuses against academic freedom, freedom of the press, and freedom of opinion committed by President Ronald Reagan's second administration.

Martin Diskin and I traveled for almost two weeks. Diskin was an anthropology professor at MIT in Boston, whom I met up with again after years of separation after we'd been neighbors and friends in San Felipe del Agua on the outskirts of Oaxaca. Those days of travel, observation, and interviews with Miskito, Black Creole, Rama, Sumo, and Garífuna citizens was a profound experience for me, one filled with immense cultural and human richness. From Diskin, who was already suffering from an advanced cancer, I learned once more from his love of all the diverse forms in which life mani-

52. Martin Diskin, Thomas Bossert, Solomóm Nahmad, and Stefano Varese, *Peace and Autonomy on the Atlantic Coast of Nicaragua: a Report of the LASA Task-force on Human Rights and Academic Freedom.* (A publication of the Latin American Studies Association, Pittsburgh, September 1986).

fests itself in this world. With his great sense of humor—very typical of Jews from the eastern part of the United States—and at one and the same time his innate sympathy and profound critique, lightened by irony, I was able to learn more about the anthropology of human rights in a multi-ethnic society than in months of theoretical classes. I saw Martin Diskin again in Boston in 1991, when he invited me to his lovely colonial house on the outskirts of Cambridge to see his wife Vilunya and children Leah and Aaron again. They had played with my own children, Vanessa and André, in the gardens and patios of San Felipe del Agua. With great generosity, Martin invited me to lecture at MIT, where I spoke in an almost hallucinatory state brought on by an attack of vertigo that threatened to conspire against my "academic prestige."[53]

In August 1997, at the age of 62, Diskin decided to cross the river and he left us with a terrible loneliness that was nevertheless filled with memories of his life. To Martin Diskin and Guillermo Bonfil Batalla, who had left us six years earlier, I dedicated an Indigenous poem by the Mazatec poet Apolonio Bartolo Ronquillo as a tribute to the utopian imagination that was their final gift.[54] It reads as follows:

> *Weaver of dreams*
> *teaching me to weave mine . . .*
> *how can I decipher the night,*
> *how can I understand the day . . .*
> *how many knots must I tie*
> *to connect with you . . .*
> *Tell me, weaver of dreams*
> *how to weave the path*
> *to connect with you.*

BETWEEN 1984 AND 1986 I bore direct witness to the genocidal policies directed against the Mayan peoples by Guatemala's military government. I

53. Stefano Varese, "The Ethnopolitics of Indian Resistance in Latin America." A Working Paper for the Center for International Studies, Massachusetts Institute of Technology, Cambridge, MA, January 1991.

54. Stefano Varese, "Crítica de la razón distópica. Homenaje a la imaginación utópica de Martin Diskin y Guillermo Bonfil Batalla" (Critique of dystopic reason. Homage to the utopic imagination of Martin Diskin and Guillermo Bonfil Batalla), in *Desacatos. Revista de Antropología Social*, CIESAS, Mexico (2002): 189-194.

made a few somewhat irresponsible family trips as well as long observational visits and did field work at the Guatemalan Maya refugee camps in the Mexican states of Chiapas, Campeche, and Quintana Roo. There, under the auspices of the United Nations High Commission for Refugees (UNHCR), the United Nations Research Institute for Social Development (UNRISD), the Colegio de México, and the Mexican Commission for Refugee Aid, along with researchers Sergio Aguayo, Hanne Christensen, and Laura O'Dogherty, I was able to observe the atrocities committed by the military government against Guatemala's civilian population. The children's drawings, their stories, and the histories I gathered from their parents were typical of the long list of atrocities that has accompanied the Indigenous peoples of all the Americas for 500 years.

I recognized a knot in my spiderweb years later when I realized that on one of my weeks-long trips through camps with more than 43,000 refugees there had been a young Maya Jacalteco from the region of the Juchumatanes who had managed to escape after having been tortured by the Guatemalan military and witnessing his brother's murder.[55] The young Víctor Montejo reappeared in my life years later at the University of California—Davis where he had a post graduate fellowship that I arranged on the recommendation of an anthropology colleague at a Midwestern university. Víctor Montejo reinvented himself as an anthropologist, intellectual, poet, novelist, cultural and political leader in two Mayan languages, English and Spanish, and as a professor in the Department of Indigenous Studies at the University of California—Davis. We accompanied one another during years of intellectual collaboration, creating a space for Mesoamerican and Mayan studies in that department.

In spite of my efforts as director of the Department of Indigenous Studies, I was unable to save Víctor from the deep ethnic-racial prejudices on the part of a Dean of Letters and Humanities during an administrative period rife with Eurocentrism; she could not understand the immense intellectual, artistic, and academic value of that wise Maya, who would later be appointed Minister of Peace and Reconciliation in Guatemala's first democratic government. That Dean, steeped in the bureaucracy and mediocrity of imported Eurocentrism wouldn't stretch the rules (rules that exist to be broken, as the poet monk Thomas Merton said), and wouldn't give the Maya professor Víc-

---

55. Víctor Montejo, *Testimony. Death of a Guatemalan Village* (New York: Curbstone Press, 1987).

tor Montejo, Minister of Peace in Guatemala, one more year off without pay in order to carry out his work in the construction of a new, democratic, and ultimately Mayan Guatemala.

Our relationship, invisible to begin with in the Mayan lands of Mesoamerica and transformed years later into a deep friendship in California, continues now that we are both retired from the University at California Davis and one of us is growing coffee in Jacaltenango while the other is drinking that coffee ever more, often in celebration of one more knot in our hammock. Or is a spiderweb divine?

CHAPTER 27

Bertrand Russell and American Indians

꙰

I DIDN'T FIND THOSE DAYS at the end of November 1980 in Rotterdam particularly cold, considering the fact that I'd arrived by plane from the suffocating heat of Veracruz and the autumn breezes of Oaxaca. I knew that Guillermo Bonfil Batalla would be coming from Mexico City and that my other friend, Robert Jaulin, would be arriving by train from Paris. During the long flight from Mexico I'd been comforted by the idea that with this surprising invitation to serve as a member of the jury at the Fourth Bertrand Russell Tribunal, "Los derechos de los pueblos indios de las Américas" (The Rights of the Indian Peoples of the Americas) I would be sharing the task with these two friends.

All the members of the Jury—I think we were eleven in all—met, got to know one another, or renew our friendships just hours before the Tribunal's inauguration. For the first time I could look into Eduardo Galeano's blue eyes and acknowledge the beauty of his writing and truth of his words. An absence of formality quickly linked Guillermo Bonfil, Darcy Ribeiro, Eduardo Galeano, and me in a quartet of joyous irony, critical revision, and lofty propositions that we hoped to bring to the Tribunal as a contribution of the Indo-American utopian tradition.

At that moment we weren't that clear about the magnitude of this international peoples' tribunal founded years before by philosophers Bertrand Russel and Jean Paul Sartre with the goal of confronting the power of the State—in all its democratic or authoritarian incarnations—and of the market with the ethical force of the world's millions of poor and oppressed.

The following morning, in an enormous auditorium, the Dutch organizers and hosts invited us up to the Tribunal before which thousands of people of

every age, university students and workers, mixed with hundreds of Indigenous delegates and representatives from North, Central and South America.

The following days were exhausting. Long hours of day and night listening
to oral testimonies in Indigenous languages translated into English, Spanish,
and Portuguese by interpreters. Hours of reading reports and denunciations
of massacres and all sort of abuses, and long interviews with Indigenous individuals and groups, left little time for reflection and rekindling of old friendships and nourishment of new ones.

There was a man of a certain casual elegance at the event. He was wearing
a tweed jacket, blue jeans, and a long pony tail, and he turned out to be the
great anthropological historian Jack Forbes, whom I knew from references as
founder of the DQU Indigenous university in California. We talked a lot, or
rather I listened at length, as he told his illustrated stories of the Indigenous
reality in the United States. His testimonies before the Tribunal revealed his
deep knowledge of "official U.S. Indian history" and the "history of the Indigenous peoples and nations." These brief moments of volatile friendship
with Jack Forbes remained with me until they reemerged some ten years later
when Indigenous professors Sarah Hutchison and David Risling of the University of California—Davis invited me to give a talk in the Program of Native Studies and I remembered that the director of the program—at the time
on a sabbatical in Europe—was the same Jack Forbes I'd met at the Russell
Tribunal in Rotterdam.

I'd encountered Eduardo Galeano several more times: through reading and
writings when, in 1984, I asked him to sign a letter I was circulating in support
of my brother Luis who was imprisoned at the time in Peru, accused of terrorism. It's hard to know, but Eduardo Galeano's name and prestige may have
had some influence, if not with the officials of State Intelligence—illiterate
by definition—with President Alan García, who a few months later had
something to do with Luis's liberation and exile. In time, and in my position
as a professor and Director of the Department of Indigenous Studies at the
University of California—Davis, I was able to extend an official invitation to
Eduardo, asking him to deliver a guest lecture at the university. More than
500 students crowded into the small classroom and listened in fascination
to that famous narrator tell fantastic stories of a beloved continent and its
peoples of all colors forever threatened by the gray monotony of a sad and
decadent empire. On another occasion he came to San Francisco. I went to
pick him up and take him to see the pine and sequoia forests, those temples

With Eduardo Galeano and my Oaxacan cat Lulá in Davis, California, circa 1995

of the Miwok and Pomo peoples about which he wanted to know everything, and I was unable to satisfy his curiosity. We ended up at my home in Davis where I had to grab his cigarette for a moment so Linda could take a picture in which Eduardo Galeano and Stefano appeared along with Lulá, our cat of Oaxacan origin. Years later, when I felt our farewell was near, with immense generosity he wrote a few lines that will forever be inscribed on the back cover of *Selva Vida*.[56]

56. Stefano Varese, Frédérique Apffel-Marglin, and Roger Rumrrill, coords., *Selva vida—De la destrucción de la Amazonía al paradigma de la regeneración* (Copenhagen, Mexico and La Habana: IWGIA, UNAM and Casa de las Américas. 2013).

CHAPTER 28

Berkeley, Stanford, and the Miskitos

🐒

T HE FIRST TIME I was a visiting professor at the University of California—Berkeley in the summer of 1972, I had received an invitation from the ethnobiologist and linguist Brent Berlin. I had met Berlin a few months before in the forest in northern Peru, in Aguaruna-Awuajún territory. He was doing research there on Indigenous agricultural ecology. I realized that he would be interested in gaining access to the Amazon country in an era of nationalist tensions. I accepted the invitation with some trepidation, tempered somewhat by the fact that the great historian of the Andean world, Professor John H. Rowe and his wife Patricia Lyons were also sponsoring the invitation. I knew of them from their studies of the Andes and the Amazon.

Those were times of heightened activism in Berkeley: that summer, inspired by the writings of Herbert Marcuse, the students had risen up in protest and resistance against the obligatory draft and the war in Vietnam. Telegraph Avenue, in the heart of Berkeley, had seen violent confrontations between anti-riot police and the young students. The police had gone onto the campus without entering its buildings, but thereby infringing on an unwritten tradition of not invading the university grounds. In May 1970, at Kent State University, four students had been assassinated by the National Guard. It had been a human tragedy of serious political consequences for President Richard Nixon and the stability of his administration. From my Latin American point of view, these military and police interventions in university life were simply a part of our "natural history."

Nevertheless, I was always excited about the possibility of participating in the Berkeley student movement and whenever I could I tried to delay my return to our apartment in San Francisco, where Linda waited for me after her day working at a bank. One night I came home with the enthusiasm of a convert, announcing to Linda that a young black man had convinced me of the prodigious benefits of garlic, a talisman of health and miraculous cure for every ill. In my ignorance I had rejected it for years in spite of my Genovese ancestors and Linda's own culinary insistence, and now she had finally been vindicated by a young black man of the Nation of Islam.

The truth is that during my weeks in Berkeley the revolution failed to materialize, and my radicalism had to resign itself to the limits of my anthropology classes where, without inhibition, my attentive students invited me to smoke marijuana and offered me little tabs of LSD. The fountain in front of Kroeber Hall was filled with happy anarchist dogs who, nonetheless, were unable to enter the building where students of the contiguous Department of Music practiced jazz or Baroque scores amplified by anthropological departmental resonance.

I returned to Berkeley eleven years later invited by professors Brent Berlin and Laura Nader. I'd met the latter (and read her work) in Oaxaca, where she had carried out her studies on communal justice among the Zapotec people of Talea de Castro in the northern Sierra Madre.

At the end of my residency at UC—Berkeley, Professor George Collier, co-director of the Joint Berkeley-Stanford Center for Latin American Studies, invited me to do a study residency at the Center, teaching a trimester in the Department of Anthropology. Our little family separated again: Linda, André who was five at the time, and Vanessa stayed once more in Santa Rosa, near Linda's parents, and I inhabited a sad, dark apartment in East Palo Alto on a street strewn with hypodermics, addicts, and police patrol cars. And yet those were months of great intellectual richness and even political activism.

I never knew exactly what roles the post-graduate student Charlie Hale and his friend and colleague Edmund Gordon had had in securing my contract at the Center for Latin American Studies. I know that Professor Collier formally assigned another post-grad anthropology student, Jeremy Narby, to be my guide and assistant, helping me navigate Stanford's intricacies. We immediately became friends and found we were both interested in the communities of the Peruvian Amazon and the "economic development" of the peoples of the Amazon. These interests soon focused on the Asháninka people and their shamanic practices. Jeremy Narby became one of the important experts and scholars of the Peruvian Amazon and an author of great narrative talent and political and cultural commitment to Indigenous peoples.[57]

The political radicalness of Charlie Hale and his colleague Edmund "Mundo" Gordon revealed itself when, somewhat mysteriously, they asked me to sign an official document donating several computers to the Indigenous and black communities of Nicaragua's Atlantic Coast. Stefano Varese, Visiting Professor at Stanford, with legal residence as academic in the United States, would defy the economic blockade imposed by the Reagan administration against Sandinista Nicaragua under the legal subterfuge of charity. A few days after complying with my role as a smuggler, Charlie Hale gave me an invitation extended by the Indigenous activist and university professor Roxanne Dunbar-Ortiz in which Stefano would enter an extremely polemical debate with Bernard Nietschmann, a geographer at the University of California—Berkeley, who at that time opposed to the Sandinistas and, somewhat naively, was in passive alignment with the *Contras* and the scandalous U.S. interventionism.

During those months I developed profound friendships with Charlie, Edmund, and Roxanne, friendships that later renewed themselves at meetings and chance encounters in Colombia, Nicaragua, Peru, Guatemala, Mexico, Honduras, and wherever else our activism took us.

57. Jeremy Narby, *The Cosmic Serpent. DNA and the Origins of Knowledge* (New York: Jeremy P. Tarcher/Putnam, 1998) and Jeremy Narby, *Intelligence in Nature* (New York: Jeremy P. Tarcher/Putnam, 2006).

CHAPTER 29

Oaxacalifornia

ༀ

¡Cuatro consciencias
Simultáneas enrédanse en la mía!
—César Vallejo, "Cuatro conciencias"

I N THOSE TIMES AND places my hammock was being woven with pres-
ences, absences, recurrences, and coincidences intertwined by my obstinate desire to enlace myself ever so tightly to a borderless community that
I knew just and necessary.

In late 1984, after four quarters of teaching at UC—Berkeley and Stanford
University, I came back to Oaxaca, this time without family, to continue my
job as director of the Regional Unit of Popular and Indigenous Cultures.
During the next two years of frenzied activities with a professional team of
social, cultural, and environmental researchers accompanied by a large group
of Indigenous intellectual and activists, I devoted my energy to bring to a con-
clusion the project of cultural and historical recuperation of the Chinantec,
Zapotec, and Mixe Indigenous communities of the Northern Sierra Madre
of Oaxaca.

The hurry was mine: I wanted to conclude the family move to California.
Linda back in Santa Rosa with her parents was dedicated full time to the
treatment and education of André, while Vanessa was in a private boarding
school in Palo Alto. I could not abandon the Oaxaca project with its thirty
Indigenous cultural promoters and more than a dozen activist researchers
without trying to consolidate the achievements and guarantee its continuation beyond the uncertainties of the political cycle of Mexico. During a few
months of 1985 Linda and André were back with me in Oaxaca to prepare

for the move out of our beloved pueblo of San Felipe del Agua and our own house that we had started to build on the North Eastern slope of San Felipe mountain.

The months of solitude in the little rented house of San Felipe were mitigated by my obsession to carry forward the Indigenous cultural recuperation project and to show concrete results: writing systems and alphabets for the linguistic variations of the Chinantec, Zapotec, and Mixe ethnicities; registration and transcription of Indigenous literature in native languages; production of theatrical and videographic Indigenous works; gathering ethnobotanical collections and organizing itinerant exhibitions of them; compilation of community histories, tales, children fables, cosmologies, and even exploration of mathematical and geometrical concepts in Zapotec language. This succinct recount, even from the distance of years, amazes me. Nothing of this could have been achieved without the commitment of the whole team. A fair tribute to this cultural and political initiative would cover pages of names, anecdotes, and life histories and would not make justice to the dedicated passion of all the participants. This is a story that is being written and told by the Indigenous intellectuals and creators that came out of the project of Popular and Indigenous Cultures and are now active in their own communities and, in some cases, are surviving in some Oaxaca cultural and educational institutions now swamped by neo-liberal trash and political opportunism.[58]

58. I must mention, however, some of the friends and collaborators that, during my years in Oaxaca, played a fundamental role in educating and re-educating me in my knowledge of Indigenous Mesoamérica and, why not, of the Americas: Nemesio Rodríguez, Argentinian political refugee totally "Mexicanized" with whom I coedited various books and texts and with whom I share a deep political affinity; Pedro Lewin, Ernesto Díaz Couder, and Teresa Pardo Brugman, ethno-linguists that built the alphabets and the writing systems of the three most complex Indigenous languages of South Eastern Mexico: Chinantec, Mixe, and Zapotec; geographer Luis Crespo, whom together with members of the Indigenous communities of the Northern Sierra Madre of Oaxaca elaborated "talking maps" in native languages that represented time/space in their own ethnic categories; ethno-biologist Carlos Gómez, who introduced in the local communities ideas and practices of endemic plant gathering, identification, and use/cultivation/reproduction; Elba Gigante, the visionary pedagogue who built the whole program of participatory teaching/learning of the project; the

In the quietness of my loneliness in the house of San Felipe, my mind was returning more and more times to the memory of my children, far away in California, to their noisy plays, their lives in this house, in this garden where now silence was master.

Vanessa was born in July 1975, just after we left Lima and came to Oaxaca. I remember she was born in the early rainy morning in the Clínica del Carmen, in an "operating room" that looked more like a kitchen. Linda, trained during weeks in the Lamaze method, resisted very well the eight hours of pains of the natural childbirth until the moment in which a plumber walked through the operating room—called pompously *quirófano* operating theater—to go fix some water pipes in the next room. I had to explain Linda in between heavy breathing and sweaty counting that she did not have a hallucination of our dog Orégano, but she was rather seeing the plumber's toolbox. The Lamaze method of respiration and relaxation collapsed into a series of very Latin American insults learned and practiced during her life in Peru.

André Luis, whom I had imagined years before of his birth with the Indian name of Grey Cloud, was born in the same hospital four year later, the 20th of June of 1979. It was at sunset. There was no rain this time, but rather a proud earthquake who gave a true Mesoamerican welcome to our child that during the first few years of his life was the owner of silence.

What can a crepuscular father say about the early years of his two children? What can I add to the list of anecdotes and stories, sometimes too short, that decorate the memory during the periodical family reunions? What philosophies give sense to those inexperienced years that stumbling we walked together, the four of us, without knowing to which harbor we would arrive?

Indigenous intellectuals who helped and collaborated with playwright Luis Villaseñor to write, produce and perform theatrical and radio/video productions based on native oral literature and knowledge; Javier Castellanos, Zapotec novelist, author of three bilingual and internationally-acclaimed novels, philosopher of his language and analyst of his Zapotec-Benn'éxon epistemology; Eucario Ángeles, video-documentarist, community activist, and promoter of Indigenous economic projects; Zapotec historian Melitón Bautista; ethno-zoologist and ethno-botanist Coastal Zapotec Sara Cruz, who began her job in Popular Indigenous Cultures as secretary and became an expert on the biodiversity of her region; and the dozens of other Indigenous activists and promoters that are enriching the emotional and intellectual life of the "México Profundo."

The questions and the amazements, the joys and the profound sadness of my children come back to resound unsolved in my memory as I try to give consistency to this flow of episodes. I remember the desperate cry of Vanessa—who Linda and I call Vani—when at three years of age, she became aware, during our road trip through the sierras of Tamaulipas, that the dinosaurs had died millions of years ago and that now did not live anymore close to Ciudad Victoria. We could not calm those tears with our Darwinist explanations about the survival of the fittest. For months, years, decades Vanessa's passion for every animal—small or big, beautiful or repugnant, flying or crawling—restored my perception of the natural world to the point that it reconfigured myself as an ethno-ecologist engaged in environmental justice. I re-encounter that same passion in her daughter, our only granddaughter Isabella, who with her music and her poetry may be walking the same path of peaceful relation with nature.

Vanessa, as a child growing up, had learned the art of flexible adaptation at the foothill of "el Cerro de San Felipe del Agua" together with her friend Emily, daughter of another foreign academic and her musician mother. In school, her condition of *güerita* positioned her in the ambiguous marginality before her little friends that expressed their Indigenous ancestry in the color of their breaded hairs and skin. But it was precisely in California, in the public school of Santa Rosa, where nine-year-old Vanessa was confronted directly with ethnic (or racist) discrimination when an Anglo-American kid insulted her with the epithet *"Mexican bitch."*

The art of survival and cultural flexibility was the best present that Vanessa could have given to her younger brother André Luis. During years of learning, in Oaxaca middle class children parties, in preschools and elementary classes, in playgrounds, in soccer games, in the gardens of the private school Carlos Gracida, Vani taught André the basic rules of self-preservation in cultural environments less than sensitive to individual differences: she taught him the unusual art of appreciate, coexist, and give yourself into diversity in all its expressions.

Vanessa with her huge Mexican flag pinned on her Davis bedroom door was teaching André to listen to Mexican popular music and rock. In exchange, Linda was teaching Vanessa to fish and fillet—an extra motivation for Vani to pay attention to her courses in biology and to the fantasy of becoming a surgeon or even a forensic coroner. In fact, Vanessa even spent some weeks of internship in the morgue of Oaxaca assisting the city coroner who was one of her boy-friend fathers. André, instead, once he had to shift from Oaxaca soccer and his Mexican team of friends to California baseball little league, insisted in turning me, sport disabled father, into a dignified coach culturally assimilated.

All these interwoven stories, callings, fantasies, and desires shaped the dramas, happiness, and nostalgias of our years of "Oaxacalifornia."

CHAPTER 30

Lie and Banishment

🜋

M Y LIFE IN PERU ended abruptly and almost violently at the beginning of 1975, when the reactionary Peruvian oligarchy dealt a death blow to the Velasco Revolution. Years later we would learn that the CIA and the United States government were behind that final push that led to Velasco being replaced by General Morales Bermúdez, in what amounted to a "bloodless countercoup" which, nonetheless, threatened the lives and meant prison for a good many on the militant left. The infamous "Condor Plan," orchestrated by the United States and loyally adhered to by the military dictatorships of Chile, Argentina, Uruguay, Bolivia, Paraguay, Peru, and Ecuador, was working as planned.[59]

For his takeover, General Moral Bermúdez put on a democratic mask and initiated a repression without fear of reprisal. Some militants and activists were deported to Argentina, where they were "disappeared"[60] by the military government and then saved at the eleventh hour by an army captain in the city of Tucumán, who interrupted their trip to Buenos Aires, which would

---

59. Operation Condor, or Plan Condor, was the name of a coordinated plan of action and mutual support among the dictatorial regimes of the of South America in the 1970s and 1980s. It included Chile, Argentina, Brazil, Paraguay, Uruguay, Bolivia and sporadically Peru, Colombia, and Venezuela, with the support and participation of the United States.

60. "Disappearance" was a particularly Latin American phenomenon of the right during the 1970s and 1980s. In Argentina alone, 30,000 people are estimated to have been taken from their homes or off the street and never seen again, their loved ones left with no body to mourn. In Guatemala, 40,000 were disappeared (translator's note).

have ended in sure death, and kept the "subversive Peruvians" in the local jail. Others, with the help of money from family and friends, left for Mexico or Europe. The great majority of activists and sympathizers of the revolution remained with the Andean and coastal settlers, workers, miners, and Indigenous peoples of the Amazon and throughout the country, confused by the dark era ushered in by a so-called liberal democracy.

Linda and I had been banished from my father's family a few years earlier. Sporadic meetings with my siblings Luis-Gigi, Chiara, and Francisco-Cecco occurred in secret and in the nondescript gray of anonymous places, far from the inquisitive gaze of my stepmother and my father's passive inertia. When my sister Ilaria came to visit from South Africa or Italy, the illusory hide-and-seek my stepmother imposed upon the entire extended family became a parody I found almost intolerable.

Cut off from my adopted family, from that space which for years I had made into a refuge from childhood abandonment, I returned to a state of depression and self-blame only alleviated in part by Linda's honest devotion. Years later, on a visit to Italy, my sister Ilaria told me that when she asked about me, my father and stepmother told her vague stories about my travels to some distant and out of touch place. The truth was that Linda and I continued to live in the little house on Hilda Street.

Near the end of years of violation and sexual abuse protected by emotional blackmail and the threat that *"Se mi lasci io dico a tuo padre che tu mi hai sedotta,"*[61] my life had lost all remnants of transparency. And I, immersed in such a lie, found comfort in my studies of "the other," my flights of exoticism, and the familiarity of the absurd. I could find no way out of the labyrinth of deception, and in the loneliness of betrayal had no one to whom I could turn for help.

What did my father know? Why hadn't he thrown me out of the house and left his traitorous wife the very somber afternoon on which, without a word, he handed me a copy of Miguel de Unamuno's *Fedra,?* that Catholic version of a wife's and stepmother's betrayal with the son with whom he had so recently been reunited? What mysteries and obscure secrets act as cover ups for incestuous betrayal? Why stand by as the two of us rolled toward the abyss, toward the spiral's final perversion? Or could it be that my father was

---

61. "If you leave me, I will tell your father that you have seduced me."

enacting some sordid version of his own Catholic guilt at having betrayed my mother Pina and abandoning his three children to postwar uncertainty?

The first act of violation, at the house on the beach, had surprised my innocence to the point where my child's mind didn't know what to do with it. That night in the servant's room I erased from my mind my adolescent body's crude movements in all their ambiguity and clumsiness; and my atrocious doubts that this price my stepmother was making me pay was the condition, explicit now, of my acceptance into my new family. In those initial moments, I did not know if I must accept the act and its secret, those repeated offerings of our bodies, and the accompanying dark and anguished terror, always attentive to the danger of being found out.

CHAPTER 31

The Body's Entanglements

꣠

*The beauty of all things
resides in the spirit of those
who contemplate them?*
—(D. Hume)

HOW TO TELL LINDA, in the beauty of her truth, in her embodiment of the eternal feminine, replete with eroticism and at a discreet remove from the dark side of sexuality, about the many years of my body's hidden tasks? How to explain the absence of spirit in those times of the body's knots?

How to tell her I lost my virginity at a beach house one night in the southern hemisphere? I was seventeen and the woman thirty-two. She almost pushed me up that narrow flight of stairs to the maid's room. There, between her hospitable breasts, in her eager mouth, agile muscles, and moist and insane convulsion, I found the unexpected quiet I'd sought for years. The following morning, the stepmother took off, warning she would find me again each time her husband's absences or supposed inattentions permitted her to do so.

And that's how it was for almost ten years of epic and uncertain meetings in the least expected places: absurd hideaways, city attics, jungle lofts, borrowed beds, pitiful apartments, every sort of terrain that bore mute testimony to our acrobatics and heartbreaking lack of tenderness. The constant risk of being discovered in our incestuous infidelity added fear and urgency to the desire that led us both to an endless chase in search of an elusive satisfaction

I knew was wrong. She took over my being until she left me helpless in a voluptuous cloud from which I could not free myself.

From time to time I betrayed her—the betrayer—in half-hearted efforts to escape the fascination of her body. But every new adventure with another woman seemed unworthy: the Argentine Jew on her way to Israel; the anthropology student, also Argentine, who was so wholesome with her Polish background and unpronounceable surname; the UNESCO interpreter who wooed me with marijuana, nighttime tales, and a thousand adventures; that other girl with the Croatian name who tried to keep me at her house with dozens of bottles of Cristal beer because we were too poor for wine; and the sweet and special Italian I reencountered after visiting my mother in Turin. None of them, or others, could make me forget those guilty and anxious celebrations of excitement.

I could never understand my lack of unease, my indifference before the opponent to whom I was linked by profound sentiments of friendship, admiration, and love. Only now, more than fifty years later, do I find in this nameless confession the liberating grief that an aging body bequeaths a spirit unraveling itself from Eros. Was that summer night a rape or did I, for years and in my anguished guilt, construct and reconstruct the act as a gift of generous hospitality, the adoption that canceled abandonment?

It was many years later, at Stanford University, that a young psychotherapist at last gave me the strength to access from the abyss of my consciousness the understanding that my decade of adulterous adventures was nothing but a prolonged reenactment of incestuous rape that profoundly threatened my spiritual wellbeing. But Linda had been healing my damaged persona from the moment we met in Peru.

CHAPTER 32

Crossroads

I BANISHED MYSELF TO MEXICO with Linda and our dog Orégano at the beginning of 1975. The Sonoran desert's immense openness dissipated my grief somewhat. Linda and I entered that desert by car after crossing the Arizona border. With a small amount of money that Linda had earned from a few months' work in California, and the savings I'd brought from Peru, we had purchased a Volkswagen van we made into a camper with a mattress on a board as its bed, and its outdoor dining room, kitchen, and bath. The monastic poverty of our new mobile home was offset by the pseudo-Hindu hippy curtains that Linda stitched and decorated. Our Andean dog, Orégano, also deported to the Mexican highlands, had adapted himself to the van easily and without complaint; he fashioned his own space at every stop. Orégano, in fact, was the first of us to emit *charro* howls, by turn festive or threatening or distraught, depending on what the circumstances demanded.

We crossed the border at night to avoid the desert heat and drive a few hours before finding a place to camp.

"Do you have weapons?" the border agent asked.

"No, should we have one?" I asked in my ignorant naïveté, inspired by stereotypical Mexican films with their pistol-packing ranchers.

That out of the way, we decided to make camp by the side of the highway that, the following morning, would take us to Tepic, in the state of Nayarit. Months later we realized how irresponsible we'd been camping out alongside a highway frequented by bandits. Once in Tepic's main square, we could add to the images of Mexico gleaned from films one of an elegant white-haired grandfather with a pistol in his belt who had taken his grandson to an ice cream stand.

With our Peruvian dog Orégano en route to Mexico,
circa 1975

From those first moments traveling through northern Mexico, I began to be conscious of the fact that in our newly adopted country all sorts of unresolved contradictions constituted ontology rather than mere attributes. And, little by little, my Peruvian Spanish began to lose its descriptive capacity as, without intending to, I began to sketch a new ontological landscape. It was a landscape of ambiguities and paradoxes, which I tried unsuccessfully to force into an Andean framework always calibrated by its millennial history of opposing and complementary halves, by its four "suyos" of the universe, the *ceq'es* that give order to earthly sanctity, and the principle of *pachakuti* that organizes time/space.

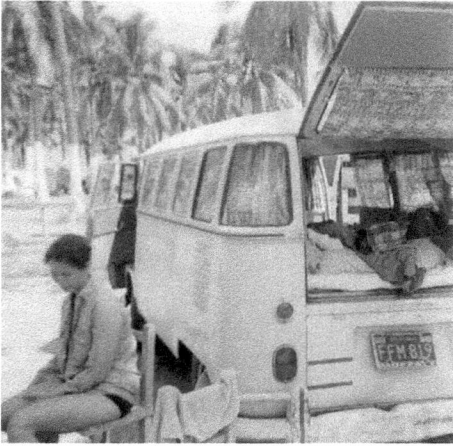

Linda en route to Mexico, circa 1975

It would take a me few years of living in Oaxaca before I could begin to understand the civilizing profundity of Mesoamerica in its complexity of symbols, hieroglyphs, writing, calendar, and its centuries of hundreds of ethnicities, each autonomous yet linked by a common cultural history.

From Tepic, we were only able to advance a few miles to the south when the old van decided its gear box needed adjustment. And it was there, in its wild north, that Mexico opened its arms in the person of an auto mechanic whose family invited us to camp in the patio of their house that also served as his shop. With the van raised on wooden stilts, surrounded by dark oils, spare parts, tires, and a pair of dogs that made friends with Orégano, we slept there for two nights. Our dining room, on the other hand, took up residence next to the kitchen where the wife, children, a little old grandmother, and the mechanic himself offered us hand-made tortillas, beans, and epic chile peppers with which Linda immediately fell in love. How could we not open ourselves up to that generosity? How could we doubt this would be the country of our exile, made bearable by its people?

I had to ask for the money to pay for the van's repair from the director of the National Institute of Anthropology and History, my friend Guillermo Bonfil Batalla. He quickly wired me what I needed, against the promise of a job that did not yet exist. The wire was signed by Attorney Leopoldo Zorrilla, the administrator of the Institute of Anthropology, who had once been an advisor and "administrator" to Che Guevara when Che was the Minister of Finances in revolutionary Cuba.

CHAPTER 33

To *México profundo* . . . To Oaxaca by Mistake

ༀ

I HAD BEEN TO MEXICO to attend academic conferences a couple of times before. Confined for a few days to university halls or a hotel room in the Zona Rosa, my vision of the country was limited to that of a middle-class tourist. Stunned by the U.S.-type modernity of its post-revolutionary nationalism, I hadn't given much thought to the profound and millennial Mexico that I reduced, in my leftist vision of the moment, to the backdrop of dramatic class struggle and worker and peasant uprisings.

The 1968 massacre at Tlatelolco was still fresh in a memory informed by articles by the Italian Oriana Fallaci. At those academic meetings, I had run into some key people in the Mexican social sciences, among them Guillermo Bonfil Batalla. Since 1968 or 1969, I had been writing to Rodolfo Stavenhagen. At the time, he was interested in learning about the Peruvian Revolution.

In 1971, at the meeting of activist anthropologists on the Caribbean island of Barbados, I met Guillermo Bonfil, who captivated me with his conceptual depth and knowledge of Mexico, masked by a sharp sense of humor, polysemy, and use of language. Years later, fully installed in the Mexico of my exile, I would once again learn the daily use of ambiguity and arcane semantics the Mexican people have assumed as arms of resistance against all oppression. In Oaxaca I reconnected with Gustavo Esteva, with whom I'd had superficial contact at an international sociology conference. He went into self-exile in the decade of the 1980s, after "leaving his profession" and abdicating academic sociology.

I met other Mexican intellectuals and the many exiled Latin Americans who had sought refuge in that country's generosity. I got to know them at lectures, occasional meetings, and eventually through the new professional relationships I made in the work that brought me to Mexico thanks to Guillermo Bonfil Batalla's opportune and life-saving invitation. It all happened very quickly at the beginning of 1975, when the Peruvian Revolution received the death blow dealt by General Morales Bermúdez's reactionary coup, aided by the proverbial support of the U.S. State Department and CIA in the finest tradition of North American intervention. Guillermo Bonfil Batalla soon went from savior to mentor and guide in my meandering through Mexico's intellectual and political life in the 1970s and 1980s.

In April 1976, Bonfil named me Visiting Researcher at the National Institute of Anthropology and History and participating member of the Seminar on National Culture. With these generous appointments, the director of the National Institute of Anthropology and History opened the doors to the most elevated spheres of Mexico's intellectual world.

My participation in a series of academic and cultural policy events, always organized by Bonfil, allowed me to get to know José Emilio Pacheco, Nicole Girón, José Joaquín Blanco, Héctor Aguilar Camín, Carlos Monsiváis, Antonio Alatorre, Arturo Warman, Jorge Bustamante, Pablo González Casanova, Alejandra Moreno Toscano, Enrique Florescano, Enrique Valencia, Leonel Durán, Sergio Aguayo, the Berber Simone Ben Sheik, the French-Egyptian intellectual Anwar Abdel Malek, French sociologist Jean Loup Herbert, Guatemalan Carlos Guzmán Bockler, Mexican-Lebanese Ikram Antaki, and dozens of other intellectuals and activists who filled and enriched classrooms and seminars at the Institute of Anthropology and History. How could I not pay tribute to that great Mexican intellectual and friend who for decades, and until his premature death in 1991, contributed to reconstructing a diverse *México Profundo*, the Indigenous and *mestizo* Mexico that has played such an important part in its civilizing and ecumenical Latin American mission?

IN 1975 GUILLERMO BONFIL Batalla had embarked on the colossal task of decentralizing the National Institute of Anthropology and History (INAH), inviting hundreds of Institute researchers and technicians to move to new INAH regional centers being inaugurated throughout the country.

"Stefano, where would you like to go?"

"Yucatán, Guillermo. I like the tropics, I like forest peoples, I want to get to know the Mayans and learn from them. And Linda is fond of hot climates."

When we started out in our van from the campground to the south of the city, we got lost after just a few blocks and ended up taking the highway going to Oaxaca instead of the one to Veracruz and the Yucatán peninsula. Acci-

Our mobile home in Mexico, circa 1975-76

dent or destiny? In Huahuapan de León, in the Lower Mixteca, besieged by clouds of flies interested in the *tamales* we were having for lunch, we realized our mistake.

We arrived in the city of Oaxaca late and, looking for a place to camp, ended up in a small mango grove at the foot of an immense hill carpeted with pine and oak trees. The next morning, we saw some urban-style houses on both sides of the little valley. Once again, the *nahuales* or some other Amazon spiritual guide had deposited us precisely in front of the house belonging to the regional director of INAH. A few days later he issued me a contract as a visiting researcher. I imagine it was on Guillermo Bonfil's recommendation.

CHAPTER 34

Spell and Panic

꣢

O AXACA SEDUCED US COMPLETELY. We made a home there,
had our daughter Vanessa and our son André Luis, adopted more
than a few cats and dogs, and became attentive and careful students
of one of the most complex, fascinating, and seductive areas of American
civilization.

The state of Oaxaca is the third poorest in the Mexican federation, and it
is ethnologically and biologically the most diverse region of the country. It
has one of the most profound histories in all Meso- and Central America. Its
seventeen Indigenous "nationalities" make up more than half the state's population. A few miles to the west of Oaxaca city, Lulá the Zapotecs call it, their
ancestors left clear evidence they'd domesticated squash (Cucúrbita pepo)
more than ten thousand years ago. Squash became one of the Mesoamerican people's most important foods. Meanwhile, a few miles to the northeast,
people from the same linguistic family as the Zapotecs—possibly Mixtecs or
Cuicatecs—domesticated corn (Zea mays), beans (Phaseolus vulgaris), and
avocado (Persea Americana).

In this way, for several millennia the Indigenous peoples of southeastern
Mexico accompanied nature's transformation and created the conditions for
one of the most elaborate, nutritious, and delicious cuisines in the world.
The civilizing principles of diversity and complimentary reciprocity are to
be found in the creation of the *milpa*—the field that combines corn, beans,
squash, and chili peppers (Capsicum), and dozens of "*quelites*"[62] that add surprising tastes to the Mesoamerican diet.

62. Quelites (from the Nahua word *quilitl*) is the generic term used in Mexico to
describe more than 200 edible herbs that grow spontaneously or semi-cultivated in

In the highlands and valleys of southeastern Mexico I found the same civilizing Indigenous principles I had intuited in the Amazon and the Andes,
and that I would revisit years later in my cultural history studies of the Indian
peoples of the Americas. The Indigenous cultural language—always rooted
in place—is built around a few concepts and a logic or topological culture
that privileges biological-cultural diversity and heterogeneity over homoge-
neity, eclecticism over dogma, multiplicity over duality. It is a language woven
in locality, in the concrete space where culture has its roots and constantly re-
produces itself upon a familiar landscape, one in which the names of things,
spaces, objects, plants, animals, living and dead beings, the underworld, and
celestial infinity evoke the total cosmic network in its mysterious and terrible
sacred edifice.

A few weeks after beginning my work as a research anthropologist at the
Regional Center, I went into panic mode. Will I have the learning needed to
be able to understand the tremendous complexity of this area of Mesoamerican civilization? Was my intention to decipher the long millennial Zapotec
history born out of innocence or stupidity?

Five hundred years before our era, the Bennexon or the Binnigula'asa had
begun the enormous work of transforming themselves from a group of small
agricultural hamlets scattered across the valleys and mountains of southeastern Mexico into a complex centralized urban state that, over eight centuries,
refined its arts and sciences, hieroglyphic writing, mathematical calculations,
astronomy, architecture, mastery of environmental biology, water, and social or practical cosmological philosophy, all rooted in principles of diversity,
complementarity, and reciprocity of the cosmic totality.

Following the centralized Zapotec state and until the arrival of the Spanish
invaders in the 16th century, there were times of fragmentation, in which the
city-states of the Zapotecs and their Mixtec neighbors coexisted in a sort of
Indian peace with other Indigenous cities, such as those in central and northern Mexico—Mexica-Tenochca—, those of the southeast, and the Mayan
peoples of the Yucatán peninsula, Guatemala, and Honduras.

---

the fields—*milpas*—of Indigenous and *mestizo* farmers. The leaves and stalks of these
herbal plants make up a fundamental part of the peasants' diet, providing vitamins,
minerals, antioxidants, fiber, and fatty acids to the "sacred triad" of corn tortillas with
beans, squash, and chilis.

As I made headway in researching archeological, historical, ethnographic, and documentary sources on the Bennexon, I found myself getting lost in thousands of references: books, articles, archival documents, colonial vocabularies, *Relaciones Geográficas de Indias*, confessionals in various languages, and codices that had survived the Inquisition. I was surrounded by, and submerged myself in, a quarter million "primary sources," meaning sources from the Zapotec people themselves. Some had advanced degrees and academic positions at the University of Mexico. Others, both men and women, had careers in medicine, architecture, and the law. Still others were writers, novelists, poets, painters, and musicians.

In comparison with the work I had done among the small Indigenous nationalities or tribal peoples of the Amazon, this new task seemed an insurmountable challenge. I had to remake myself as a student of agrarian societies, a specialist in peasant communities and cultures, an ethno-historian and anthropologist of complex societies. During two years of profound nostalgia for Peru and my work in the Amazon, attempts at learning some elements of the Zapotec language—what arrogance, believing I was a polyglot simply because I knew a few Indo-European languages!—and more or less systematically reading studies on Mesoamerica, Oaxaca, and contemporary Mexico, I was able to produce a manuscript of about one hundred pages which I conceived as the first two chapters in a book to be called *The Village and the State. Zapotec History*.

I had thought I could decipher 3,000 years of Bennexon social history with a combined methodology: a long-term approach (the long-term study suggested by Fernand Braudel) and a Marxist analysis of the political economy of the resistance and continuity of the Zapotec peoples when up against the pre-Colombian Indigenous State, the Spanish imperial-colonial state, and finally the liberal authoritarianism of the post-revolutionary Mexican state.

I believe this study confirmed my hypothesis that the Zapotecs, through many centuries of existence as an ethnicity and from their position of constitutive units as efficient, highly integrated, productive, and "democratically" governed communal villages, had been able to negotiate forms of coexistence with the various manifestations and expressions of power on the part of pre-colonial, colonial and Republican administrations.

There was little the centralized pre-Colombian or colonial state could do to totally subjugate the village, except demand tribute or decide on its elimination as a social entity, deporting its inhabitants and destroying its land. No

State, and even less the autocratic modern Mexican State, had put forth such a radical solution. In fact, I could argue that each successive governing formation that came into being, developed and imposed itself upon the Zapotec village, and was interested in maintaining the village autonomy since, economically and politically, the whole system depended on the limited sovereignty of each local unit and its integration into the totality of the pre-Colombian, colonial, or Republican system.

I put the manuscript in one of my desk drawers, afraid of submitting it to be reviewed by my Mexican colleagues and terrified of giving it to my Zapotec friends. After a few years, I timidly handed a fragment to the Zapotec historian and poet from the Isthmus, Víctor de la Cruz, who accepted it for publication in the Zapotec bilingual magazine *Guchachi Reza*.

I had gotten to know Víctor de la Cruz at the end of the 1970s, when he directed the Culture House in Juchitán, on the Isthmus of Tehuantepec. Víctor introduced me to the world of Zapotec literature, suggesting I interview Macario Matus and the professor of Zapotec language and literature Andrés Henestrosa, who had been struggling to elevate the Zapotec language written in the Latin alphabet to academic and publishing levels since the 1930s.

Henestrosa, of Zapotec and Huave parents, had founded a magazine called *Neza* (The Way) and years later *Neza Cubi* (The New Way), encouraging the resurgence of a Zapotec Indigenous language and literature. When I interviewed him at his home in Mexico City, I was surprised by his deep knowledge of other Indigenous Latin American languages. He referred to the work of José María Arguedas—who wrote in Quechua and Spanish—as an example of the "new Latin American literature" that could be traced to the beginning of colonial times with Inca Garcilaso de la Vega, Guamán Poma de Ayala, and the Nahuatlatos who survived the conquest and occupation of the Aztec state.

Little by little, from my new world in southeast Mexico, I began transforming my concepts of indigeneity, which is to say, "of being Indigenous in modern day Latin America." At last I understood that modernity's systemic totality is nothing more than a sum of unequal and combined developments, of savage capitalisms and shameless pillage, racism and ethnic discrimination, political repression and economic class exploitation—all phenomena normalized or naturalized under the nebulous rhetoric of electoral democracy and a materialist science or way of knowing devoid of any ethical restriction.

CHAPTER 35

Article 33

ॐ

Foreign persons are those who do not possess the qualities put forth in Article 30 of the Constitution or enjoy the human rights and guarantees recognized by this Constitution. The Executive branch of the Union, through a judicial hearing, may expel from the national territory foreign persons when there is basis in the law, and will designate the administrative procedures, as well as the place and duration of detention.

Under no conditions may foreigners participate in the country's political matters.
—Mexican Constitution.

IN HIS NOVEL *The Old Gringo* Carlos Fuentes attributes the phrase "Ah, to be a gringo in Mexico, that is euthanasia" to the American writer and journalist Ambrose Bierce. Bierce, who had joined Pancho Villa's troops—at the age of 71—as a war reporter in 1914, disappeared from Chihuahua City without leaving a trace.

Although we didn't go to such extremes, some of us Latin American foreigners of the 1970s and 1980s who were exiled in Mexico, tended to think of ourselves as permanent *gringos* in that country. During the years I lived there, each time I opened my mouth in a store, restaurant, gas station, or police checkpoint on the highway, they "didn't understand my Spanish" and were hard put to accept the fact that I was Latin American. This ethno-racial and national barrier on the part of every good Mexican citizen functions as a defense mechanism and protection against Mexico's long history of having been repeatedly invaded and occupied by foreigners for centuries.

Since the Iberian invasion, passing through French intervention and half a dozen attempts at invasion and occupation on the part of the United States, the Mexican people have had to teach themselves the acquisition of a sort of

defensive nationalism that reveals itself in the permanent suspicion that foreigners have ulterior motives for wanting to be in their country. Once this suspicion is assuaged, acceptance flourishes, and the warmest and most generous
hospitality is offered. But Article 33 of the Mexican Constitution lives in the
minds of all foreigners, along with the terrifying threat of being deported and
losing forever the human warmth of this beautiful people.

It must have been a morning in April or May of 1979 when Linda, who
was seven or eight months pregnant with our son André, went to the front
gate of our rented house in San Felipe del Agua and found two Federal Police agents asking for Señor Estefano Barrese. They had an order to bring that
federal employee to headquarters, accused of having embezzled government
funds assigned to Oaxaca's Regional Center of Anthropology and History.
Linda invited the two policemen in, offered them coffee and, in her *gringa*
innocence, explained that she didn't know where her anthropologist husband
was traveling:

> He's always going off without telling me where, and I'm left here waiting
> for him with my daughter Vanessa. We don't have a telephone, but you can
> ask at the Regional Center for Anthropology and History. They'll know
> where to reach him.

The truth was, I had gone to Mexico City at the request of my colleagues
at the Center, to meet with members of the National Institute of Anthropology and History's researchers and workers union. They wanted me to try
to resolve a labor dispute between the workers and the Center's director, a
man with a rather tortured personality, an ex-priest whose personal demons
had turned him into an authoritarian alcoholic. There were four foreign researchers at Oaxaca's Regional Center and we assumed, in our naiveté, that we
had the same labor rights as the Mexicans. We had simply forgotten Article
33: Under no conditions may foreigners participate in the country's political
matters.

Sometime later I understood why, of all the foreigners working at the
Center of Anthropology, I was privileged by the director to head the small
workplace rebellion. In his historic missionary's memory, the ex-priest must
have found remnants of the Spanish colonial practice of isolating someone
he deemed responsible and sacrificing him to save the rest of the rebels from
a collective punishment that would have been too costly to implement. Or, if
he couldn't find a leader, he would have to invent one. And that is how I hap-

pened to be in Mexico City, at the welcoming home of my new friend, Nemesio Rodríguez Mitchell, political refugee and survivor of Argentina's worst repression, when I heard I must avoid the Federal Police, go into semi-hiding and ask for help from my "political sponsor" Guillermo Bonfil Batalla, so as not to incur the wrath of Article 33.

It wasn't an easy situation. Bonfil Batalla was off on an official visit to Cuba, accompanied by another of my possible saviors, my friend the anthropologist Salomón Nahmad Sittón. Desperate, I remembered an exchange of letters a few years earlier with the prestigious intellectual and social scientist Rodolfo Stavenhagen, member of the Colegio de México and initiator, at that moment, of a new federal program of support for the Indigenous peoples in their projects of cultural and linguistic recuperation.

In a matter of hours, this respected Mexican intellectual—himself the son of a German Jewish refugee who had fled to Mexico during World War II—extended me a contract as an anthropologist at the recently created General Office of Popular and Indigenous Cultures. The continuation of my residency and that of my family was now guaranteed by a contract at a Mexican federal government research institution. The generosity, solidarity, and modesty that that great Mexican intellectual, along with Guillermo Bonfil Batalla and many other friends or simple acquaintances, offered me and other Latin American exiles, was unconditional. I understand it as an allegory of the profound and age-old Mexican Indigenous practice of never denying hospitality or solace to a visitor.

CHAPTER 36

The Miseries of Oil

꙰

P OPULAR WISDOM THROUGHOUT LATIN America has it that the
worst misfortune one of our countries can have is to possess oil and
minerals. If these are beneath communal and Indigenous lands, it is a
death sentence for people who have lived for millennia on those lands of forests, waters, and seas.

My small internal exile began immediately after receiving my contract from
the General Office of Popular and Indigenous Cultures, the headquarters of
which were in Mexico City. Following a brief interview with Leonel Durán,
its director and an anthropologist in the same line as Bonfil and Stavenhagen,
I went home to Oaxaca, spent a few peaceful days with Linda and our daughter Vanessa, retrieved what I had at the office of the Center of Anthropology,
said a quick goodbye to a few friends and colleagues, packed a bag, and took
the night bus to the Isthmus of Tehuantepec, to my new assignment at the
Regional Unit in Acayucan, Veracruz.

Acayucan is one of the saddest, most miserable places I came to know in
southeastern Mexico. Situated on the coast of Veracruz state, not far from
the Gulf of Mexico's warm waters, I had imagined my new workplace to be
a tropical paradise surrounded by jungle and transparent rivers. I'd nurtured
this fantasy during that twelve-hour bus ride. After all, I thought, the labor
union defeat hadn't turned out that badly.

The bus dropped me on the main street. I asked directions and, carrying
my small bag, began to walk, sweating for all I was worth. In one night, I had
come down from Oaxaca's central valley at 1,400 meters of altitude to coastal
plains, savannahs, and tropical woods completely devastated by overgrazing,
oil exploitation, and industrial incursion. I was now at sea level. Instead of the
tropical landscape that the ancestors of the Olmec, Zoque, Mixe, Populuca,

Mayan, and even the later Nahuas must have seen many centuries before the Conqueror Hernán Cortés sent Pochteca merchants and occupying soldiers, now there was nothing left. Only suffocating heat magnified by a lack of trees, earth paved over with broken cement and asphalt, and puddles of water in suspicious colors and reflections.

I arrived soaked in sweat and depressed at the Unit's office, which also turned out to be the residence of a couple of young anthropologists. In the house's uncared for back yard there was a single immense tree, lone survivor of an ancient primary forest that must have existed two hundred years before. Right away the young anthropologist in charge of the office told me that tree "suffered" at night, that I shouldn't be alarmed because during the Revolution as many revolutionary men and women as federal soldiers had been hanged from its branches. That night, after taking a shower in a bathroom of precarious hygiene, I fell asleep hoping I wouldn't have visions of tree ghosts. The following morning, I awoke, both eyes swollen and infected.

"We forgot to tell you to shower with your eyes closed, because the water is contaminated with who knows what . . . " Welcome to Mexico's petroleum exploitation, where nature is assassinated and dollars flow to fiscal paradises right over there on the Caribbean islands on the other side of the Gulf. I was beginning to doubt my good luck, but as the Mexicans say, "*ni modo* . . . what's done is done."

I began reading all the Unit's documentation, going over the budget, analyzing the program carried out by the previous director, and finally calling Mexico City to request another researcher to be able to fulfill the proposed investigation and practical application with the Indigenous communities of the region, to which the Mexico City office had assigned me.

The Andean *Apus* or Mesoamerican *Nahuales* must have taken pity on me, because a few days later a woman arrived from the capital. She was around thirty, had an Italian look about her—she could have been one of my cousins from Piamonte—and spoke with the rich Córdoba accent of Argentina. This told me she was an Argentine political refugee who had survived her husband's extra-judicial assassination and a stretch of imprisonments and tortures before being rescued and seeking asylum at the Mexican Embassy. "Mexico, Mexico . . . so close to the United States . . . so far from God . . . " and yet so generously open to the thousands of political refugees fleeing the Fascist dictatorships of Brazil, Uruguay, Paraguay, Argentina, Chile, and one or another lesser pseudo-dictatorship, all financed, sustained, and blessed by the co-governance of the United States and the multinational corporations.

Aside from standing up to the military dictatorship, Elba Gigante had been a professional instructor in the field of popular education and an expert in the teachings of the Brazilian Paulo Freire. But what impressed me about her from the moment we met was her great ability to constantly reinvent pedagogical techniques and methods, adapting them to the diverse learning communities she encountered. For me, up to then, to learn meant repeating the didactic formulae I'd been taught at school in Italy and at the university in Peru: intake of information, memorization, acritical and partial storage of canned knowledge, and oral and written techniques that allowed for archiving, distributing, and reproducing this baggage and its protocols.

None of that modern European pedagogical formula is of any use to us, Elba Gigante said, if we want to draw out the millennial historic memories of the Indigenous peoples and communities, with their cultural roots, ethical principles, philosophies of life, languages, ethnic ways of relating to the universe, the world, their own natures, their landscapes, and other neighboring national or international communities.

If the new mission of Indigenous policy—or pro-Indian policy, as they called it in Mexico—, employed by the Office of Popular Culture, proposed to do away with the old government practices of culturally assimilating the Indian peoples into that of the generic *mestizo* México, then dialogue with the Indigenous communities had to be carried out according to a pedagogy (teaching/learning) that was socially horizontal, ideologically transparent, based on an equivalence in civilizing forms, and open to diversity's fertilizing function. Immersed in Mexico's nationalist authoritarianism, a proposal of this sort seemed like a utopian fantasy or, as the Peruvian novelist Mario Vargas Llosa would call it years later, "an archaic utopia," referring to similar cultural ideals that emerged in Peru.

At the Acayucan Unit we worked with communities of Zoque, Popoluca, Mixe, and Nahuatl ethnicities, trying to complete a collection of oral narratives in native languages and in Spanish that had been started by a woman anthropologist from Mexico City. The work of gathering these oral histories from women, men, children, and especially from the narrators who lived in the communities, opened our eyes to the different modalities of knowledge and its transmission among the four ethnicities of the region. It goes without saying that the greatest obstacle in this phase of the investigation was our ignorance of the native languages spoken by these four ethnicities. We could only overcome this by having bilingual children and adults—especially men—in the communities.[63]

After a few months in Veracruz, I obtained my transfer to the Unit in Oaxaca, and my internal exile was over. I convinced the central Mexico City Office to hire Elba Gigante for Oaxaca if they wanted to start a program of "linguistic-cultural rebirth and retrieval" of the Indigenous ethnicities in the state to which I was assigned.

Bureaucratic labyrinths always have their surprises: from Mexico came the news that I had been named Director of the Oaxaca Regional Unit for Peoples and Indigenous Cultures. Director Leonel Durán, a generous humanist anthropologist, even authorized contracting numerous linguists, anthropologists, geographers, ethnobiologists, and theatrical and visual communicators. Within a few months, the URO—Oaxaca Regional Unit—became a beehive of research activities, cultural retrieval, teaching/learning, promotion, and ethno-political activism in more than forty communities of the Zapotec, Mixe, and Chianteca ethnicities in the areas of northern mountains, the Isthmus of Tehuantepec, central valleys, and southern mountains.

The state of Oaxaca is the size of South Korea. More than half its population is Indigenous, representing sixteen native nationalities, the *mestizo* population, and a substantial number of Afro-Mexicans. Faced with the vastness of this demographic and cultural challenge, the Unit had to be careful to limit its radius of action and focus on the social and cultural depth of its intervention.

I am not the one to evaluate the social and cultural achievements of more than forty researchers—professionals as well as women and men from the Indigenous communities—who committed themselves to studying, understanding, and retrieving from oblivion and marginalization the deep linguistic and civilizing roots of the three Mesoamerican nationalities with which we lived and worked for years. What should make all members of that multiethnic and multidisciplinary team proud was to have broken with the anthropological, historical, linguistic, biological, and pedagogical molds that for almost ten decades contributed to concealing and suppressing modes of

63. Técnicos Bilingües de la Unidad Regional de Acayucan y Stefano Varese, coord., *Agua, mundo, montaña. Narrativa nahua, mixe y popoluca del sur de Veracruz* (Puebla, Mexico: Premiá Editores, 1985).

Indigenous knowledge, its creative imagination, the profound ethical values of its cosmologies, and its hopes of reconstituting itself in viable civilizing and harmonious forms for the third millennium.

At the time, the Indian philosophy of Kumak Kawsay-Sumak Qamaña hadn't yet reawakened. That philosophy postulates a radical revolution of values for all the earth's living beings, but says the old Indigenous struggles would continue as in colonial times: in defense of their territories, to preserve and consolidate their collective property, for self-governance and state independence, to decide when and where to speak their languages, construct their own systems of training and education, and live in harmony with their own spiritual beings.

I do not presume to be the chronicler of this cultural and humanist enterprise of "Indian" Mexico, because in the end I remain a foreigner from the east and south who lived for a few years in the heart of Mesoamerica. Someone else should write this history and leave it to float in the blue air of Oaxaca's mountains so that the new peoples of Ixtepeje, Comaltepec, Xelató, Tlahuitoltepec, Huixtepec, Tabáa, and all the other Indigenous communities will be able to collect and keep it in their memories. Nevertheless, in my head and heart are the names of the Chinantec poet Hermenegildo; the Zapotec novelist and poet Javier Castellanos, who has published three bilingual novels; the Zapotec historian Melitón Bautista Cruz; the naturalist Sara Cruz—also a Zapotec from the southern mountains—; the filmmaker and theatrical director Eucario Ángeles; the silk weavers Silvia and Estela of the Zapotec region of the Caxonos mountains; and so many others who have left their indelible marks on Oaxaca's cultural landscape.

My return to the little rented house in San Felipe del Agua, where Linda, Vanessa, André, my Andean dog Orégano, my Oaxacan cat Lulá, our new dog Diana who came from a nearby working-class neighborhood to give birth to a multitude of puppies at the edge of our garden, and finally the anarchist parrot Kropotkin, was the greatest prize I could have received from my Mexican friends. We stayed there our remaining years in Mexico, until we could buy a piece of land in the foothills of San Felipe mountain, and build, brick by brick and with spoons of cement, the home where Linda and I hoped to retire and live out our later years.

CHAPTER 37

More than Forty Years of Silence

🦟

"Whereof one cannot speak, thereof one must be silent."
—Wittgenstein's *Tractatus* (quoted in F. David Peat's *Synchronicity*)

I HAD TO WAIT FOR more than forty years before daring to write about my encounter with Poshano, the shirpiari-shaman of the Gran Pajonal who accompanied me on my walk back to my Asháninka family's hamlet, appearing several times as a friendly woodpecker. My academic formation in models of scientific materialist knowledge, exclusively based on empiric proof, had imprisoned me in the fear of accusations of esotericism or irrationality from the anthropological community, and especially from those leftist activists to whom I had vowed my loyalty. We academics are "people of reason," not "people of custom," as the Indigenous peoples of southeastern Mexico would say, based on their precise taxonomic dichotomy. Cartesian and Newtonian reason cannot accept a return to the occult and the admission that mystery exists and requires an epistemological change from "calculative" to "contemplative" thought.

I don't dare say that my walk through the Chenkári hills, in the company of Poshano transformed into a woodpecker *torónkoti* or *chamanto* was really a mystic episode or numinous experience, that it was an inexplicable brush with the occult, a brief unconscious descent into the profundity of the Asháninka world inhabited by Kamétza goodness, the Amatsénka, our spiritual siblings and the mysterious and hidden Manínkari. Nevertheless, I can find no explanation in "modern reason," nor can I satisfy the logic of the materialist empiricism of psychoanalysis that allows me to assume and understand the dream that came to me in the month of July 1991, a few hours after my friend

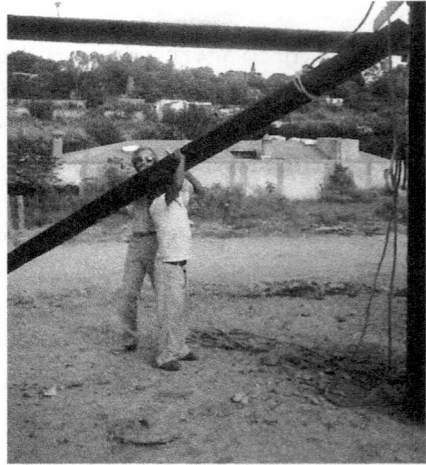

With my daughter Vanessa, Orégano, and Don Andrés starting the building of our house brick by brick, Oaxaca, circa 1977 through 1988

Guillermo Bonfil Batalla's death in an automobile accident when he was driving along the broad avenue of the pyramids of Sun and Moon in Teotihuacan on his way to see me.

The two of us wore contemporary clothing and walked slowly, surrounded by pre-Colombian Mesoamerican Indians wearing light-colored cotton tunics knotted at the shoulders in the manner of the Aztecs. We talked as we

had been doing for decades, somewhat indifferent to the people of Teotihuacan who milled about us as if they were celebrating a long and intense friendship. I was in the bedroom of my house in Oaxaca, almost four hundred miles
from Mexico City, immersed in the indolence of a warm nap that made it
difficult for me to recompose myself from that ghostly oneiric visit, and even
more difficult when my friend Salomón Namad called on the phone to tell
me that Gillermo Bonfil had died early that morning.

The anthropology of the senses is enjoying a resurgence for reasons already
explored in the first half of the twentieth century by C. G. Jung, Wolfgang
Pauli, Paul Radin, Ernesto de Martino, and other thinkers intrigued by the
fact that in many societies throughout the world the human use of the senses
receives an attention that is both individualized and selective.[64] I am not interested, now, in entering the labyrinth of empirical science that attempts to
resolve these paradoxes in laboratories through statistical research that ends
up discarding as relics all manners of perceptions and representations of reality that don't respond to the West's sensory hierarchy. Mine is a hermeneu-
tical rather than heuristic interest: I look for meanings and senses more than
"rational" or causal explanations. Which of my senses did Poshano and Guillermo Bonfil make use of to say goodbye without being physically present?
Which of my senses served as hosts to my visitors?

My para-sensory experiences with Poshano and Guillermo Bonfil were separated in time by a quarter of a century and in space by thousands of miles and
landscapes that were dramatically different, although culturally analogous.
And throughout the rest of my secular life in Peru, Mexico, Central America,
and California similar phenomena marked my life.

During one of the first nights I spent with my wife Linda at the small house
in Chaclacayo at the foot of the Andes, as I lay in deep sleep at her side, the
silent vision of an ethereal elongated figure woke me suddenly. It floated up-

---

64. Ernesto De Martino, *Il mondo magico. Prolegomeni a una storia del magismo*
(Torino: Einaudi, 1948), Paul Radin, Carl Gustav Jung & Karl Kerenyi, *Il briccone
divino* (Milan. V. Bompiani, 1965; English edition: Paul Radin, *The Trickster: A
Study in Native American Mythology* [New York: Schocken Books (commentaries by
K. Kerenyi and C. G. Jung), 1965]. My references to C. G. Jung and Wolfgang Paul
are based on my reading of F. David Peat, *Blackfoot Physics. A Journey into the Native
American Universe* (Boston, MA: Weiser Books, 2002) and F. David Peat, *Synchro-
nicity. The Marriage of Matter and Psyche* (Pari, Italy: Pari Publishing Sas, 2014).

ward and disappeared through the roof. Neither of us had an explanation for this. It had nothing to do with recently encountered friends or lovers, except for the fact that Linda had moved a few days earlier to my rented house and had insisted on sealing its entire perimeter with coarse salt.

To my surprise, she said she didn't feel safe in this one-room house. Linda, whose maternal ancestors could have been Indians from the U.S. state of Montana or western Canada, had been traveling through the Amazon looking for, and studying, Indigenous medicinal plants. In the region of Pucallpa, she had gotten to know an eminent *ayahuasquero* or healer, who had given her a bottle of ayahuasca, the powerful enteogenic Banisteriopsis caapi that she was supposed to share with me, a man she still didn't know that well. The *ayahuasquero*—or perhaps a different reincarnation of the same man— reappeared in my life some time later through the writings of the Amazon poet and novelist César Calvo, who describes how "Don Hildebrando and/ or Don Javier" reveals that the healer from the Amazon does not need to personally know an individual or author to know and understand what they think and say:

> I have never seen that book but I know it, I know it well ... good peoples' thoughts live in the air, they lodge themselves in the air as we do in our homes. Before being taken into books, when they are merely thoughts and although they have not been written down, they already live in the air ... an eternal beginning ... Because the air belongs to everyone, perhaps the only thing that truly belongs to everyone today ... the voice of life ... And without our knowing it, without our heads being aware, the ideas that in- habit the air like spirits feed us ... I have never seen this book you tell me about, by your friend Varese, and yet I have read it several times. And let us suppose that one sad day they burn every copy of that book, it will not matter because the thoughts, doubts and certainties of the person who wrote it, the same as of other kind, great, and true spirits, live in the air and belong to us ...[65]

65. César Calvo, *Las tres mitades de Ino Moxo y otros brujos de la Amazonía* (Iquitos: Proceso Editores and Editorial Gráfica Labor, 1981); English edition: César Calvo, *The Three Halves of Ino Moxo. Teachings of the Wizard of the Upper Amazon* (translated from the original Spanish by Kenneth A. Symington), (Rochester, Ver- mont: Inner Tradition International, 1995).

The book and César Calvo's poetic description of the way in which the shamanism[66] of the Amazon understands humanity's position in space-time can be interpreted as an alternative and complementary elucidation of the complex and debated phenomenon of synchrony proposed by C. G. Jung and others as "a non-causal connective principle in which events that take place in the external world can line up with " an individual's experience," reflecting personal emotions, thoughts, or whole combinations of events. Our spiritual Amazon experiences, in the specificity of their personal life lessons, although separated in precise times and spaces, came together in our fortuitous meeting in Peru. It was a coincidence or the foreshadowing synchrony of a friendship and love sealed by Don Hidelbando and/or Don Javier, and his gift of a bottle of ayahuasca, the Teacher Plant we finally drank in the seclusion of our Andean home, that allowed us to live the mystical experience of the Unity of Ontological Totality.

In the mid-sixties, during two long nights of *masateada* and dances with the Asháninka on the Chitani River, completely drunk on the fermented yuca—*piárintzi*—I suffered the worst tobacco intoxication of my life: not exactly the mystical epiphany I was hoping for when I ingested the Master Plant: the shirpiari/shamán's "wife." For two days, the whole world spun around me, no matter what position I assumed: standing, sitting, or sprawled on the floor in the midst of my own vomit.

Toward the end of the second day I was able to drag myself along a trail that led to the evangelical mission, in search of some allopathic medicine capable of alleviating my misery. The response from the ILV missionary was a firm refusal to my plea for help; the faithless sinner, who preferred to spend his time in the company of savage Indians rather than with Christians, could pay for his sins. My disillusionment, however, wasn't as much with the evangelical's harsh attitude as with the toughness of the Shiri, the wife of the shaman that my innocence had imagined would be a sacred plant filled with compassion and powerful knowledge open to the spiritual questions and concerns of this young and honest *wiracocha*.

After those two days of chaotic and uncontrollable sensations, and disquieting visions caused by ingesting the *shiripiári*'s tobacco juice, Nicotiana rus-

---

66. I use the term shaman/shamanism with care, conscious of the deterioration this semantic field of profound historic roots has suffered at the hands of commercial popularizations.

tica, I never again tried Amazon tobacco, least of all that of the Asháninkas, until the first years of the third millennium when another shaman from the Amazon blew tobacco smoke over my head and my entire body while singing three *icaros*—sacred songs—, the purpose of which was to show me the path back to my place in the cosmos.

Should I discern a sign of synchrony—non-causal coincidence—in my ambiguous and traumatic initial contact with the *shiripiári*/shaman's Nicotiana rustica and my decision to give up smoking profane commercial tobacco—Nicotiana tabacum—after years of youthful addiction and Linda's gentle prodding? At the same time, she invited me to reconsider the spiritual power of salt that surrounded the home of our ethereal and physical body with its impenetrable protective shield. Why did I focus my understanding of the Asháninka people's life and history on *tzivi*—salt, the salt of the mountain[67]—a decade before I met Linda?

In the month of August 2015, I had another encounter-separation-reencounter with *tzivi*—salt. During a nine-day diet—*ieta*, as they say in the Spanish of the Amazon—I completely deprived myself of salt and food twice a day. It was a strict one-meal regimen of watery rice and boiled plantains accompanied by three drinks a day of infusions made from three Teacher Plants. The shaman explained to me that not eating salt would open my physical and spiritual body to the curative properties of the Teacher Plants I was ingesting. At the same time, the lack of salt's protection would leave me vulnerable to negative energies that circulated in the forest—and in the world—and therefore it would be necessary for me to protect my body/spirit with tobacco or *shiri*, Nicotiana rustica.

My separation from *tzivi* and renewed friendship with *shiri* accompanied the spiritual regeneration and emotional healing I had gained through the ritual ingestion of the Master Plant, ayahuasca. When, on the ninth day of my retreat, I tasted the first meal with salt, I felt I was surrounding myself and my retrieved memories with the protective energy that *tzivi* had given to me, Linda, and our children, from the times I had spent with the Asháninka people in Tzivíniki and Tziviriani.[68]

---

67. Varese, *La sal de los cerros. Resistencia y utopia en la Amazonia peruana*, op. cit. There are three more editions in Spanish (Lima, Lima, Havana), one in English (University of Oklahoma Press), and one in French (L'Harmattan, Paris).

68. *Tsivíniki* is the Asháninka name for the Mountain of Salt, and *Tsiviriani* the Asháninka name for the River of Salt.

CHAPTER 38

Small Deaths

꙼

DEATH HAS VISITED ME from time to time in dreams and visions, and especially in an apparition aided by the Master Plant uspawashasanango at Takiwasi, the House of Silence and Song, surrounded by friendly trees, a few monkeys and birds, and numerous, loud, and ever-present *cicadas*. In the middle of the night, the small, obscure yet familiar figure of a woman who had died a couple of years before, came to see me, standing silently in a direction diagonal from where I was looking, near the door to my cabin. She didn't speak, but simply stood there, faceless but recognizable, reminding me of her presence in the depth of my memory.

How could uspawashasanango, the Teacher Plant—memory of the heart—bring her to me? How could the Plant convoke, animate, and give corporeal substance to someone who had died physiologically two years earlier and had emotionally departed many years before that? How can the spirit acquire substance, such that my sensory vision could be the vehicle for my perception? When I had this vision, I was following a strict Amazon diet of Teacher Plants, in total isolation and silence. The rules of the cure do not allow for the use of a watch or any other electronic device, only writing and reading materials. My devotion to western rationality was left intact by that shamanic cure, and I even took advantage of the isolation and silence to finish some intellectual work.

From early childhood, I associated death with animals and other non-human beings. The memory of the pig that had been sacrificed on those peasant planks at Prato Sopra la Croce followed me throughout my life as a symbol of human arrogance in its conditioned alienation from other living beings. I think I tried to compensate for those separations and expiate my infantile vision of that butchery by spending time with animals or accompanying as intimately as I could what I perceived to be the multiverse. Still, the massacre of innocent animals pursued me from the northwestern part of the Amazon where the young awajún's hunting dogs became the executioners of the capybara, all the way to Mexico City where I was forced to participate in the cruel death of a rooster that had been buried alive as the victim in a supposed ritual meant to bring fealty to a lover who was given to adultery. My Brazilian friend never got her lover back, perhaps confirming that the supposed Nahuatl shaman was really a vulgar and malevolent witch.

Once again, in Oaxaca's northern mountains, the Zapotec peasants burdened me with the dubious honor of offering up the life of a bull at community festivities. The bull's eyes were terrified. My confused carnivorous consciousness took one more step in the direction of the growing vegetarian commitment I had never been able to fully achieve. It's a paradox that my anthropological calling had taken me to the Amazon, where most people farm and forage but also depend on hunting and fishing for their animal fats and proteins.

Much of animal butchery is as violent and cruel as our western practices of industrial slaughter. The only difference is scale; the intense work involved in obtaining meat from the hunt and the complex rituals which in many cases require a diet of salt, hot chile, and sugars, sexual abstinence, and a sacred and reciprocal agreement with the "owners" of the animals. Hunting—like all Indigenous peoples' agricultural activity and foraging—is a repeated celebration of each individual's membership in the broad system of kinship relations that includes humans, non-humans, and all other visible and invisible beings who populate the universe.

For the last fifty years of my life I have lived with dogs and cats rescued from desperate situations of abuse, cruelty, or indifference. All our family's animals lived to enjoy years of wellbeing and serene transitions into death. Of my first dogs, the Andean Orégano who accompanied us in our exile to Mexico and the feisty little Oaxacan dog, Chaparro, who insisted on adopting us, are buried in the garden of the house at San Felipe del Agua. The rest of our animals were cremated and we keep their ashes on the depths of my bookcases as if they were one more volume of history. So, death and transition have been a constant in our family, and Linda and our children—as toddlers and adults—have been participants in final farewell rituals somehow adopted from the ways in which Indigenous and *mestizo* people honor the lives and memories of their dead.

The Day of the Dead ceremony, at the beginning of November, has become a part of our ritual calendar. It includes an altar of the dead, with offerings of food, drink, and tobacco, and yellow cempazuchil flowers adorning a path to that altar which holds their favorite foods and drinks. In the past two decades, the altar honoring our real or imagined dead has paid tribute to far too many. It seems as if my community of those who have gone is larger than the community that accompanies me here in the Americas. The challenge of my Days of the Dead is how to evoke these memories with smiles and laughter, slaps on the shoulders, warm hugs, great feasts, and wine, beer, mescal, pisco, tequila, constant political irony, and taunts, and the bittersweet sensation of knowing we are all mortal, without distinctions of any sort.

The belief that the dead return to visit us every year on the first and second of November, became more than a creed one night more than thirty years ago when Linda and I decided to visit San Felipe del Agua's cemetery with our two children and participate with other members of the community in the festive celebration. It was a cold night, illuminated and made a bit warmer by the many fires lit among the graves that were covered with cempazuchil flowers, colored cloths laden with all manner of food, fruit, glasses filled with beer and mescal, and children playing board games on the tombs. San Felipe's traditional music band was there, along with a quasi-rock electronic ensemble made up by some of the town's youth.

That night Linda and I took a whole roll of color pictures, especially of Don Tomás and Doña Candelaria's family. These were old friends who had received us warmly when we'd first arrived. We wanted to record for our children the scene of this first experience of deep Mexico. A few days later, when I went to retrieve the pictures from the only serious photographic lab that existed in Oaxaca, we could see a grayish elongated aura in the background of every image.

Two Aprils ago, Linda and I returned to Oaxaca, to the house in San Felipe for a brief visit. The house's old dog, Señora Josefina's loyal protector Chaparro, was suffering so with old age and illness that we decided to put him down. That night we helped Señora Josefina hold the vigil for Chaparro just as we keep watch over all our loved ones when they leave: we surrounded his body with cempazuchil flowers, candles, and some of his favorite foods. We turned off the patio lights and, seated in a circle, had hot drinks and a light repast as we remembered Chaparro's happy life, the ferocious male dog who could tell which people were good and identify those with bad intentions, "like that time when he wouldn't accept the presence of a worker who, days later, turned out to be a thief."

While Josefina and her two sons shared these stories with us, we heard a noise coming from the patio roof and saw an animal the size of Chaparro—was it a fox?—walking calmly across the top of the wall in the direction of the garden where Chaparro had spent the last few days of his life. It stopped for a moment and looked, almost with curiosity, at the scene of Chaparro's wake, and then continued to his doghouse. We all saw the animal, thinking it must be a type of fox. It turned out to be an animal that was exceptionally rare in that part of Mexico, and under threat of extinction: the cacomixtle (Bassariscus sumichrasti), an omnivorous nocturnal tree creature completely out of place in this part of the country and more so in a semi-urban area contaminated by the sounds of cars and human presence.

My rational explanation was that the cacomixtle had taken to visiting Chaparro at night so he could eat what was left of his dinner. Josefina, on the other hand, coming as she did from Indigenous Zapotec ancestry in the Ixtepeji mountains, and being the daughter of an herbalist and healer, had a more "synchronic" explanation in line with Mesoamerican Nahuatl and Tonal concepts: alter egos that accompany all living beings through life and death.

CHAPTER 39

Our Struggle in California

O N JULY 19, 1979, the guerrilla columns of the Sandinista National Liberation Front entered Managua, the capital of Nicaragua, and were welcomed by thousands of people who had been on a general strike for several weeks, participating in the final defeat of more than forty-five years of the Somoza family's bloody dictatorship.

In the internationalist column of the Southern Front, that had advanced from the Costa Rican border across the Lake of Nicaragua, past the archipelago of Solentiname and the cities of Granada and Masaya, was an internationalist guerrilla fighter by the name of Luis David Varese Scotto: my younger brother and Christian poet who had devoted years of his life to the Trappist community of the poet Ernesto Cardenal on the island of Solentiname. Following victory, the Sandinistas offered Luis the opportunity of remaining in the army, with an officer's rank, and a position in the revolutionary government. In Oaxaca, Linda and I knew little of Luis's recent adventures, except for fragmentary news that came from friends who were war reporters and filmmakers traveling between Mexico and Nicaragua.

On June 20, 1979, precisely a month before Nicaragua's liberation, our son André Luis was born at the Clínica del Carmen in the city of Oaxaca. As almost renegade lukewarm Catholics, Linda and I had been talking for years about naming our first boy Grey Cloud in honor of an unknown U.S. Indian leader. The Christian tradition won the day, and we ended up using the hybrid names André and Luis. In Italian the name is Andrea, and in Spanish and English it's a girl's name. Andrés, with an "s" at the end, created a certain cacophony with Varese, and so a phonetic aesthetic dictated our use of the French hybrid. André would be André from then on. The name Luis was a

My daughter Vanessa and my son André in our house in
San Felipe del Agua, Oaxaca, circa 1989

nominal link to my Papá Luigi and to my half-brother Luis, now an officer in
the Sandinista army and a perpetual wandering poet.

It had been more than three years since André's birth, when Luis sent
me word through a Mexican filmmaker friend that he would be visiting us
in Oaxaca. The old VW van had been rehabilitated and I drove it to Mexico City to pick up this revolutionary brother whom I baptized from that
moment on as "the poet who took up arms." Back then, the highway from
crowded Mexico City to Oaxaca went through the Mixtec mountains. It was

Vanessa and André, Pacifica Grove, CA, circa 1990

the old Pan-American Highway that, in theory, links Alaska with Tierra del Fuego.

Luis and I had traveled the Pan-American highway several times in different parts of Central and South America: Chile, Peru, Ecuador, Colombia and recently Luis had done so in a Nicaraguan military caravan. In the van we headed south, passing Cuautla, sugarcane fields, peasant milpas, and hundreds and then thousands of miles of goats, the historic cause of the Mixtec land's erosion, until we arrived at Izúcar de Matamoros. At that small town in Tehuitzingo, in a startling display of military force for a country at peace, we were met by a group of plain clothed armed men, their faces angry. With rude

Our granddaughter Isabella and mom Vanessa
at our Oaxaca house, circa 2002

gestures, they indicated we should get out of the van. Our Spanish surprised
them: "Shit, man, we thought you were French! Where do you come from,
where are you going, and what do you have in the van?"

My terror increased as I saw Gigi's rage rising to his eyes and accumulating
around his eyebrows and in his hoarse voice that declared, with the relative
diplomacy he's always been known for: "In the first place, we aren't French

André, our dog Camilla, and me at the beach
in Monterey, CA, circa 2003

or fucking *gringos*. Our California license plate has nothing to do with our nationality. I am an officer in the Sandinista Liberation Army of Nicaragua, and I'm on vacation visiting my anthropologist brother who works for Mexico's federal government."

The van's inspection was rapid and didn't have the result the judicial police had hoped for: a few marijuana roaches, or "mota" as it's called in middle-class

Mexico. All they found were the remnants of the bed that had belonged to old Orégano, some plastic toys and rag animals, and the backpacks of two poor travelers.

Once installed in the rented house on Calle Eucaliptos between San Felipe and the working-class neighborhood of Colonia Volcanes, Gigi could relax and give us some censored news of his experiences of the Nicaraguan war. He was the first and only member of either of our families who had come to see us in our Mexican exile of more than seven years. After his visit, Linda's parents and brother and sister came, my sister Giliola came from Italy with her partner of those years, Mario, and much later Papá and stepmother Rita came with my youngest brother Francisco-Cecco. Our family in exile would finally acquire legitimacy, and our children Vanessa and André Luis take up their precarious positions in the Varese kinship system and their full and legitimate places in the Ayre family of California.

Luis-Gigi's visit lasted only a few days, enough to reconnect memories, hopes, and fantasize about our uncertain futures. But the most meaningful thing for Linda and me, isolated from our parents and nearby relatives, was the verification of what we had felt from André's first year: the development of his speech was too slow and hesitant. In our ignorance, we had thought this was because we spoke both Spanish and English at home, even though we had practiced the same bilingualism with Vanessa who, at the age of three, was fluent in both languages. Gigi called our attention to what was later misdiagnosed as apraxia.

For us, André's parents, this was the beginning of a long and uncertain pilgrimage of days that sometimes seemed not to have any defined direction, frustrating itineraries ending in ambiguity and confusion, with dark and depressing answers revealing an extreme poverty on the part of the social sciences when it came to understanding the infantile mind, its language skills, intelligence, and emotions. Our child of only a few years, and his four-year-old sister, became the center of all the existential decisions we made about our small nuclear family. No one else among family members, nearby or faraway neighbors, friends or even acquaintances, professionals, doctors, educational specialists, and linguists could alleviate the profound pain and intimate loneliness that came from not knowing what lay in store for André.

What could have caused this delay in the development of our child, whose birth had been normal in every way? A Catholic sense of guilt floated in our gnostic consciences. Could it have been the ayahuasca from the Amazon we'd taken so many years before, or the more recent peyote ceremony in a little Na-huatl village near Tepoztlán, or those few tokes of marijuana I'd smoked in a social setting, or one of the medicines or vaccinations given free in Mexico's Seguro Social hospital?

Or was it that trip to Mexico City when André, three months old at the time, didn't wake up the entire way, and we had to blow on his pale face to revive him and take him immediately to a doctor who knew nothing, didn't even question the fact that in a single day André had gone from 5,000 to almost 10,000 feet above sea level, and to a city where "the air was no longer transparent" but rather thick with lethal gases? Who or what could we blame? Why must there always be someone or something to blame when there is some rupture in the natural order of things, especially if that order is our Judeo-Christian theocentrism?

No one in Oaxaca or Mexico City could tell us anything we could trust. Language therapy was the most innovative and advanced that medical science could offer us, including a crude and doubtful surgical procedure that involved cutting some of the tissue below the tongue in André's little mouth. With the hope of finding a viable solution, we got a bit of money together, I requested some time off work, we asked Linda's family for help, and the four of us plus Orégano got in the van and went north, to California, to Stanford University, where someone told us there was an important specialist in cases of apraxia, aphasia, or the neurological inability(!) to form words.

After an extremely expensive consultation, we left the office of this "famous" university professor and scientist incredibly depressed. According to the professor, André would never speak, and communication between him and the rest of the world would only happen using an electronic device that was relatively new on the computational market.

Linda refused to accept this diagnosis. With the stubbornness, will, and strength of a mother cornered by some mysterious danger, she gave herself totally to the task of finding an answer and a solution. In the early 1980s, we didn't yet have access to cybernetic information, to a computer that in real time was able to scan thousands if not millions of bits of data that existed regarding these symptoms.

No one had told us that in the 1940s the child psychiatrist Leo Kanner had identified a kind of highly functional autism by the name of Asperger Syndrome in children who exhibited symptoms associated with late and partial language development. Later, the Austrian pediatrician Hans Asperger himself had linked this syndrome to a series of other symptoms: extreme sensitivity to noise, an almost obsessive need to keep things ordered, a limited focus in certain areas of knowledge and mental activities, and a difficulty in interpreting the body language and particularly facial expressions of others, and the inability to respond accordingly.

After a few weeks we decided that Linda, Vanessa, André, Orégano, and the van would stay in California at her parents' home, while I returned to Oaxaca and back to work. Our last pilgrimage began, this time to find a place where our André could live. A place where the warmth and love of family might add to his knowledge and social and cultural understanding, an ambience we hoped might be better prepared to decipher and treat this type of autism that had invaded our home.

The fear of having to leave Oaxaca, where we had just finished building a home, of taking Vanessa out of school and away from her circle of friends, of having to say goodbye to all our friends, our adopted sister/daughter Nana Pina, all our trees and flowers and what little furniture we possessed, after years of uncertain wanderings, brought me to the very edge of desperation. Linda, in contrast, possessed the irrevocable determination to find a solution to our challenge, and from that moment on set her sights on a cure and return to normalcy.

For the next three years, our family was divided: Linda and André searching for a cure in California and occasionally Mexico City, and Vanessa and Stefano first in Oaxaca and then in California, where I obtained a series of visiting professorships at the University of California—Berkeley and Stanford. For Vanessa, I think the transition from life in the countryside surrounded by attentions and friends and Mexico's popular creativity to the gray and insipid discipline of a middle-class public school in California was too traumatic. Only years later, did Linda and I realize how painful it had been for her, at eight or ten years of age, to have to leave the warmth of her world because of the excessive attentions needed by her brother André.

We spent more than four years of fragmented lives and residencies, between Santa Rosa, Berkeley, Stanford, Palo Alto, and Oaxaca, during which Linda and André were dedicated to full-time study, understanding and navigating the several ways forward and how to live creatively with Asperger Syndrome. While Vanessa attended a private, and later a public, middle school, I went from university to university where I had temporary visiting professorships, always on the lookout for a stable job that would provide the income needed to keep us afloat in California's giddy 1990s economy.

The dream of returning to Oaxaca to live in a house—now our own—grew more and more distant as we struggled to find a creative coexistence with André's process of development who now, at the age of nine, spoke English and understood Spanish, read and wrote with difficulty but did so, rode his bicycle to the dentist or to school in Davis, played a very deficient game of baseball (my fault), and mastered all the things a typical nine-year-old does. Linda did all this intense formative and educational work with André, while working full-time as a bilingual teacher at a public high school in California, and completing a Master's degree in Pedagogy and Educational Administration.

Stability finally arrived for us all when three Indigenous intellectuals and academics (Dave Risling, Sarah Hutchinson, and Jack Forbes) of the University of California—Davis took the risk of hiring me for a year as a Visiting Professor in the Native American Studies Department. The following year, the same school offered me a full professorship of Indigenous Studies in that Department. I cannot entirely rid myself of the suspicion that the Amatzénka or perhaps the hidden Maninkari of the Asháninka forest, or maybe Poshano himself, were my and our protectors. Or could it have been the Nahuales from the mountains of Oaxaca, who came down to the feet of San Felipe Hill one day to see how that child André was doing?

CHAPTER 40

Cosmic Dialogues

ERRORS IMPRISON US IN our pride. My pilgrimage between the material and the spiritual, the secular and sacred, was marked by small insinuations, allusions, diminutive epiphanies, revelations, and a few brief encounters with the unknown and inexplicable which, when woven into an integrated vision, make up the symbolic cloth of the hammock of my life. I find myself now, in these twilight years, living and resting, reflecting and imagining space and time in a network of unrelated and non-causal events that speak of mysteries more than of algorithms, and that convoke my emotional intelligence more than my Cartesian logos.

I wouldn't have been able to anchor life's uncertainties in the company of animals, plants, other non-human beings, and the quantum ontology of the cosmos, if I hadn't shared years of my life with the Asháninka men and women of the Gran Pajonal, the Quechua peoples of the Amazon and the Andes, the Miskito, Garífuna, and Creole peoples of Nicaragua and Honduras, the Zapotecs, Chinantecs, and Mixes of southeastern Mexico, the Guatemalan Mayans—including those in Mexican refugee camps—, the rural undocumented Mixteco and Trique workers in the agricultural fields of California, and all the Indigenous colleagues, friends, and students I met throughout my years of teaching at California universities.

The coming together of activism and the social sciences, my way of practicing anthropology, has opened multiple windows of perception which might otherwise have remained obscured by modernity's obsessive epistemology of materialist empiricism. Without explicit intention, I have journeyed—a bit unconsciously, I admit—the same epistemological path that emergent post-materialist science has been proposing with quantum mechanics for the past one hundred years.

In my own experience—not in my logos but in my pneuma, my soul in the Socratic sense of "close to the heart" like the Mayan *ch'ulel*—knowledge became ever more a process analogous to the Indigenous way of knowing: recognizing that we humans, animals, plants, mountains, rocks, water, air, sun, moon, stars, and all other uranic entities, as well as all invisible beings, are linked in an existential cosmic contract written at the beginning of time which the Asháninkas call *poerani*, the *in illo tempore* of my own Mediterranean tradition, when all manifestations of life began.

It is a cosmic pact that implies a cosmic ethics, linking all and every entity—tangible and intangible, visible and invisible—in a complex polyphonic dance that looks for harmony beyond and even through conflicts, and ignores classifications and hierarchies created by humans or immutable laws invented by scientists. A few years ago, after an epistemological crisis, I began to use my own personal cosmocentric neologism to describe the radical difference between modern Western cosmology, that I identify as anthropocentric, and the American Indian cosmologies that I have called polycentric or cosmocentric.

But my consciousness continued to resist liberating itself from the hegemony of impartial and "objective" observation that years of Eurocentric study imposed. It resisted the humility, respect, and openness required by perceptive consciousness and the consequent difficulty in believing in a universal truth, an objective universal science. Therefore, as I continued to get closer to the Indigenous ways of knowing, to the Indian epistemologies, I have had to face the demons of my intellectual and emotional formation that are deeply rooted in monotheistic Judeo-Christian cosmology, Aristotelianism philosophy, and modern Cartesian and Newtonian science.

Anthropocentrism meant the separation of humanity from nature, man's hierarchical position at the top of an unquestioned universal order, and a divine or secular mandate ruling all forms and manifestations of existence. This hierarchy is accompanied by a growing commercialization of the universe, which has been emptied of its sacred nature and of all ethical consideration. Neither does the capitalist economy's so-called "self-regulating market" answer to any moral statute; it is amoral by definition. Consequently, it lacks any obligation to humans and their cosmic relatives. Can we be surprised by the tragedy of global warming and criminal indifference on the part of those in power when faced with a possible apocalyptic outcome?

After living for a few weeks in the embrace of an Indigenous community, one becomes aware that any social practice based exclusively on materialist principles is essentially destructive of nature, now reduced to the level of "resources": a series of unrelated commoditized entities that lack the intelligence or cosmic reason to exist. I can go on making the argument that ever since modernity and its capitalist economic expression has taken possession, first of Euro-America and then of the rest of the world, the cosmological representation of life and its social practices have abandoned all vestiges of spirituality, sacredness, and even humanism. Modernity has reduced our contemporary value system—our axiology—to a parody of the post-Marxist binary option of "use value" or "exchange value," filling our minds with a limited egotistical code of conduct guided exclusively by individual monetary interests.

The long individual—gnostic or humanistic?—pilgrimage through a world dominated by exchange value and the predominant commoditization of everything, makes it hard for the contemporary individual to perceive and recognize the unitary and interrelated totality among the apparently disparate entities that populate the universe. This is true unless one has had the privilege of living for a time among the Indigenous peoples of the Americas, sharing their material scarcities but also the richness of their knowledge, which in its omnipresence can be understood as invoking heart and mind, soul and spirit, and the mystic visions induced through meditation and the Teacher Plants or by dreams experienced in the communal *maloca*. The Indigenous world—that cosmocentric world—is inhabited by animals and immaterial beings committed to a cosmic conversation that recognizes in each entity an interlocutor with intelligence, free will, feelings, and awareness of its own teleological participation.

In the last decade, I have had the privilege and good fortune of being able to return to visit and live with communities in the Amazon. With them, and with others in Sarayaku, Keweriono, Apaika, Huaycu, Lamas, Tziviriani, and other villages, I once again travel this existential itinerary that always takes me farther toward the integrated and total cosmic unity in a personal experience I hesitate to call "theistic" or religious but rather humanist and gnostic.

The language and ethics of the different cosmocentric manifestations—the many Indigenous communities with their historic profundities in tangible and intangible landscapes—can be analyzed by us in line with our "relativist" or "perspectivist" modalities as anthropologists, outside observers conditioned by our binary code of nature/culture or culture vs. nature. My journey, in search of meanings more than practical results, spirituality rather than material things, tells me that as part of humanity I am not standing in some space of anthropocentric and insular power separated from cosmic totality. Nor am I engaged in a struggle with animals, plants, rocks, waters, amoebas, subatomic particles, and other invisible "rivals." Rather, I find myself attentive to the whisperings of the universe, the sound and smell of wind in the leaves, the barking of my dogs, the howls of coyotes, and answers of crows. And even more to the sound of my soul when I wake in the night, touch Linda's shoulder, and feel grateful for my life well-lived in her company and in that of the cosmos.